Phonics and Word Study for the Teacher of Reading

Programmed for Self-Instruction

Eleventh Edition

Barbara J. Fox

North Carolina State University, Emerita

PEARSON

Boston   Columbus   Indianapolis   New York   San Francisco   Upper Saddle River
Amsterdam   Cape Town   Dubai   London   Madrid   Milan   Munich   Paris   Montreal   Toronto
Delhi   Mexico City   São Paulo   Sydney   Hong Kong   Seoul   Singapore   Taipei   Tokyo

Vice President and Editor in Chief: Aurora Martínez Ramos
Associate Sponsoring Editor: Barbara Strickland
Editorial Assistant: Laura Marenghi
Director of Marketing: Margaret Waples
Executive Marketing Manager: Krista Clark
Production Project Manager: Liz Napolitano

Manager, Central Design: Jayne Conte
Cover Designer: Suzanne Behnke
Cover Image: (c) Julie Vanec/Shutterstock
Full-Service Project Management: Suganya Karuppasamy, Element LLC
Composition: Element LLC
Printer/Binder: LSC Communications
Cover Printer: LSC Communications

Credits and acknowledgments borrowed from other sources and reproduced, with permission, in this textbook appear on the appropriate page within text.

11   17

ISBN 10: 0-13-283809-5
ISBN 13: 978-0-13-283809-2

About the Author

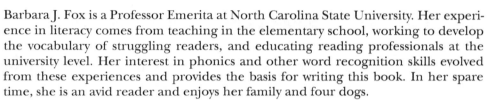

Barbara J. Fox is a Professor Emerita at North Carolina State University. Her experience in literacy comes from teaching in the elementary school, working to develop the vocabulary of struggling readers, and educating reading professionals at the university level. Her interest in phonics and other word recognition skills evolved from these experiences and provides the basis for writing this book. In her spare time, she is an avid reader and enjoys her family and four dogs.

Brief Contents

Contents

Part Three Consonant Digraphs and Consonant Blends   71

Part Four Vowels   93

Part Five A Review of Phonemes   143

Part Six Onsets and Rimes   157

Part Seven Syllable and Accent Patterns   167

Part Eight Morphemes, Prefixes, Suffixes, Contractions, and Compound Words   193

Preface

This book presents the letter–sound relationships of phonics, syllable and accent patterns, onsets and rimes, and the meaningful units, morphemes, which are the building blocks of complicated words, as well as phonological and phonemic awareness skills. Classroom teachers, reading teachers, and special education teachers who understand the content in this book will have the background to make sound instructional decisions and to implement effective instructional practices. This book also will be a resource teachers may consult in future years when making decisions about the teaching of word identification skills.

New to This Edition

My intention in revising this book is to facilitate the study of phonics and word study so that all teachers enter the classroom or continue in their current teaching positions with the knowledge they need to be effective in a variety of settings. To this end, I have addressed the Common Core State Standards in English Language Arts (National Governors Association Center for Best Practices and Council of Chief State School Officers, 2010) as they apply to the content of this book. Other goals for this revision are to update the research on teaching phonics, further strengthen this book as an effective learning tool, and provide more information on phonological and phonemic awareness.

Each bulleted item describes one of the many new features of this edition:

- A new section addresses the Common Core State Standards in English Language Arts in phonics, word recognition, and phonological awareness. This section is intended to provide readers with an overview of relevant standards and an explanation of how these standards pertain to word recognition and apply to the content of this book.
- Interleaved throughout this new edition are the Common Core State Standards in English Language Arts that apply specifically to phonics, word recognition, and phonological awareness. Each applicable standard appears in the book where the information on the standard is addressed. The goal is to help teachers connect the material they are studying with grade-specific learning expectations for word recognition.
- With a view toward strengthening this book as a learning tool, the answers to the pre- and posttests are now cross-referenced with the pages in the book where the information is addressed. Cross-referencing will assist teachers in using this book as a study resource.
- A new section describes how to use this book. The section describes how to read and respond to the instructional frames and explains the use of reviews and assessments. This information will make the book easier for teachers to use independently. As a consequence, teachers will bring greater knowledge of phonics

and word study to the teacher education setting, be better prepared to discuss the content, and be more confident in the implementation of teaching practices.

- In order to assure that this book presents bite-size amounts of information, a large section on consonants in the previous edition has been separated into two smaller parts. These smaller parts provide a logical and manageable focus to the study of the consonants.
- The literature review has been revised and updated. The updated overview of research will help teachers better understand the research on teaching word recognition and apply research findings to their own teaching practices.
- This new edition includes more attention to phonological and phonemic awareness. Phonological awareness and phonemic awareness, now covered in a separate subpart in Part One, will help teachers better understand these language-based skill sets and, additionally, provide them with knowledge of skill-specific learning and behaviors specified in the Common Core State Standards.

How Is This Book Organized?

Phonics and Word Study for the Teacher of Reading is a self-paced program of instruction that has proven a useful technique for presenting background on two word-recognition skills: (a) skill at associating sounds with letters, letter patterns, and syllables so as to pronounce unfamiliar words and (b) skill at using the meaningful parts in complex words to identify words and discover word meaning. The book guides teachers through a series of small steps that help them learn the information needed to be effective teachers of phonics letter–sounds, syllable patterns, and the meaningful units in words.

 Acknowledgments

I would like to thank the reviewers of this text. I appreciate their insightful guidance: James Gaggini, Clarion University of Pennsylvania; Leslie Hopping, The Columbus Academy, Gahanna, Ohio; Marsha Jane Jackson, Centerville Abington Elementary, Centerville, Indiana; Dorothy Morrison, Ohio State University; Charlotte L. Pass, SUNY, Cortland; Donna Schweitzer, Forwood Elementary School, Wilmington, Delaware; and Kayla S. Zimmer, St. Bonaventure University.

Self-Evaluation I

A Pretest

This is a test designed to give an indication of your present knowledge of phonics and the structure of long words. Read each item, including **all** the choices. Indicate the answer you consider best by circling the appropriate letter (a, b, c, d, or e) or marking the appropriate letter on an answer sheet. Be sure to respond to every item. The answers for the pretest (pp. 228) cross-reference the page in the text that addresses the correct answer for each test item. Time: 30 minutes.

I. **Multiple Choice.** Select the best answer.

1. A requirement of a syllable is that
   a. it contain at least one consonant letter.
   b. it contain no more than one vowel letter.
   c. it contain no more than one vowel phoneme.
   d. it contain no more than one phoneme.
   e. All of the above.

2. Which of the following most adequately completes this sentence? The consonant speech sounds in the American-English language are represented by
   a. the distinctive speech sounds we associate with the 21 consonant letters of the alphabet.
   b. 18 of the consonant letters of the alphabet plus certain digraphs.
   c. the single-letter consonants plus their two- and three-letter blends.
   d. The American-English language is too irregular to represent the consonant speech sounds with any degree of accuracy.
   e. the consonant–vowel combinations.

3. The letter *y* is most likely to be a consonant when
   a. it is the first letter in a word or syllable.
   b. it is the final letter in a word or syllable.
   c. it follows *o* in a syllable.
   d. it has the sound of *i* as in *might.*
   e. None of the above.

4. Generally, when two like consonants appear together in a word or syllable,
   a. only one is sounded.
   b. one is sounded with the first syllable and the other with the second.

1

    c. both are sounded when the preceding vowel is *i*.

    d. both are sounded when the following vowel is *e*.

    e. neither is sounded.

5. The second syllable of the nonsense word *alithpic* would be expected to rhyme with

    a. *aright*.

    b. *brick*.

    c. *kith*.

    d. *pyth* (as in *python*).

    e. *hit*.

6. The open syllable in the nonsense word *botem* would most likely rhyme with

    a. *coat*.

    b. *hot*.

    c. *rah*.

    d. *low*.

    e. *gem*.

7. We usually double the final consonant before adding a suffix to

    a. a one-syllable word that ends in a single vowel followed by a single consonant.

    b. a one-syllable word that ends in two consonants.

    c. a one-syllable word that has two vowels.

    d. a one-syllable word that ends in a final *e*.

    e. Both a and b.

8. The sound of the schwa is represented by

    a. the *a* in *baited*.

    b. the *e* in *early*.

    c. the *e* in *happen*.

    d. the *w* in *show*.

    e. All of these.

9. How many phonemes are represented in *knight*?

    a. one   **b.** two   **c.** three   **d.** four   **e.** six

10. An example of a closed syllable is

    a. *desk*.

    b. *hot*.

    c. *help*.

    d. All of these.

    e. None of these.

11. The consonant blend, or cluster, is illustrated by

    a. the *sh* in *shirt*.

    b. the *ng* in *thing*.

    c. the *ph* in *graph*.

    d. the *br* in *brought*.

    e. a, c, and d.

12. Which of the following has an incorrect diacritical mark?

  a. cắll   **b.** sĕll   **c.** ĭll   **d.** hŏt   **e.** ŭp

13. Which of the following has an incorrect diacritical mark?

  a. mād̄e   **b.** sēe   **c.** tīme   **d.** lōve   **e.** ūse

14. When the single vowel *i* is followed by a single consonant and a final *e* in an accented syllable, the *i* would most likely have the sound of

  a. the *i* in *active*.
  b. the *y* in *my*.
  c. the *i* in *easily*.
  d. the first *e* in *bee*.
  e. None of the above.

15. If *o* was the only vowel in an accented, open syllable, that *o* would most likely represent the same sound as

  a. the *o* in *nothing*.
  b. the *a* in *wanted*.
  c. the *o* in *do*.
  d. the *ew* in *sew*.
  e. None of these.

16. The letter *q* could be removed from the alphabet because it could adequately and without conflict be represented by

  a. the soft sound of *c.*
  b. *ch* as in *chair*.
  c. *k* as in *keep*.
  d. All of the above.
  e. The idea is foolish; *qu* represents a distinctive consonant sound.

17. If *a* was the single vowel in an accented syllable ending with one or more consonants, that *a* would most likely represent the same sound as

  a. the *ai* in *plaid*.
  b. the *ay* in *ray*.
  c. the *a* in *all*.
  d. the *a* in *any*.
  e. None of these.

18. When *o* and *a* appear together in a syllable, they usually represent the same sound as

  a. the *o* in *bottle*.
  b. the *o* in *labor*.
  c. the *o* in *toil*.
  d. the *o* in *come*.
  e. None of these.

19. The symbol *s* is used in the dictionary to show the pronunciation of the sound heard in

  a. *shall*.
  b. *his*.
  c. *sugar*.
  d. *seem*.
  e. Both b and d.

20. If *e* was the only vowel in an open syllable, that *e* would most likely represent the same sound as

    a. the *e* in *pine*.
    b. the *ea* in *meat*.
    c. the *y* in *my*.
    d. the *e* in *set*.
    e. None of these.

21. The word *if* ends with the same sound as

    a. the *ph* in *graph*.
    b. the *f* in *of*.
    c. the *gh* in *enough*.
    d. the *gh* in *ghetto*.
    e. Both a and c.

22. The letter *c* followed by *i* is most likely to represent the same sound as

    a. the *s* in *sent*.
    b. the *c* in *cello*.
    c. *c* followed by *o*.
    d. *c* followed by *e*.
    e. Both a and d.

23. The letter *g* followed by *o* is most likely to represent the same sound as

    a. the *j* in *joke*.
    b. the *g* in *ghost*.
    c. the *g* in *swing*.
    d. *g* followed by *e*.
    e. Both a and d.

24. The final *y* changes to *i* before a suffix is added to a word that

    a. ends in a consonant followed by the letter *y*.
    b. ends in two consonants.
    c. ends in a vowel followed by the letter *y*.
    d. has two or more syllables.
    e. consists of no more than one syllable.

25. A free morpheme is illustrated by

    a. *-ing*.
    b. *-un*.
    c. *-ous*.
    d. *fame*.
    e. *-ment*.

26. A word that includes both a free and a bound morpheme is illustrated by

    a. *unhappy*.
    b. *easily*.
    c. *famous*.
    d. None of these.
    e. All of these.

27. Add *-es* to a word that ends in
    a. the letter *s*.
    b. the letters *sh*.
    c. the letters *ch*.
    d. the letter *x*.
    e. All of these.

28. A suffix may
    a. change the meaning of a word.
    b. make the meaning of a word more specific.
    c. change the part of speech.
    d. Both a and b.
    e. All of the above.

29. Which word(s) includes a derivational suffix?
    a. *furious*.
    b. *camels*.
    c. *enjoyment*.
    d. *laughed*.
    e. Both a and c.

30. Double the final consonant before adding a suffix to a one-syllable word to indicate that the
    a. vowel represents a long sound.
    b. vowel is a diphthong.
    c. vowel represents a short sound.
    d. vowel sound changes from short to long.
    e. All of the above.

31. The guideline for adding a suffix to a word that ends in an *e* is illustrated by
    a. *timely*.
    b. *nicer*.
    c. *replacing*.
    d. *largest*.
    e. All of the above.

32. Which word includes an inflectional suffix?
    a. *serious*.
    b. *rabbits*.
    c. *statement*.
    d. *childhood*.
    e. None of these.

33. Which underlined item illustrates a free morpheme?
    a. *play<u>ful</u>*.
    b. *<u>il</u>legal*.
    c. *dis<u>appear</u>*.
    d. *<u>re</u>appoint*.
    e. a, b, and c.

34. A contraction is illustrated by

   a. *Sue's.*
   b. *teachers'.*
   c. *could've.*
   d. *Jones's.*
   e. *cannot.*

35. Which word below shows the correct syllable division?

   a. *en' erg y.*
   b. *gin' ger snap.*
   c. *journ' al.*
   d. *rem' ed y.*
   e. None of these.

36. A compound word is illustrated by

   a. *cheekbone.*
   b. *rattled.*
   c. *disability.*
   d. *chickadee.*
   e. *playful.*

37. *They'd* is composed of which of the following two words:

   a. *They should.*
   b. *They will.*
   c. *They would.*
   d. *They had.*
   e. Both c and d.

38. *W* is part of a diphthong in

   a. *which.*
   b. *tower.*
   c. *throw.*
   d. *hawk.*
   e. *were.*

39. Which nonsense word below illustrates a closed syllable?

   a. clom.
   b. phry.
   c. prue.
   d. twa.
   e. stroi.

40. The VCe (vowel–consonant–e) pattern is best illustrated by

   a. *agree.*
   b. *cave.*
   c. *ample.*
   d. *rattle.*
   e. *aisle.*

41. The VV (vowel–vowel) pattern is illustrated by

   a. *crowd.*
   b. *steep.*

   c. *tale.*
   d. *awful.*
   e. All of the above.

42. As a diphthong, when *ou* appears in a syllable, it represents the same sound as

   a. the *oi* in *coin.*
   b. the *ow* in *towel.*
   c. the *ow* in *grow.*
   d. the *oy* in *boy.*
   e. None of the above.

43. The VC (vowel-consonant) pattern is illustrated by

   a. *toy.*
   b. *match.*
   c. *me.*
   d. *two.*
   e. *toe.*

44. *Y* as the only vowel and final letter in a one-syllable word is most likely to represent the same sound as

   a. the *ee* in *see.*
   b. the *a* in *play.*
   c. the *i* in *ice.*
   d. the *oi* in *boil.*
   e. None of the above.

45. When *oi* appears in an accented syllable, it represents the same sound as

   a. the *oy* in *boy.*
   b. the *ow* in *cow.*
   c. the *ou* in *mouse.*
   d. the *ew* in *new.*
   e. the *ie* in *piece.*

II. **Multiple Choice.** Where does the accent fall in each of the words or nonsense words given below? Indicate your answer by selecting the last two letters of the accented syllable found in the same row as the word.

   Look at the example: *showboat.* The first word in a compound word is generally accented: ***showboat.*** Look for the last two letters of *show, ow,* in the row to the right. You would circle b or mark b on your answer sheet.

   Example:

showboat	**a.** ho	**b.** ow	**c.** bo	**d.** at	
46. contract (noun)	**a.** co	**b.** on	**c.** nt	**d.** ra	**e.** ct
47. frottomly	**a.** ro	**b.** ot	**c.** to	**d.** om	**e.** ly
48. plargain	**a.** la	**b.** ar	**c.** rg	**d.** ga	**e.** in
49. cidaltion	**a.** ci	**b.** id	**c.** da	**d.** al	**e.** on
50. phight	**a.** hi	**b.** ig	**c.** gh	**d.** ht	

III. Multiple Choice. Three words are provided for each item (a, b, c). Select the word in which you hear the same sound as that represented by the underlined part of the word at the left. You may find that the sound is heard in all three words; if so, mark d. If none of the words contains the sound, mark e.

51. men<u>ti</u>on	**a.** special	**b.** sugar	**c.** machine	**d.** All	**e.** None
52. <u>th</u>en	**a.** third	**b.** mother	**c.** think	**d.** All	**e.** None
53. <u>j</u>et	**a.** gnome	**b.** gentle	**c.** sang	**d.** All	**e.** None
54. in<u>t</u>o	**a.** thick	**b.** watch	**c.** hoped	**d.** All	**e.** None
55. su<u>cc</u>ess	**a.** cheese	**b.** knee	**c.** queer	**d.** All	**e.** None
56. <u>h</u>ome	**a.** honor	**b.** night	**c.** who	**d.** All	**e.** None
57. t<u>a</u>ll	**a.** talk	**b.** fault	**c.** gnaw	**d.** All	**e.** None
58. f<u>oo</u>d	**a.** look	**b.** blood	**c.** bought	**d.** All	**e.** None
59. b<u>oi</u>l	**a.** mouse	**b.** employ	**c.** riot	**d.** All	**e.** None
60. <u>w</u>ould	**a.** whom	**b.** once	**c.** cow	**d.** All	**e.** None
61. sa<u>ng</u>	**a.** ranger	**b.** ponder	**c.** thinker	**d.** All	**e.** None

IV. Multiple Choice. Select the letter(s) at the right that represents the onset in each one-syllable word.

62. spell	**a.** s	**b.** ell	**c.** ll	**d.** sp	**e.** spe
63. chat	**a.** ch	**b.** at	**c.** a	**d.** t	**e.** hat

Select the letter(s) at the right that represents the rime in each one-syllable word.

64. steam	**a.** ea	**b.** eam	**c.** st	**d.** team	**e.** ste
65. dress	**a.** ess	**b.** dr	**c.** dre	**d.** ress	**e.** ss

V. Multiple Choice. Select the word in each row that is **incorrectly** divided into syllables.

66.	**a.** ro bot	**b.** rod ent	**c.** ro bust	**d.** ro tor	**e.** rouge
67.	**a.** let hal	**b.** rab bit	**c.** re cov er	**d.** mer cy	**e.** con nect
68.	**a.** un der line	**b.** un e qual	**c.** unt ie	**d.** pre dic a ment	**e.** re mit
69.	**a.** home work	**b.** book man	**c.** eye ball	**d.** now here	**e.** egg nog

VI. Multiple Choice. Complete each sentence by selecting the word for which the correct pronunciation is indicated.

70. I went to the park for a
    a. pĭc'nĭc. **b.** wôk. **c.** rəst. **d.** pär' tē. **e.** rĭd.

71. When I picked my vegetables, I dropped a
    a. lĕt' ĭs lēv. **b.** kūk' ŭm bər. **c.** kär' ŏt. **d.** kăb' ĭg. **e.** bēt.

72. The tree we planted was a
    a. pälm. **b.** wĭl' ou. **c.** māp' le. **d.** kŏt' ən wŭd. **e.** sĭk' ə môr.

73. I went to the men's store to get (a)

     a. sŏgz.   **b.** sho͞oz.   **c.** trou′sərs.   **d.** chərt.   **e.** nək′ tī′.

74. The wall is

     a. krăkt.   **b.** smo͞oth.   **c.** rôf.   **d.** pānt əd′.   **e.** thĭk.

75. The committee was composed of

     a. klûr′ gĭ měn.   **b.** bŭk mĭn′.   **c.** băngk′ ərz.   **d.** tē zhərs.   **e.** jŭd′ jĭs.

     (See pp. 228 for answers to Self-Evaluation I.)

Number correct _____

Part One

General Knowledge and Concepts

What kind of background do you have in phonics and word analysis? To help determine the depth of your present knowledge or lack of knowledge, and to aid in evaluating your growth, this text includes a pretest and a posttest. Do not examine the posttest now. Turn to page 1 and take the pretest now. Correct it. At your next sitting, turn back to this section and continue reading. Now that you have completed the pretest, you are ready to continue with this program.

Events That Shaped English Spelling

The English language did not exist in the middle of the fifth century when three Germanic tribes—the Angles, the Saxons, and the Jutes—sailed across the North Sea and marched onto the shores of the British Isles. There they found the Celts, a peace-loving people who were overwhelmed by the invaders. The Saxons became the dominant tribe, and eventually, distinctions among the tribes disappeared. As the Anglo-Saxons settled down to life in their new homeland, their Germanic-based language began to change. These naturally occurring changes marked the beginning of the English language.

The early Anglo-Saxons were relatively illiterate (Bryson, 1990). Their meager use of the runic alphabet left few records, save for inscriptions on stones used in religious ceremonies. All this changed at the end of the sixth century when monks made their way into Great Britain, bringing with them the Christian religion, the Roman alphabet, and literacy (Burnley, 2000). As literacy spread across Great Britain, scribes used the Roman alphabet (with some modifications) to create a written record of regional dialects.

The imported Roman alphabet had only 26 letters to represent approximately 44 English sounds (phonemes). The problem of having too few letters could have been solved by inventing new letters or using diacritical marks to indicate pronunciation. Rather than adding letters or using diacritical marks, English made up for the shortfall by combining letters (*oi* and *oo*, for instance), forming letter patterns (the final silent *e* indicating that the preceding single vowel is long, as in *hope* and *late*), and using one letter to represent more than one sound (the *o* in *hot*, *doll*, and *for*, for example).

The spellings of many English words had not yet been established when the French-speaking Normans conquered Great Britain in 1066 and legions of French-speaking scribes poured into England. When asked to spell English words, a language they did not know, the scribes turned to letter combinations related to French spelling, introducing into the English spelling system combinations such as *qu, ou,* and *ch.* The Normans more or less ignored English, a second-class language spoken only by the working classes. The Norman French indifference created a fertile climate in which many different English dialects developed. Dialectical variation is significant because it affected English spelling when the speakers of one dialect adopted the spellings of another (Bryson, 1990).

Wholesale borrowing from classical languages also affected English spelling. In the 17th century, zealous scholars borrowed words from the Latin and Greek languages, perhaps in the belief that these two respected languages would raise the stature of English. Not only did the scholars borrow from Latin and Greek, but also they changed the spelling of some existing English words to suggest a Latin influence, even though the spellings were not particularly consistent with English pronunciation.

By the mid-17th century, the English language spelling system was more or less standardized. Unfortunately, this standardization was quickly followed by a shift in pronunciation (Burnley, 2000). For example, the initial *k* and the initial *g* when followed by *n* (*knight, gnat*), some instances of the initial *w* (*write*), and the *l* in some positions (*chalk*) were no longer pronounced. As a consequence, some contemporary spellings represent 17th century pronunciation (Bryson, 1990).

English spelling continues to change and evolve in the 21st century (Burnley, 2000). Pronunciation is changing, and foreign words (such as *peso*) are finding their way into English. Yet in spite of military intervention and social change, the use of only 26 letters to represent 44 sounds, and a plethora of foreign words entering the English language, phonics still gives readers insight into pronunciation. This brings us to a discussion of research on the teaching of phonics.

What the Research Says about Teaching Phonics

Written English is based on the alphabetic principle—the use of letters to represent sounds. **Phonics** is the relationship among the letters of the alphabet and the sounds in spoken words, as well as an approach for teaching these relationships. Phonics helps readers (1) identify and learn unfamiliar words (Beech, 2010; Ricketts, Bishop, Pimperton, & Nation, 2011), (2) develop a large reading vocabulary (Cunningham, Nathan, & Raher, 2011), (3) spell, and (4) read independently (National Reading Panel, 2000), regardless of children's social or economic background (Schwanenflugel, Hamilton, Kuhn, Wisenbaker, & Stahl, 2004).

Children who learn phonics early and well are better readers in the early grades than children who struggle with phonics (Cunningham et al., 2011). High and average beginning readers know more about phonics than below-average readers, irrespective of whether English is their first or second language (Brice & Brice, 2009). There is a strong, positive association among word recognition, fluency, and comprehension in the early elementary grades (Duke & Carlisle, 2011). Phonics instruction increases the achievement of struggling readers (Ehri, Satlow, & Gaskins, 2009; Macaruso & Rodman, 2011) and English language learners who have incomplete knowledge of letter and sound relationships (Torgesen, 2004; Vadasy & Sanders, 2010; Vadasy & Sanders, 2011). Phonics instruction also helps to prevent reading problems in children at risk of becoming struggling readers and to close the achievement gap between struggling and average readers (Duff, Hayiou-Thomas, & Hulme, 2012; Jeynes, 2008).

Some phonics knowledge appears to be necessary for beginning readers to take advantage of the context clues in sentences (Tunmer & Nicholson, 2011). Above-average first graders use context to support accurate reading throughout the school year, average readers develop this skill during the year, and less-skilled readers do not appear to develop this ability in first grade (López, Thompson, & Walker-Dalhouse, 2011). Researchers speculate that less-skilled beginning readers do not recognize enough words to make it possible for them to use context clues to support accurate reading. These readers pay excessive attention to word identification, which limits their ability to attend to clues in the reading context. Beginning readers who have some knowledge of phonics use this information to learn words. The more words beginning readers instantly recognize, the greater the likelihood that these readers will use context clues to support accurate reading. Effective teachers give beginning readers many opportunities to use phonics to learn words and encourage them to pay attention to meaning while identifying the new words in text (Cunningham et al., 2011; Tunmer & Nicholson, 2011).

An extensive body of research shows that **phonemic awareness**—the ability to separate words into sounds and blend sounds into words (explained later in Part One)—is necessary for using phonics and contributes to success in learning to read (Melby-Lervåg, Lyster, & Hulme, 2012). Children with high phonemic awareness are better at using phonics than their classmates with low phonemic awareness (Gilbert, Compton, & Kearns, 2011). The majority of struggling readers in the early elementary grades have low phonemic awareness (Duff et al., 2012; Fletcher et al., 2011).

Teaching phonics along with phonemic awareness is more effective than teaching either of these skills alone (Tunmer & Nicholson, 2011). There is a reciprocal relationship among phonemic awareness, phonics, and success in learning to read (Foy & Mann, 2006). An increase in one—phonemic awareness, phonics, or reading achievement—coincides with an increase in the others (Castles, Wilson, & Coltheart, 2011; Torppa et al., 2007). Greater awareness of the sounds in words—phonemic awareness—helps children make sense of the letter–sound relationships of phonics. Learning phonics, in turn, improves awareness of sounds and the ability to learn new words. A large and growing reading vocabulary is, of course, necessary for increasing reading achievement.

While phonics instruction is important, the same amount and intensity of instruction is not equally beneficial for all children. Children who begin school with good letter knowledge are likely to require less intense instruction than their classmates who have relatively limited knowledge (Juel & Minden-Cupp, 2004). Beginning readers with low reading achievement learn best in classrooms where the teacher directly teaches phonics, models how and when to use phonics, and gives children feedback on their use of phonics to identify words while reading (Connor, Morrison, & Katch, 2004; Connor, Morrison, & Underwood, 2007; Sonnenschein, Stapleton, & Benson, 2010).

Phonics instruction is most effective when it is (1) done early, intensely, directly, and systematically (National Reading Panel, 2000; Schwanenflugel et al., 2004); (2) combined with instruction in reading comprehension (Berninger et al., 2003;

Blachman et al., 2004); (3) taught throughout the day; and (4) integrated with on-going reading, writing, and spelling instruction (Rupley, Blair, & Nichols, 2009). In order for you, the teacher, to be effective in teaching phonics, you need to understand how written English uses the 26 letters of the alphabet to represent as many as 44 different speech sounds.

 # Phonics, Word Recognition, and Phonological Awareness in the Common Core State Standards for English Language Arts

The Common Core State Standards for English Language Arts describe expectations for reading literature, reading informational text and developing foundational skills, K–5 (National Governors Association Center for Best Practices & Council of Chief State School Officers, 2010). The Foundational Standards for Reading consist of four standards: 1. Print Concepts, 2. Phonological Awareness, 3. Phonics and Word Recognition, and 4. Fluency. Phonological Awareness—standard 2—and Phonics and Word Recognition—standard 3—apply to the content you will study in this book. There is one standard for Phonological Awareness and one for Phonics and Word Recognition. There are more explicit standards that apply to specific grades. These grade-specific standards describe learning expectations for different grades.

To assist you in your study, all of the standards for Phonological Awareness and select standards for Phonics and Word Recognition are reproduced and interleaved throughout this book. This will help you connect the material you are studying to the expectations for learning in each grade. Phonological awareness impacts achievement when children are learning to read. Consequently, these standards apply only to kindergarten and first grade. Phonics and Word Recognition standards apply from kindergarten through fifth grade. However, not all of the standards for Phonics and Word Recognition are relevant to the content you will be studying. For simplicity, only the applicable standards are reproduced. By and large, the Phonics and Word Recognition standards describe the sequence in which reading is taught, K–5. Children in kindergarten through second grade are expected to develop proficiency using phonics. The third grade standards do not mention letters and sounds. The third through fifth grade standards focus instead on reading long and complex words. Third graders are expected to decode multisyllable words and use prefixes and suffixes to read new words. Fourth and fifth graders should be able to use syllables, prefixes, suffixes, and other word parts to read multisyllable words in and out of context. A child who does not meet the standards one year and moves on to the next higher grade should meet the standards for the previous grade, as well as the standards for the current grade.

Consistent with best practices, effective teachers provide systematic, explicit instruction in the foundation skills (International Reading Association Common Core State Standards (CCSS) Committee, 2012). Instruction should be ongoing, integrated with the classroom language arts curriculum and in proportion to children's needs. The standards are not intended to list everything that makes up a successful classroom reading program. In fact, the Foundational Standards for Reading are silent on teaching methods and teaching materials. Teachers decide (a) what to teach beyond the standards and what is important for developing good readers, (b) what instructional methods and materials to use, and (c) how to assess learning. You will be a better decision maker when your decisions are based on an understanding of phonics, syllable and accent patterns, and the meaningful parts in words.

 How to Read This Book

This book is arranged in frames. Each frame requires a response. The left portion of the frame indicates the expected response. To avoid glancing at the left column, cut the mask from the back cover of this book and place it over the left-hand column to conceal the correct response. When you have studied and written your response to the first frame, move the mask down to reveal the answer. The frames are designed to guide you to the correct responses. You will find that there is a good deal of repetition. There are also many opportunities to review the information you are learning. The repetition and review will help you fix the important points in your mind. The pretest and posttest will help you gauge your learning. The answers are cross-referenced with the text to give you ready access to material that is addressed by questions.

   Now cover the left-hand column below. Study the first frame. Make the required response. Then move the mask down to reveal the answer to the frame. Compare the two so that your learning is immediately reinforced. If your answer is correct, study the second frame, and fill in the blank. If you are incorrect, review; then write the correct answer.

 Basic Elements of Phonics

spoken	**1.** The language of any people is the **sound** system by which the individuals communicate with one another. The written language is merely a system of **symbols,** a code, used to represent the _____ language. (written, spoken)
code (or symbols)	**2.** Therefore, one of the basic steps in the reading process is **decoding:** translating the _____ into the sounds of the spoken language.
symbols (or code)	**3.** We study phonics to learn the code so that we can translate the written _____ into the spoken sounds. But to our regret, the code is not perfect; part of our study involves its inconsistencies. We shall begin our study by examining the basic elements of the code, the **phoneme** and the **grapheme.**
phoneme	**phoneme** **grapheme** **4.** *Phon* (tele<u>phon</u>e, <u>phon</u>ograph, etc.) refers to voice or sound. The suffix *eme* denotes a unit of language structure. Therefore, one speech sound is called a _____ (*phon + eme*).

sound	**5.** These word pairs illustrate the phoneme. As you pronounce each pair, notice the sound that makes the top word different from the one beneath it. p<u>i</u>n pin pin pin <u>t</u>in p<u>e</u>n pi<u>t</u> <u>ch</u>in **A phoneme is the smallest unit of _____ that distinguishes one word from another.**
t	**6.** To attain a better understanding of a phoneme, let us examine these words more closely. For example, how does *pin* differ from *tin?* The sounds **represented** by the *p* and the _____ are the smallest units of sound that distinguish *pin* from *tin.*
sound i, e	**7.** Compare the phonemes represented by the underlined letters in the set of words below. p<u>i</u>n p<u>e</u>n Remember that the phoneme is a _____ , so say the words aloud. The sounds that are represented by the _____ and the _____ are the smallest units that distinguish *pin* from *pen.*
n, t	**8.** Pronounce the words below. pi<u>n</u> pi<u>t</u> The sounds that are represented by the _____ and the _____ are the smallest units that distinguish *pin* from *pit.*
/r/, /p/	**9.** We can hear sounds, but we cannot write sounds. For example, we cannot write the sound of *l.* We can say, "the sound represented by *l*" or "the phoneme recorded by *l.*" There is also a symbol, / /, which indicates that we are referring to the phoneme of the specific letter or letters enclosed with slashes: /l/. How will we write symbolically the phoneme we associate with the letter *r?* _____ The phoneme represented by *p?* _____
grapheme	**10.** Sounds cannot be written! Letters do not speak! We use a letter or letters to **represent** a phoneme. *Graph* means "drawn, written, recorded." The _____ (*graph* + *eme*) is the written representation of the phoneme. It is the unit in the written code.
p, i, n p, i, n	**11.** When you say the word *pin,* you hear three phonemes. We represent these three phonemes with the graphemes _____ , _____ , and _____ . Put another way, the three letters in *pin* are _____ , _____ , and _____ . **The grapheme is the written representation of the phoneme. As the phoneme is the unit in the sound system, the grapheme is the unit in the written code.**

phonemes one	**12.** Reread frame 5. We used word pairs to illustrate the definition of a phoneme. When you said the word *chin,* you heard three _____. *Ch* represents **one** unit of sound; you cannot divide it. Since the grapheme is the written representation of the phoneme, *ch* is _____ grapheme(s). <div align="right">(How many?)</div>
ch, i, n ch	**13.** We represent the three phonemes in *chin* with the graphemes _____ , _____ , and _____ . The sounds represented by the *p* and the _____ are the smallest units of sound that distinguish *pin* from *chin.*

Box 1.1

Green Glass or Green Grass?

Two English Phonemes

Use your knowledge of the phonemes in the English language to answer the three questions below. Read each question aloud, and write the answer on the line.

1. The second phoneme in *glass* and the second phoneme in *grass* are _____.
(the same, different)

2. The first phoneme in *late* is _____ the first phoneme in *rate.*
(the same as, different from)

3. *Fire* and *file* are _____ English words.
(the same, different)

The /r/ and /l/ phonemes (here presented between two slashes) are distinctly different in the English language. Therefore, you hear two separate phonemes and, by extension, two different words when you pronounce *glass* and *grass.* These phonemes, which are entirely distinct to you, a fluent speaker of the English language, are not so distinct and so simple to differentiate for native speakers of the Japanese language.

The Japanese language does not have an equivalent phoneme for the English /r/. Because the Japanese *r* is a combination of the English /r/ and /l/, speakers of Japanese may perceive the /l/ and the /r/ as variations of the same phoneme. Not only do speakers of the Japanese language have difficulty in distinguishing the English language /r/ from the /l/, but also they may well confuse these two phonemes when pronouncing English words, perhaps saying "grass" when the intended word is "glass."

We listen for and perceive those phonemic differences and similarities that are particular to the language that we speak. Not all languages share exactly the same phonemes, however. Children bring to your classroom—and to the speaking, reading, and writing of the English language—an awareness of the phonemes in their home, or native, languages. You can, therefore, anticipate that some children who speak Japanese as their first language may occasionally confuse the /r/ and /l/ when pronouncing, reading, and spelling English words. When children who are English language learners have opportunities to hear, speak, read, and write English in your classroom, they develop greater sensitivity to the English language sound structure and, in so doing, create mental categories for those English phonemes that differ from the phonemes in their native languages.

phoneme ch	**14.** A **grapheme** is the written symbol of the _____. It may be composed of one or more letters. We represent the first phoneme in the word *chart* with the grapheme _____.
grapheme phoneme graphemes k, c, q	**15.** A **phoneme** is a speech sound. A _____ is composed of the symbols we use to picture the sound on paper. Say the words <u>keep</u>, <u>come</u>, and <u>quit</u>. In each one, you will hear the _____ that we commonly associate with the underlined grapheme. Three different _____ are used to represent this phoneme. They are _____ , _____ , and _____ .
   three three w a, sh sh	**16.** The words **grapheme** and **letter** are not synonymous. A grapheme never consists of less than a letter, but it may consist of more than one letter. The grapheme represents the phoneme. Examine the word *wash: w a sh.* Say it aloud. *Wash* consists of _____ (How many?) phonemes. Therefore, it consists of _____ graphemes—one grapheme to represent each phoneme. The graphemes are _____ , _____ , and _____ . What letters comprise the final grapheme of the word *wash*? _____

phonemes (or speech sounds)
	17. Although there are hundreds of different speech sounds (consider the variations due to dialect, individual speech patterns, change in stress, etc.), for all practical purposes, in the task of teaching reading,
	
	     we can consider the American-English language to contain
	
	     44 separate _____ .

 phoneme, grapheme	**18.** If the code were consistent (that is, if we had one grapheme for each _____ and one phoneme for each _____), the task of teaching children to read would be much simpler than it is now.
26 phonemes	**19.** The truth is that we have only _____ letters in our alphabet, only 26 symbols to represent 44 _____ .
 phonemes	**20.** We add symbols to our system by using combinations of letters (such as *ch*) to represent the _____ not represented by the 26 letters of the alphabet.
 phoneme, a	**21.** We also add symbols by using one letter to represent more than one _____ . The letter _____ , for example, represents three different phonemes in the words *ate, pan,* and *all.*

k, g, h	**22.** Another of the many complications is the use of symbols that do not represent any sound: *Knight* has three letters that do not represent sounds: _____ , _____ , and _____.
gh, ph phoneme	**23.** Besides lacking a one-to-one correspondence between the letters of the alphabet and the phonemes needed, the spelling of the English language is further complicated by its many inconsistencies. One of the greatest of these is the use of different symbols to represent the same phoneme. For example, the sound we associate with *f* is represented by *f* in *fine,* by _____ in *cough,* and by _____ in *elephant.* This is an example of three graphemes representing one _____.
grapheme (or letter)	**24.** Sometimes when a grapheme represents more than one phoneme, there are clues within the word to indicate which sound the _____ represents. A teacher of reading should be able to recognize these clues.
phoneme phonemes, graphemes	**25.** Our alphabet represents speech at the level of the _____. Therefore, learning the code requires that readers separate (segment) spoken words into _____ and associate _____ with the phonemes.

 # Phonological Awareness and Phonemic Awareness

Common Core State Standards for English Language Arts
Reading Standards: Foundational Skills—Phonological Awareness

Standard 2   *Demonstrate understanding of spoken words, syllables, and sounds (phonemes).*

KINDERGARTEN
a. Recognize and produce rhyming words.
b. Count, pronounce, blend, and segment syllables in spoken words.
c. Blend and segment onsets and rimes of single-syllable spoken words.
d. Isolate and pronounce the initial, medial vowel, and final sounds (phonemes) in three-phoneme (consonant–vowel–consonant, or CVC) words. (This does not include CVCs ending with /l/, /r/, or /x/.)
e. Add or substitute individual sounds (phonemes) in simple, one-syllable words to make new words.

FIRST GRADE
a. Distinguish long from short vowel sounds in spoken single-syllable words.
b. Orally produce single-syllable words by blending sounds (phonemes), including consonant blends.
c. Isolate and pronounce initial, medial vowel, and final sounds (phonemes) in spoken single-syllable words.
d. Segment spoken single-syllable words into their complete sequence of individual sounds (phonemes).

rhyme	**1. Phonological awareness** is the understanding that spoken language consists of words, syllables, rhymes, and phonemes, and ability to act on this understanding. For example, children who have developed phonological awareness know that the words *man, pan,* and *van* _____.
phonemes (or sounds) phonemes	**2. Phonemic awareness** is a much narrower term than word awareness. Phonemic awareness refers *only* to the understanding that spoken words are composed of _____ and the understanding that individual phonemes, when blended together, form meaningful words. Phonemic awareness includes the ability to (a) separate words into phonemes and (b) blend _____ together to pronounce words.
segmenting	**3.** Let us begin by defining two terms that pertain to phonemic awareness: segmenting and blending. **Segmenting** is separating a large unit of spoken language into smaller units. Separating /*pig*/ into /*p*/, /*i*/, and /*g*/ is an example of _____. (segmenting, blending)
blending	**4. Blending** is combining smaller units of language together to pronounce a larger unit. Combining /*f*/ with /*ell*/ to pronounce /*fell*/ or combining /*p*/ + /*i*/ + /*g*/ to pronounce /*pig*/ illustrates _____. (segmenting, blending)
words	**5.** Children who have developed **word awareness** can separate a sentence into words. The child who separates /*Throw the ball*/ into /*throw*/, /*the*/, and /*ball*/ is aware of the _____ in spoken language.
syllable	**6.** The ability to separate words into syllables and blend syllables into words demonstrates **syllable awareness**. Counting the syllables in words or tapping for each syllable is an indication the child has developed _____ awareness. (Standard 2b, kindergarten)
rhyme phonological awareness	**7.** Children who have developed **rhyme awareness** can recognize or think of rhyming words. Rhyme is the vowel and ending consonant sounds common to several words, as /*sat*/, /*mat*/, and /*hat*/. The child who says that /*man*/, /*fan*/, and /*ran*/ "belong together," while /*bat*/ does not belong, demonstrates the ability to recognize words that _____. (Standard 2a, kindergarten) Rhymes consist of more than one sound. Therefore, rhyme awareness is a _____ skill. (phonological awareness, phonemic awareness)

blend	**8. Beginning sound awareness** often develops at the same time as or shortly after rhyme awareness. Children who are aware of beginning sounds understand that /s/ is the beginning sound in /sat/. Children who apply their awareness of beginning sounds and rhyming sounds to pronounce /s/ and /at/ and then to pronounce /sat/ demonstrate the ability to _____ (segment, blend) beginning and rhyming sounds. (Standard 2c, kindergarten)

Box 1.2

Spanish Phonemes

Different languages use different phonemes and different graphemes. Let us consider four Spanish phonemes that do not have exact English language equivalents and the graphemes that represent them.

1. The Spanish *ñ* is pronounced like the *ny* in the English word *canyon* and is represented by the grapheme *ñ*. We hear this phoneme in the Spanish loan words *El Niño* and *La Niña*.

2. The Spanish trilled *r* is pronounced by rolling the *r* on the upper palate. A single *r* is the grapheme that indicates a slightly trilled pronunciation; a double *rr* represents a strongly trilled pronunciation. The Spanish word for *dog, perro,* is pronounced with a strongly trilled *rr.*

3. In Latin America, the *ll* is the grapheme that represents the sound of the *y* in *yellow*. In Spain, the *ll* is pronounced like the *lli* in *million*. *Tortilla,* a cornmeal flat bread used in tacos and other dishes, is an example of a Spanish loan word in which the *ll* is pronounced like the *y* in *yellow* or the *lli* in *million*.

4. The Spanish *j* is pronounced like the English /h/ in *happy,* only farther back in the throat and with more emphasis. *Javelina,* the wild pig of the southwestern United States, is an example of a Spanish loan word in which the letter *j* represents /h/.

The native speaker of English who wishes to speak the Spanish language must learn to pronounce the four Spanish phonemes that are not among the 44 American-English phonemes. English language learners whose first language does not include some English sounds may have a bit more difficulty developing phonemic awareness (Brice & Brice, 2009). In this situation, begin to develop phonemic awareness with the sounds that are common to English and the language spoken in children's homes. Bear in mind that English language learners and English-only children develop phonemic awareness in the same way. Consequently, you will not need special material to develop the phonemic awareness of the English language learners in your classroom. However, you may want to spend extra time to develop children's ability to speak English. English language learners benefit from many and varied opportunities to speak and listen to English, to participate in phonemic awareness and other classroom teaching activities, to participate in English conversations, and to hear English books read aloud.

segment blend	**9.** Reread frame 2. Phonemic awareness requires attention to the individual phonemes or sounds in words. Phonemic awareness has two components: (1) the ability to _____ spoken words into individual phonemes and (2) the ability to _____ individual phonemes into words.
hear see	**10.** Phonemic awareness makes it possible for children to realize that the sounds they _____ in spoken words are represented by the letters (hear, see) they _____ in written words. (hear, see)
three four segment (or separate)	**11.** Pronounce the word *tip.* /*Tip*/ is composed of _____ phonemes. (How many?) Now say *trip.* /*Trip*/ is composed of _____ phonemes. (How many?) When you count the phonemes in a word, you _____ the word into individual sounds.
/d/, /c/ /o/	**12.** Say the last sound in /*red*/: _____. Say the first sound in /*cat*/: _____. What sound do you hear in the middle of /*rock*/? _____ You have demonstrated the ability to isolate the individual phonemes in words. (Standard 2d, kindergarten and Standard 2c, first grade)
/p/ /i/ /n/, segment	**13.** Pronounce *pin* aloud. /*Pin*/ begins with the phoneme _____. The phoneme in the middle of /*pin*/ is _____. /*Pin*/ ends with the phoneme _____. You have demonstrated the ability to _____ (segment, blend) the word /*pin*/ into phonemes. (Standard 2d, first grade)
	14. We will now consider three other activities that the teacher of reading may use to help beginning readers develop and demonstrate phonemic awareness: phoneme addition, phoneme deletion, and phoneme substitution. In **phoneme addition,** children attach one or more phonemes to a word or word part. Combine the phonemes below to pronounce a word. Write the new word on the line beside each activity.
/man/	**A.** Add /m/ to /an/. The new word is _____. **B.** Start with the word /*bike*/. Add /s/ to the end. What is the new word?
/bikes/ /sit/	_____ **C.** What word do we make when we add /s/ to /it/? _____ (Standard 2e, kindergarten)

	15. Phoneme deletion is removing one or more phonemes from a word. Complete the phoneme deletion activities below. Write the new word on the line beside each activity.
/at/	**A.** Say /fat/. Now say it again without the /f/. The new word is _____.
/top/	**B.** What is left when we take the /s/ from /stop/? _____
	C. Say /seat/. Now say it again without the /s/. What is the new word?
/eat/	_____

16. In **phoneme substitution,** children remove one or more phonemes from a word and replace them with one or more different phonemes. Complete the phoneme substitution activities below. Write the new word on the line beside each activity. Be sure to use slashes to indicate that we are referring to sounds.

A. Say /can/. Say it again, but this time say /m/ instead of /c/. The new word is

/man/   _____.

/pin/   **B.** Say /pan/. Change /a/ to /i/. What is the new word? _____

/fat/   **C.** Begin with /fan/. Change /n/ to /t/. What is the new word? _____
(Standard 2e, kindergarten)

17. We have studied phonological awareness, and phonemic awareness, and activities the teacher of reading may use to help beginning readers develop or demonstrate awareness. The phonemic awareness activities we have demonstrated require children to intentionally count phonemes; note the positions of phonemes in words; fully segment words by pronouncing their phonemes one by one; and add, delete, and substitute phonemes. Write the name of the activity on the line beside the description. Read all the descriptions before answering!

deletion

A. Removing the /s/ from /sat/ to form the new word /at/ is an example of

phoneme _____.

noting the positions of phonemes in words

B. Pronouncing the middle phoneme in a three-phoneme word is an example

of _____. (Standard 2d, kindergarten and Standard 2c, first grade)

substitution

C. Exchanging /h/ for /f/ in /fat/ to pronounce the new word /hat/ is an

example of phoneme _____. (Standard 2e, kindergarten)

D. Telling how many phonemes are in a spoken word is an example of

counting   _____ phonemes.

E. Adding /b/ to /at/ to pronounce the new word /bat/ is an example of

addition   phoneme _____. (Standard 2e, kindergarten)

segmenting (or separating)

F. Saying each phoneme in /mat/ one by one (/m/ /a/ /t/) is an example of

fully _____ a spoken word into phonemes. (Standard 2d, first grade)

blend	**18.** We will now turn our attention to the second aspect of phonemic awareness: the ability to _____ individual phonemes into meaningful spoken words.
/l/ /a/ /f/ no	**19.** Use your knowledge of phonics to say the phoneme represented by each grapheme in the word *laf*. The grapheme *l* represents the phoneme _____. The grapheme *a* represents the phoneme _____. The grapheme *f* represents the phoneme _____. You have now pronounced each phoneme in isolation. Have you pronounced a word? _____
blend	**20.** To identify the spoken word that the graphemes in frame represent, you must associate a phoneme with each grapheme, and then you must _____ the phonemes together. (segment, blend)
laugh *quit* decoding (or sounding out words)	**21.** Now blend the phonemes together. Say the phonemes aloud as you blend. The phonemes /l/ + /a/ + /f/ form a word you recognize in speech. Write the word the way that you would normally spell it. _____ Now blend /k/ + /w/ + /i/ + /t/. What word did you pronounce? _____ Blending is an essential aspect of _____. (Standard 2b, first grade)
phonemic awareness, segment blend	**22.** Children who are successful using phonics to recognize new words have developed _____. These children _____ words into phonemes (sounds) and _____ phonemes (sounds) together to pronounce words.

Review 1

Close your eyes and summarize the information contained in Part One. On another piece of paper, write the answers to this review without looking back. Complete the entire review before you check the answers.

1. The smallest unit of sound that distinguishes one word from another is called

    a _____.

2. For all practical purposes, the American-English language contains

    _____ phonemes.
    (How many?)

3. Phonemic awareness consists of the ability to (1) _____ words into their individual phonemes and (2) _____ individual phonemes together to form meaningful spoken words.

4. Separating the word /*sat*/ into its individual phonemes (/*s*/, /*a*/, and /*t*/) is an example of _____.

5. Combining the three phonemes /*s*/ + /*a*/ + /*t*/ to pronounce the word /*sat*/ is an example of _____.

6. A _____ is the written representation of a phoneme.

7. Children who tell their teacher that /*man*/, /*can*/, and /*tan*/ "belong together," while /*fin*/ does not belong, demonstrate _____ awareness.

8. Complete these sentences:

    a. _____ , in combination with phonics, makes it possible for children to read and spell new words.

    b. Children who have developed phonemic awareness realize that the _____ they hear in spoken words are represented by the _____ they see in written words.

    c. We can conclude that _____ is essential for using _____ to read and spell new words.

Turn to the Answers to the Reviews section, page 230, and check your answers. You should have answered all the questions correctly. If you did not succeed, analyze your study procedure. Is your mind active? Are you writing all the answers? Do you complete a frame before you move the mask down? Did you summarize your learning before you started the review? Study the appropriate parts of Part One again. Congratulations to those who had a perfect score! Your learning should be very profitable.

References

Beech, J. R. (2010). Young readers' strategic approaches to reading unfamiliar words in text. *Reading & Writing Quarterly: Overcoming Learning Difficulties, 26*(3), 264–284.

Berninger, V. W., Vermeulen, K., Abbott, R. D., McCutchen, D., Cotton, S., Cude, J., Sharon, T. (2003). Comparison of three approaches to supplementary reading instruction for low-achieving second-grade readers. *Language, Speech, and Hearing Services in Schools, 34*, 101–116.

Blachman, B. A., Schatschneider, C., Fletcher, J. M., Francis, D. J., Clonan, S. M., Shaywitz, B. A., & Shaywitz, S. E. (2004). Effects of intensive reading remediation for second and third graders and a 1-year follow-up study. *Journal of Educational Psychology, 96*, 444–461.

Brice, R. G., & Brice, A. E. (2009). Investigation of phonemic awareness and phonics skills of Spanish-English bilingual and English-speaking kindergarten students. *Communication Disorders Quarterly, 30*(4), 208–225.

Bryson, B. (1990). *Mother tongue: English and how it got that way.* New York, NY: William Morrow.

Burnley, D. (2000). *The history of the English language: A source book* (2nd ed.). Edinburg Gate, England: Pearson.

Castles, A., Wilson, K., & Coltheart, M. (2011). Early orthographic influences on phonemic awareness tasks: Evidence from a preschool training study. *Journal of Experimental Child Psychology, 108*(1), 203–210.

Connor, C. M., Morrison, F. J., & Katch, L. E. (2004). Beyond the reading wars: Exploring the effect of child-instruction interactions on growth in early reading. *Scientific Studies of Reading, 8*(4), 305–336.

Connor, C. M., Morrison, F. J., & Underwood, P. S. (2007). A second chance in second grade: The independent and cumulative impact of first- and second-grade reading instruction on students' letter-word reading skill growth. *Scientific Studies in Reading, 11*(3), 199–233.

Cunningham, A. E., Nathan, R. G., & Raher, K. S. (2011). Orthographic processing in models of word recognition. In M. L. Kamil, P. D. Pearson, E. B. Moje, & P. P. Afflerback (Eds.), *Handbook of Reading Research* (Vol. 4, pp. 259–285). New York, NY: Routledge.

Duff, F. J., Hayiou-Thomas, M. E., & Hulme, C. (2012). Evaluating the effectiveness of a phonologically based reading intervention for struggling readers with varying language profiles. *Reading and Writing, 25*(3), 621–640.

Duke, N. K., & Carlisle, J. (2011). The development of comprehension. In M. L. Kamil, P. D. Pearson, E. B. Moje, & P. P. Afflerback (Eds.), *Handbook of Reading Research* (Vol. 4, pp. 199–228). New York, NY: Routledge.

Ehri, L. C., Satlow, E., & Gaskins, I. (2009). Grapho-phonemic enrichment strengthens keyword analogy instruction for struggling readers. *Reading & Writing Quarterly: Overcoming Learning Disabilities, 25*(2–3), 162–191.

Fletcher, J. M., Stuebing, K. K., Barth, A. E., Denton, C. A., Cirino, P. T., Francis, D. J., & Vaughn, S. (2011). Cognitive correlates of inadequate response to reading intervention. *School Psychology Review, 40*(1), 3–22.

Foy, J. G., & Mann, V. (2006). Changes in letter sound knowledge are associated with development of phonological awareness in pre-schoolchildren. *Journal of Research in Reading, 29*(2), 143–161.

Gilbert, J. K., Compton, D. L., & Kearns, D. M. (2011). Word and person effects on decoding accuracy: A new look at an old question. *Journal of Educational Psychology, 103*(2), 489–507.

International Reading Association Common Core State Standards (CCSS) Committee (2012). Literacy implementation guidance for the ELA Common Core State Standards [White Paper]. Retrieved from http://www.reading.org/Libraries/association-documents/ira_ccss_guidelines.pdf

Jeynes, W. H. (2008). A meta-analysis of the relationship between phonics instruction and minority elementary school student academic achievement. *Education and Urban Society, 40*(2), 151–166.

Juel, C., & Minden-Cupp, C. (2004). Learning to read words: Linguistic units and instructional strategies. In R. B. Ruddell & N. J. Unrau (Eds.), *Theoretical models and processes of reading* (5th ed., pp. 313–364). Newark, DE: International Reading Association.

López, F. A., Thompson, S. S., & Walker-Dalhouse, D. (2011). Examining the trajectory of differentially skilled first graders' reading fluency of words in isolation and in context. *Reading & Writing Quarterly: Overcoming Learning Difficulties, 27*(4), 281–305.

Macaruso, P., & Rodman, A. (2011). Efficacy of computer-assisted instruction for the development of early literacy skills in young children. *Reading Psychology, 32*(2), 172–196.

Melby-Lervåg, M., Lyster, S. A. H., & Hulme, C. (2012). Phonological skills and their role in learning to read: A meta-analytic review. *Psychological Bulletin, 138*(2), 322–352.

National Governors Association Center for Best Practices & Council of Chief State School Officers. (2010). *Common Core State Standards for English Language Arts & History/Social Studies, Science, and Technical Subjects: Reading Standards: Foundational Skills—Phonological Awareness, Phonics and Word Recognition.* Washington, DC: Authors. Retrieved May 15, 2012, from http://www.corestandards.org/assets/CCSSI_ELA%20Standards.pdf

National Reading Panel. (2000). *Report of the National Reading Panel. Teaching children to read: An evidence-based assessment of the scientific research literature on reading and its implications for reading instruction: Reports of the subgroups* (NIH Publication No. 00-4754). Washington, DC: U.S. Government Printing Office.

Ricketts, J., Bishop, D. V. M., Pimperton, H., & Nation, K. (2011). The role of self-teaching in learning orthographic and semantic aspects of new words. *Scientific Studies of Reading, 15*(1), 47–70.

Rupley, W. H., Blair, T. R., & Nichols, W. D. (2009). Effective reading instruction for struggling readers: The role of direct/explicit teaching. *Reading & Writing Quarterly: Overcoming Learning Difficulties, 25*(2–3), 125–138.

Schwanenflugel, P. J., Hamilton, A. M., Kuhn, M. R., Wisenbaker, J. M., & Stahl, S. A. (2004). Becoming a fluent reader: Reading skill and prosodic features in the oral reading of young readers. *Journal of Educational Psychology, 96*, 119–129.

Sonnenschein, S., Stapleton, L. M., & Benson, A. (2010). The relation between the type and amount of instruction and growth in children's reading competencies. *American Educational Research Journal, 47*(2), 358–389.

Torgesen, J. K. (2004). Lessons learned from research on interventions for students who have difficulty learning to read. In P. McCardle & V. Chhabra (Eds.), *The voice of evidence in reading research* (pp. 355–382). Baltimore, MD: Paul H. Brookes.

Torppa, M., Poikkeus, A. M., Laakso, M. L., Tolvanen, A., Leskinen, E., Leppanen Paavo, H. T., Luytinen, H. (2007). Modeling the early paths of phonological awareness and factors supporting its development in children with and without familial risk of dyslexia. *Scientific Studies of Reading, 11*(2), 73–103.

Tunmer, W. E., & Nicholson, T. (2011). The development and teaching of word recognition skill. In M. L. Kamil, P. D. Pearson, E. B. Moje, & P. P. Afflerback (Eds.), *Handbook of Reading Research* (Vol. 4, pp. 405–431). New York, NY: Routledge.

Vadasy, P. F., & Sanders, E. A. (2010). Efficacy of supplemental phonics-based instruction for low-skilled kindergartners in the context of language minority status and classroom phonics instruction. *Journal of Educational Psychology, 102*(4), 786–803.

Vadasy, P. F., & Sanders, E. A. (2011). Efficacy of supplemental phonics-based instruction for low-skilled first graders: How language minority status and pretest characteristics moderate treatment response. *Scientific Studies of Reading, 15*(6), 471–497.

Part Two

Single-Letter Consonants

Common Core State Standards for English Language Arts
Reading Standards: Foundational Skills—Phonics and Word Recognition

Standard 3 *Know and apply grade-level phonics and word analysis skills in decoding words.*

KINDERGARTEN

a. Demonstrate basic knowledge of one-to-one letter–sound correspondences by producing the primary or many of the most frequent sounds for each consonant.

d. Distinguish between similarly spelled words by identifying the sound of the letters that differ.

FIRST GRADE

b. Decode regularly spelled one-syllable words.

Meeting kindergarten standard 3a calls for phonemic awareness. All things being equal, we would expect kindergarten children who meet Phonological Awareness standard 2d (page 19) to also meet the standard 3a. From the perspective of teaching phonics, we would consider kindergarten standard 3d to apply when words differ in consonant letter–sounds, such as *fan* (/fan/) and *man* (/man/). In this example, children would tell their teacher that *fan* and *man* differ because these words begin with different letters and the letters represent different sounds. That is, the *f* represents /f/ and the *m* stands for /m/. The first grade standard 3b would apply in situations where children use their knowledge of single-letter consonants along with vowel letter–sounds to decode short, regularly spelled words.

Place the mask over the left-hand column. As you work through these sections, it will be necessary for you to make sounds out loud. Be sure that you are seated where this is possible. Now work out the first frame, move the mask down to check your response, and proceed as you did in Part One. Keep an active mind! You may need to study the entire frame before you make your response.

Introduction

consonants	**1.** The 26 letters of the alphabet can be divided into two major categories: vowels and _____.
consonants	**2.** There is, however, a degree of overlap between these categories. Certain letters—notably, the *w* and *y*—sometimes function as vowels and at other times function as _____.
consonants, 21	**3.** Recognizing the fact that we are oversimplifying the situation, we shall, in this part of the program, consider all letters except *a, e, i, o,* and *u* to be _____. There are then _____ consonant letters. (How many?)
is not	**4.** We have noted previously that in the American-English language, there _____ a consistent one-to-one correspondence between letter and (is, is not) phoneme. Let us now see how this applies to consonants.
21, 25 is not	**5.** There are (for our purposes in the teaching of reading) 44 phonemes, 25 of these being consonant phonemes. There are _____ consonant letters and _____ consonant (How many?) (How many?) phonemes. There _____ one letter for each phoneme. (is, is not)
grapheme	**6.** There are more phonemes than letters. We gain seven additional phonemes through the use of the two-letter _____ (grapheme, phoneme)
digraph	**7.** We call these two-letter combinations digraphs. Note the spelling—*di* for two; *graph* referring to writing. The two-letter combination *ch,* as in *chair,* is called a _____.
not	**8.** Pronounce the word *chair* as though <u>each</u> consonant were sounded. You said either "s-hair" or "k-hair." Now pronounce *chair* as it should be pronounced. Note that you hear neither the sound represented by the *c* nor the sound represented by the *h.* The combination *ch* represents a phoneme _____ represented by (already, not) a single consonant letter. It functions like another letter of the alphabet.

c *h*	**9.** A digraph is a two-letter combination that represents a single speech sound. The digraph *ch* does not represent the sound of the _____ and the _____ with which it is spelled.
is not	**10.** The phonemes of our language are very familiar to us, but to prepare ourselves to teach others to read, it is necessary to identify *each* of the 44 phonemes. Since there _____ a one-to-one correspondence between sound and (is, is not) letter, it will be helpful to designate a key symbol for *each* phoneme. In this way, we will know the sound to which we are referring no matter how it is represented in the word (that is, no matter how it is spelled).
yes	**11.** When possible, the key symbol will be the same as the letter we ordinarily associate with the sound. For example, *b* will serve as the key symbol for the sound we hear at the beginning of the word *boat*. Would you expect *d* to serve as the key symbol for the sound heard at the beginning of the word *dog*? _____
44 25 phonemes	**12.** There are 44 phonemes; 25 of these are consonant phonemes. We will, therefore, identify _____ key symbols altogether, of which (How many?) _____ will be consonants. (How many?) **There will be one key symbol for each phoneme.** **Each phoneme will have one key symbol.** There will be a one-to-one correspondence between key symbols and _____.
symbol letter *boat*	**13.** Most of the consonants are reliable with respect to sound. Therefore, in most cases, the key _____ that designates a certain phoneme heard in a word will be the same as the consonant _____ seen in that word. For example, *b* will serve as the key symbol for the initial sound we hear in the word _____. (boat, comb)
no (The final *b* represents no phoneme: It is a silent letter.)	**14.** Will *b* serve as the key symbol for the final sound we hear in the word *comb*? _____

four, four	**15.** The word *graph* has _____ phonemes and therefore _____ (How many?) (How many?)
g, r, a, ph	graphemes. They are _____, _____, _____, and _____. So that we have a clue to its pronunciation, the logical key symbol to assign to the final
f	phoneme in *graph* is the letter _____.
ph f	**16.** Pronounce *photo*. The initial grapheme is _____. The key symbol to represent this sound is _____.
	17. We can divide the 25 consonant phonemes into two major groups: (1) 18 consonant phonemes identified by key symbols composed of single letters and
key symbols digraphs	(2) 7 consonant phonemes identified by _____ composed of two-letter combinations called _____.

Review 2

Summarize your learning. What new words have you learned thus far? Define them.

1. Is there a one-to-one correspondence between the consonant letters and the consonant phonemes? _____

2. We shall learn to identify a key symbol for each of the consonant _____ of the American-English language.
(letters, phonemes)

3. The *m* is a very dependable letter; it is the key symbol for the initial sound heard in *man*. We would expect the key symbol representing the sound heard at the end of the word *jam* to be _____.

4. Dictionaries also use _____ as the key symbol to represent the sound heard at the beginning of the word *man*.

5. Most of the key symbols will be single letters; however, seven of the consonant symbols will be composed of _____ letters called _____.

6. We can divide the consonant phonemes into two groups according to whether the key symbol representing the phoneme is composed of one or two _____.

7. *Ch,* a _____, represents how many phonemes? _____

See the Answers to the Reviews section for the answers to Review 2, page 230.

Key Symbols and Key Words for Single-Letter Consonants

a̶	**1.** Place the mask firmly over the responses at the left. Do not move it until the entire frame is completed. _____
b	_____
c̶	**A.** Write the 26 letters of the alphabet, in order, in the column at the right. _____
d	
e̶	**B.** Draw a diagonal line through each of the five vowel letters. _____
f	
g	**C.** Three of the 21 consonant letters do not represent distinctive sounds. Draw a horizontal line through each of the three unnecessary letters. _____
h	
i̶	_____
j	A puzzle? Clue: Say the words below, listening for the sounds that are represented by the underlined consonant letters. _____
k	_____
l	*city* and *cold*
m	*antique* and *quiet* _____
n	*exam* and *reflex* _____
o̶	**As single letters, c, q, and x do not represent distinctive phonemes.**
p̄	When these words are spelled so that each consonant letter represents a distinctive phoneme, the words look like this: _____
q̶	_____
r	*sity* and *kold* _____
s	*antikue* and *kuiet*
18 t	*egzam* and *refleks* _____
u̶	Eliminating the three unnecessary letters leaves us with _____
18 v	_____ single consonant letters that have distinctive sounds. In other words, our alphabet supplies us with _____
phonemes w	_____ single-letter graphemes to represent 18 of _____
x̶	the 25 consonant _____ of our language. _____
y	_____
z	_____

phonemes	b	boat
three	d	dog
	f	fish
	g	goat
	h	hat
	j	jeep
	k	kite
	l	lion
	m	moon
	n	nut
	p	pig
	r	ring
	s	sun
	t	table
	v	van
	w	wagon
	y	yo-yo
	z	zipper

2. As you repeat the letters of the alphabet, write the 18 consonant letters (the **key symbols**) that represent 18 distinctive _____.

You will omit the _____ consonant letters that do not represent distinctive phonemes.

How can we know exactly which phoneme has been assigned to each of the key symbols? We use a key word that has that phoneme as its initial sound. The selected key words follow, but they are out of order. Write each key word next to its key symbol.

Key Words

kite	pig	van	boat	goat	dog
ring	moon	wagon	zipper	jeep	yo-yo
sun	lion	table	fish	nut	hat

Key Symbols	Key Words
_____	_____
_____	_____
_____	_____
_____	_____
_____	_____
_____	_____
_____	_____
_____	_____
_____	_____
_____	_____
_____	_____
_____	_____
_____	_____
_____	_____
_____	_____
_____	_____
_____	_____
_____	_____

3. Which key symbol and key word should be used to identify the initial phoneme (or sound) heard in each of these words? Refer to frame 2 for the key words.

m	moon	g	goat
y	yo-yo	h	hat
s	sun	r	ring

mats _____ _____   got _____ _____

yellow _____ _____   have _____ _____

city _____ _____   ride _____ _____

4. Which key symbol and key word should be used to identify the initial sound heard in each of the following words? Use frame 2 for the key words.

j	jeep	f	fish
j	jeep	k	kite
k	kite	b	boat
g	goat	g	goat

jelly _____ _____   fat _____ _____

gerbil _____ _____   candy _____ _____

cat _____ _____   book _____ _____

ghost _____ _____   gone _____ _____

Now check your answers. If you missed any, say aloud the key word you selected while you listen carefully to the first phoneme. Substitute that sound in the specific study word above. Correct it so the initial sound in the study word is the same as that in the key word.

girl *gym* *goat*	**5.** Now, when we use a key symbol such as *g*, we will know that we are referring to the sound heard in _____ and not to that heard in (girl, gym) _____. (girl, gym) Check yourself. Is the phoneme you have selected the same as that heard in the key word _____?
key	**6.** As we study each consonant letter, we need to ask certain questions: **A.** How reliable is it? Does it always represent the sound we associate with its _____ symbol? Are there patterns of reliability? Patterns of inconsistencies? **B.** Does it have distinctive characteristics? The consonant letters have been grouped to facilitate our study in answering the above questions.

m, q, r, v

symbol *m moon* *r ring* *v van*	**1.** Four of the 21 consonant letters are extremely dependable: *m, q, r,* and *v*. When we see *m, r,* or *v* in a word, we can be sure it represents the phoneme we associate with its key _____ and is the initial sound heard in its key word. Fill in the columns at the right with the key symbols (2) and the key words (3). Select the words from the following: *van queen fish ring kite moon* **1** **2** **3** *m* _____ _____ *r* _____ _____ *v* _____ _____
k kite	**2.** Since *q* is an unnecessary letter, how can we call it dependable? When we see *q*, we know it represents the sound we associate with the key symbol *k*. In other words, /q/ = /k/. We can depend on it! Now write the key symbol and key word for *q* above. *q* _____ _____

k *kite*	**3.** We did not use *q* for a key symbol because the sound it represents had already been assigned to the letter _____. We have selected one symbol to represent each of the 25 consonant sounds of our language. The key word we have selected to help identify /k/ is _____.
k *k, u* *e*	**4.** Study the words below. The *que* combination at the end of a word, as in *antique*, represents the phoneme we associate with the key symbol _____. Or we might say that the *q* represents the sound we associate with _____, while the _____ and _____ are silent.

opak, unik
 	
plak, antik
	Rewrite these words using the proper key symbol to stand for each of the consonants. Omit the silent *ue* combination and the silent consonants. Copy the vowels as they are, pronouncing them as they would sound in the real word.
	
	     opaque _____ *unique* _____
	
	     plaque _____ *antique* _____

u *k*	**5.** The letter *q* is almost always followed by the letter _____. In *unique*, the *u* that follows the *q* is silent. There are a few words that begin with *q* in which the *u* is also silent, as in *quay*, or the *u* is pronounced as *u*, as in *queue*. We may miss this point because we may be mispronouncing these words. *Quay* is pronounced as though it were spelled *key*; *queue* is pronounced as though it were spelled *cue*. The first phoneme in both *key* and *cue* (therefore in *quay* and *queue*) is represented by the key symbol _____. Pronounce *quay* and *queue* correctly several times (*quay* as *key*; *queue* as *cue*). Practice reading this: *The people boarding the ship formed a queue on the quay. Three of them wore queues.*
k *w*	**6.** More commonly, the *u* following the letter *q* becomes a consonant and represents the sound we associate with the key symbol *w*. Say these words: *quilt, equal, quiet, quill.* In these words, the *q* represents the sound we associate with _____, and the *u* represents the sound we associate with _____.

kwote, kwit kwiz, kween k consonant, w	**7.** Pronounce the words below aloud. Rewrite each word below using the proper key symbols to show the pronunciation of the *qu* combination. quote _____ quit _____ quiz _____ queen _____ In these words, the letter *q* represents the sound we associate with the key symbol _____, and the letter *u* represents the sound of the _____ letter _____. _(consonant, vowel)
k u consonant, w	**8.** Let us summarize: **The letters *m, q, v,* and *r* are very dependable. The *m, v,* and *r* represent distinctive sounds of their own.** **The *q* always represents the same sound as the _____.** The letter *q* has a distinctive characteristic: It is almost always followed by the letter _____. This *u* may be silent or represent the sound of the _____ _____. _(consonant, vowel)

Box 2.1

How Would a Duck Quack without Q?

Without a sound of its own, the letter Q is tantamount to an alphabetical orphan in the modern English alphabet. Let us take a look at how we got this extra letter in our alphabet (Ouaknin, 1999). The letter Q, known as *koppa* in the archaic Greek alphabet, fell out of use and did not survive long enough to become part of the classical Greek alphabet. We would not have the letter Q in our own alphabet today had not the Etruscans revived the Q. They passed it along to the Romans, who used Q to spell /kw/ words (*quake, question*). Western languages inherited the Latin alphabet, although the Anglo-Saxons did not borrow this letter from Latin. The French language did borrow the Latin Q, however, and it was the French who added the Q to the English alphabet. After the Norman Conquest in 1066, French scribes began to use Q when spelling English words. By sometime around 1500, the letter Q had become part of the English alphabet, where it remains today. If the letter Q were to disappear from our alphabet as it did from the classical Greek alphabet, we would use the letters *kw* and *k* in its place, depending on the sounds in the words to be spelled, such as *kwest, technik, kwiz, kwilt, opak, kwip,* and *kwit.* Consider this *kwestion:* If you could choose, would you discard the letter Q or keep it as the 17th letter of the English alphabet?

Review 3

1. How many phonemes are there in *panda?* _____ How many graphemes? _____

2. How many phonemes are there in *chat?* _____ How many graphemes? _____

3. We do not have a sufficient number of consonant letters in our alphabet to represent all the consonant sounds. Rather, we supplement the single letters with seven _____.

4. Which letters have not been assigned key symbols of their own? Why?

5. To establish our code, we select key _____ and key _____ to represent each phoneme.

6. What key symbol represents /m/? _____ /q/? _____ /r/? _____ /v/? _____

7. Q is followed by _____ in English words. The *u* may be _____, as in *antique,* or have the sound of the consonant _____, as in *quilt.*

8. Using our code, how would we write the consonants in these words? *mover* _____ *quiver* _____

9. What do we mean when we say, "The *v* is a very dependable letter"?

See the Answers to the Reviews section for answers to Review 3, page 231.

b, h, k, l, p

b	b	boat
h	h	hat
k	k	kite
l	l	lion
p	p	pig

1. The five consonants *b, h, k, l,* and *p* are very dependable except for the fact that on occasion they represent no phonemes. When you see one of these letters in an unknown word, you expect it to represent the sound you hear in its key word. Complete the table at the right with the letter (1), key symbol (2), and key word (3) for each.

1	2	3
_____	_____	_____
_____	_____	_____
_____	_____	_____
_____	_____	_____
_____	_____	_____

Select the key words from the following:

lion   cat   hat   pig   queen   boat   kite

boat	**2.** You will associate *b* with the sound heard at the beginning of the key word _____. Can you say that sound aloud? It is very difficult. Many consonant phonemes cannot be pronounced easily without adding a bit of a vowel sound. Some teachers, trying to pronounce the initial phoneme in *boat,* say "buh." Adding an "uh" when pronouncing the consonant sound will not help the child to identify the word *boat: buh-oat* is not *boat!* Keep in mind that
consonant	it is very difficult to pronounce some _____ phonemes in isolation. <div align="center">(consonant, vowel)</div>
vowel	**3.** Try pronouncing /*m*/, /*v*/, /*l*/ and /*r*/. Listen to the sounds you give them in *hum, dove, call* and *car.* Say them aloud again. These are fairly easy to pronounce in isolation. Now say /*b*/, /*k*/ and /*p*/ aloud. Listen to them in the words *tub, back* and *help.* Do not hang on to the sound (as you can in *hummmmmmm*); just softly expel your breath. Try to sound them with as little of the _____ phoneme (the /*uh*/) as possible.
silent *silent*	**4.** Sometimes these consonant letters have no phonemes. It is common practice to call them "_____ letters." Certain patterns help determine whether these letters represent a phoneme or are _____ in an unknown word.
one *muffin, mufin, letter,* *purr, leter, pur, ribbon,* *ribon, happen,* *hapen, less, les*	**5.** One pattern is very common to almost all consonants: <div align="center">**Two like consonants appearing together in a word generally represent one phoneme.**</div> Say these words aloud. How many phonemes do the two like consonants represent? _____ Make a slash through the second like consonant to depict the silent letter. Then rewrite the words omitting the silent consonant. <div align="center">*muffin* _____ *letter* _____ *purr* _____ *ribbon* _____ *happen* _____ *less* _____</div>
clim, lam *bom, number* *b, m*	**6.** Pronounce the words below. Rewrite these words, omitting the silent letters. (Do not be concerned with the vowel sounds at this point. We will indicate the vowel sounds later.) <div align="center">*climb* _____ *lamb* _____ *bomb* _____ *number* _____</div> The _____ is silent when it follows an(a) _____ in the *same syllable.*
syllable, m	**7.** In frame 6, the *b* is not silent in *number* (*num ber*) because it is not in the same _____ as the _____.

is	**8.** Pronounce the words *bomb* and *bombard.* The *b* when it follows the *m* in *bomb* _____ silent. (is, is not)
is not	The *b* when it follows the *m* in *bombard* _____ silent. (is, is not)
syllables	The second *b* and the *m* in *bombard* (*bom bard*) are in different _____.
dout, det obtain, sutle	**9.** Pronounce the words below. Rewrite the words, omitting the silent consonants. doubt _____ debt _____ obtain _____ subtle _____
t	The *b* is silent when it is followed by a _____ in the *same syllable,* with a few exceptions, of course!
subtle	Which word does not belong in the set? _____
t	Notice that the *b* is silent even though the *b* and the _____ are in different syllables (*sub tle*).
b	**10.** Let us summarize: **When b follows m or precedes t in the same** **syllable, the _____ is usually silent.**
/h/, hat final	**11.** *H,* as a single letter (phoneme / /, key word _____), has a distinctive characteristic: It is never heard as the _____ sound in a (initial, final) word or syllable.
oh̸, hurrah̸, shah̸, cheetah̸ no	**12.** *H* is silent when it follows the vowel in a word or syllable. Put a slash through the silent *h* in each of the following words: oh hurrah shah cheetah Check carefully. Do you hear the /h/ at the end of each word? _____
heir, hour, honest	**13.** The *h* may even be silent when it appears as the initial consonant of a word. There are no clues to tell us whether the initial *h* represents a phoneme. In fact, some people consider the *h* to be silent in *homage, humble,* and *herb.* Circle the words below in which the initial *h* is silent. here heir hour happy honest

g *k, r*	**14.** Study the words below. *ghost khaki rhyme ghastly khan rhino* The letter *h* is silent when it *follows* the consonants _____, _____, and _____.
gost, kaki, ryme, *gastly, kan, rino*	**15.** Rewrite the words in the preceding frame, omitting the silent consonants: _____, _____, _____, _____, _____, _____.
khaki, ghost, rhino *hurrah* *hour*	**16.** Review by filling in these blanks. Use the words below to assist you. *hurrah khaki hour ghost rhino* **The letter *h* is silent when it follows the consonants** *k* (as in _____), *g* (as in _____), or *r* (as in _____). *H* is silent when it follows a vowel (as in _____). Sometimes *h* is **silent at the beginning of a word (as in _____).**
six (or five. You would not be incorrect if you omitted *wh* /hw/.) *lau<u>gh</u>, wi<u>sh</u>, <u>ph</u>one <u>ch</u>ange, <u>wh</u>ite, <u>th</u>orn*	**17.** Aside from the fact that *h* is often silent, as a single letter grapheme, it is reliable. However, we cannot say that whenever we see an *h* in a word, we know it will either be silent or represent the initial sound heard in *hat*. *H* is a component of several digraphs (two-letter combinations that represent single speech sounds). Study the words below. How many digraphs contain the letter *h* but not /h/? _____ Underline them. *laugh wish phone change white thorn*
phoneme kite	**18.** Except when silent, the *k* is a very dependable letter. Let us be sure we understand: There are other graphemes that represent the sound we associate with the key symbol *k* (<u>qu</u>een, <u>ch</u>oir, <u>c</u>oat), but when we see the letter *k* in a word, we can be quite sure that when we hear the word, we will hear the same _____ as that heard at the beginning of its key word, _____.
nob, nown *nit, nee* *n*	**19.** Study the words below to discover the "silent *k*" pattern. Rewrite these words, omitting the silent *k* in each. knob _____ known _____ knit _____ knee _____ **The *k* is silent at the beginning of a word or syllable** **when followed by _____.** Pronounce aloud the words you have written.

nife, buble, hero clim, onor, nee	**20.** Rewrite the following words, omitting the silent consonants. knife _____ bubble _____ hero _____ climb _____ honor _____ knee _____
lion /l/	**21.** The consonant *l* is another very reliable letter. To help distinguish its phoneme, we have chosen the key word _____. We can represent its phoneme thus: / /.
baloon, dolar jely, bel	**22.** However, the *l* may be silent. Study the words below to see if this generalization applies. **Two like consonants appearing together in a word generally represent one phoneme.** Rewrite these words, omitting the silent consonants. balloon _____ dollar _____ jelly _____ bell _____
cam (kam), pam, yok chak, woud, shoud	**23.** To discover another pattern, study the words below. **The letter *l* is sometimes silent when followed in the same syllable by *m*, *k*, or *d*.** Rewrite these words, omitting the silent consonants. calm _____ palm _____ yolk _____ chalk _____ would _____ should _____ (Do you hear the /l/ when you say *calm* and *palm?* If so, this is a regional difference in pronunciation and a natural variation in the way we pronounce words.)
no gold, tak, film milk, caf, wak	**24.** Is this a completely dependable pattern? _____ Rewrite the words below, omitting the silent consonants. gold _____ talk _____ film _____ milk _____ calf _____ walk _____ (Pronouncing the /l/ in *gold*, *film*, and *milk* is not a consequence of regional differences. These are true exceptions to the pattern.)
p help	**25.** Next we turn our attention to the consonant *p.* In this study, we are establishing a key symbol for each phoneme in our language. The logical key symbol to use to identify the first phoneme heard in *pig* is _____. It is the last phoneme heard in _____. *(help, graph)*

p	**26.** We establish a key symbol and a key word to help distinguish this phoneme from any other. *Pig* is the key word we have selected to identify the sound represented by _____.
p	**27.** Next we examine its dependability. *P,* as a single consonant, is very reliable. When we see *p,* we can expect to hear the sound we are associating with the key symbol _____.
no f	**28.** Do we expect to hear the sound we associate with the key symbol *p* in *phone?* _____. The two-letter grapheme *ph,* a diagraph, represents the sound we associate with the key symbol _____.
silent aple, hapy pupet, pupy	**29.** Sometimes, however, the *p* has no phoneme; it is _____. Rewrite the following words, omitting the consonant letters that represent no phonemes. apple _____ happy _____ puppet _____ puppy _____
no p	**30.** Is *p* sounded in the following words? _____ *pseudo psychology psalm pterodactyl pneumonic pneumonia* We can generalize: **When *p* is followed by *s, t,* or *n* at the beginning** **of a word, the _____ is usually silent.**
silent	**31.** **The consonants *b, h, k, l,* and *p* as** **single letters are very reliable.** However, they are not always sounded; each has "_____ letter" patterns.

Study Guide

Consonants *b, h, k, l, m, p, q, r, v*

Consonant	Key Symbol	Key Word
b	*b*	*boat*
h	*h*	*hat*
k	*k*	*kite*
l	*l*	*lion*
m	*m*	*moon*
p	*p*	*pig*
q	no key symbol	no key word
r	*r*	*ring*
v	*v*	*van*

Bb   is usually silent when it follows *m* or precedes *t* in the same syllable (*climb, doubt*).

Hh   is silent when it follows the consonant *g* (*ghost*), *k* (*khaki*), or *r* (*rhino*). *H* is also silent when it follows a vowel in a word or syllable or is a final letter (*hurrah*). Sometimes *h* is silent at the beginning of a word (*hour*). There are no clues to tell us whether the *h* at the beginning of a word is silent (*heir*) or represents a phoneme (*had*). *H* is also part of several digraphs (*th, sh, ch, gh, ph, wh*).

Kk   is silent at the beginning of a word or syllable when followed by *n* (*knee*).

Ll   is sometimes silent when followed, in the same syllable, by *m* (*calm*), *k* (*chalk*), or *d* (*should*). If you hear an /*l*/ in *calm,* this is a regional difference in pronunciation. There are exceptions (of course!) to this generalization, such as *film, milk,* and *gold*.

Mm   is a very dependable letter. When we see *m* in a word, we can be sure that it represents the phoneme we associate with the key word *moon*.

Pp   is usually silent when followed by *s* (*psychology*), *t* (*pterodactyl*), or *n* (*pneumonia*) at the beginning of a word.

Qq   has no key symbol. The *q* may represent /*k*/ (*antique*). *Q* is almost always followed by the letter *u*. The *u* may be silent or represent the sound of the *w*. When the *u* represents the sound of *w*, the *qu* stands for *kw* (*kween*).

Rr   is a dependable letter. When we see *r* in a word, we can be sure that it represents the sound we associate with the key word *ring*.

Vv   is a dependable letter. When we see *v* in a word, we can be sure that it represents the sound we associate with the key word *van*.

Silent Consonants

Two like consonants appearing together in a word generally represent one phoneme (*bubble, puddle, waffle, jelly, summer, dinner, puppet, carrot, buzz*).

Review 4

1. Phonics is used to decode unknown words. The pronunciation of each of these nonsense words is unknown to you. Using the generalizations you have studied, decide which key symbol should represent each of the underlined consonants. Rewrite the "words," omitting the silent consonants. Copy the vowels as you see them in the "words."

   a. _knoh_ **b.** _psaph_ **c.** _mell_ **d.** _plarrah_ **e.** _ghaeve_ **f.** _kheph_ **g.** _psimb_

   h. _ptovom_ **i.** _rolk_ **j.** _rhimb_ **k.** _quimmel_ **l.** _kloppem_ **m.** _voubt_

2. Make a slash through the silent consonants in the words below.

   a. _blossom_ **b.** _dumb_ **c.** _knob_ **d.** _doubt_ **e.** _ghastly_ **f.** _pollen_

3. Why is it difficult to pronounce /b/, /k/, and /p/ aloud?

4. Why did we omit _q_ in our list of key symbols?

See the Answers to the Reviews section for the answers to Review 4, page 231.

d, f, j, n, z

				1	2	3
_d_	_d_	dog	**1.** Each of the five consonants _d, f, j, n,_ and _z_ has minor irregularities. Complete the table at the right with the letter (1), key symbol (2), and	___	___	___
_f_	_f_	fish	key word (3) for each of these consonants.	___	___	___
_j_	_j_	jeep	Select the key words from the following:	___	___	___
_n_	_n_	nut		___	___	___
_z_	_z_	zipper		___	___	___
			jeep nut fish gerbil dog zipper moon			

_f_	**2.** Say the word _fish._ Now start to say the word again but hold the first sound.
	This is the sound we represent by the key symbol _____. The _f_ is, in general, a reliable letter. Write the key symbol for the sound represented by _f_ in each of the words below. Listen carefully!
_f, f, f_	fiesta _____ fan _____ effect _____
_f, v, f_	off _____ of _____ if _____
_v_	**3.** The _f_ represents the sound we associate with the key symbol _____ in the word _of._ (Try to pronounce _of_ using /f/.)

silent off	**4.** One *f* in the word *effect* is not sounded. It is clear then that *f* can be a _____ letter. Another example of an unsounded *f* in the list in frame 2 is in the word _____.
f */v/* *gh* *ph*	**5.** We have noted that *f* is, in general, a reliable letter: When we see *f* in a word, we expect, when the word is spoken, to hear the sound represented by the key symbol _____. Exception: in *of,* the *f* is pronounced / /. However, there are other letters that are used to stand for the sound represented by the key symbol *f*. We will digress to study them here. What letters represent the */f/* in the word *enough?* _____ In the word *phonics?* _____

touf, nit, dou
 	
enouf, gost, lam
 	
throu, taut, hi
	6. The *gh* digraph can be silent. Rewrite the words below using key symbols for all consonants and omitting silent letters. Copy the vowels as they are, pronouncing them as they would sound in the original word.
	
	    tough _____ knight _____ dough _____
	
	    enough _____ ghost _____ lamb _____
	
	    through _____ taught _____ high _____

b r t, s t, t t	**7.** Study the words below. What consonants are sounded in these words? bright _____ sight _____ ought _____ The *gh* digraph is usually silent when followed by _____.
gh */f/* beginning, h	**8.** Pronounce these words: *ghost, high, rough*. The digraph _____ is silent or represents / / when it appears after the vowel in a syllable. When *gh* appears at the _____ of the syllable, the _____ in the two-letter combination is silent.
ph	**9.** Study these words: *phone, graph, phrase*. The digraph _____ can be found at the beginning or end of a syllable (that is, both before and after the vowel).

foto, fork, foneme
 	
alfabet, foot, graf
 	
f
	10. Rewrite the words below to indicate their pronunciations. Use the key symbols for the consonants. Copy the vowels as they appear.
	
	    photo _____ fork _____ phoneme _____
	
	    alphabet _____ foot _____ graph _____
	
	       The digraph *ph* represents the sound we associate
	
	          with the key symbol _____.

first, laugh, phone *after, cough, nephew* *lift, enough, graph* *f f f* **silent**	**11.** We have identified three graphemes that represent /f/. Pronounce each of the words below. Underline the grapheme in each word that represents /f/, and write the key symbol on the line below. first laugh phone after cough nephew lift enough graph _____ _____ _____ **The *gh* may represent /f/, or it may be _____ (as in *high*).**
j *jeep*	**12.** Say *jeep* out loud. Now pronounce the first phoneme in that word. We will represent the initial sound heard in *jeep* with the key symbol _____. *J* is a very reliable letter. When we see a *j* in a word, we will use the same sound as that in its key word _____.
y	**13.** There is one exception! Pronounce *Hallelujah*. You see a *j*, but you do not say /j/. Can you determine what key symbol you would use to represent the *j*? _____
juj, nowlej, ej	**14.** It might be well at this time to look at a combination of letters that represents /j/, *dg*. Rewrite these words to indicate their pronunciations. Omit each silent *e* and copy the other vowels as they are. judge _____ knowledge _____ edge _____ Perhaps you hear the /d/, but try pronouncing the words as though /dg/ = /j/. It comes out the same, does it not?
no *j*	**15.** Study the one-syllable words below. Does the *dg* digraph occur at the beginning of English words? _____ fu<u>dg</u>e bu<u>dg</u>et do<u>dg</u>e pi<u>dg</u>in ju<u>dg</u>e ga<u>dg</u>et **The diagraph *dg* is very reliable. What key symbol do we** **use to represent the phoneme?** _____
d	**16.** We shall represent the initial phoneme heard in *dog* with the key symbol _____. Say *dog* aloud. Listen carefully as you say the initial phoneme in *dog*.
lader, suden	**17.** The *d* is fairly dependable. It, however, may be silent, as in *ladder* and *sudden*. Rewrite these words, omitting silent consonants. ladder _____ sudden _____

	18. But let us examine more closely the sounds the *d* represents. The key symbol represents the sounds heard in *doll*, *did*, *day* and *led*. Now read these words out loud to discover another sound that the *d* represents: *jumped*, *clipped*, *hoped*, *missed*.
	Here *d* represents the sound we associate with the key symbol
t	_____.
	19. Study each word below. Note that each word ends in the suffix *–ed*.
	missed _mist_
hopt	hoped _____
jumpt	jumped _____
slipt	slipped _____
	Missed, for example, has four phonemes. Rewrite each word showing the pronunciation of the consonants by using key symbols. In spite of their
one	appearance, these are all _____-syllable words.
	<div align="center">(one, two)</div>
	20. We have noted that the *d* sometimes is pronounced as though it were
t	_____ (as in *kissed*). Now examine the words below.
	played smiled called
one	They are also _____-syllable words. The final consonant represents
d	the sound we associate with the key symbol _____. (You will learn more about the -ed suffix when you study suffixes in Part Eight.)
	21. We have noted that *dg* forms a special combination representing phoneme / /. Occasionally, a *d* or *di* represents the /j/. Perhaps you hear /j/ when you pronounce *graduation*. Rewrite these words using key symbols to represent the consonant sounds and omitting any silent consonant letters. Copy the vowels as they are.
/j/	
soljer, fuje	soldier _____ fudge _____
sudden	**22.** We have seen that *d* can be silent, as in _____. *D* can represent
	<div align="center">(sudden, debt)</div>
jumped, soldier	/t/, as in _____, and /j/, as in _____, and /j/ as a part
	<div align="center">(jumped, pulled) (gem, soldier)</div>
fudge	of the combination *dg*, as in _____.
	<div align="center">(fudge, handgrip)</div>

nut	**23.** The /n/, identified by the first phoneme in the key word _____, can be silent, as in *running,* and when preceded by *m,* as in *hymn.* Rewrite these words, omitting the silent letters.
colum, maner	column _____ manner _____
one, yes	**24.** *N* is very reliable with one common but confusing exception. First, let us note that *n* is a part of the digraph *ng* as heard in *sing.* (Recall that a digraph consists of two letters that represent one phoneme.) The *n* and the *g* represent _____ phoneme(s) in *sing.* Is *ng* a digraph in *bring?* _____ (How many?) We will study the *ng* digraph (as in *string*) further in Part Three. For our purposes in studying *n* as a single-letter consonant, we will now consider *n* as it represents the /ng/ phoneme.
yes *think*	**25.** Say *thing.* Is the *ng* a digraph? _____ Add the phoneme represented by /k/ to *thing* (*thing* + k). We do not spell this word *thingk:* We spell it _____. The letter *n* represents /ng/ in *think!*
thang + k	**26.** There are many words in which you hear /ng/ but see only *n.* These words follow a pattern: Generally the letter following the *n* is either *k* or *g.* Pronounce *thank.* Which of these "keys to pronunciation" is correct? _____ than + k thang + k
pingk, autum, swing, thangk *shringk, ring, tunel, trungk*	**27.** Say the words below. Then rewrite the words to show pronunciation. Write the vowels as they appear. Work carefully. This takes careful listening! pink _____ autumn _____ swing _____ thank _____ shrink _____ ring _____ tunnel _____ trunk _____
autumn, *tunnel, swing, ring* *pink, thank, shrink, trunk*	**28.** Reread the words in frame 27. The *n* is silent in _____, only one *n* is pronounced in _____, following *ng* is a digraph in _____ and _____, and, as a single letter, *n* represents /ng/ in _____, _____, _____ and _____.
    fing ger	**29.** Pronounce the "words" below. This is hard! fin ger fing ger fing er Which set of key symbols (consonant sounds only) indicates the correct pronunciation of *finger?* _____

ng *g*	**30.** In *finger,* the *n* represents the sound we associate with the key symbol _____. The *g* represents the sound we associate with the key symbol _____. To show pronunciation, we need both the *ng* and the *g*.

nut
 	
solemn, tunnel
 	
banker
	31. We have seen that the letter *n* often represents the phoneme we associate with the /n/ in its key word _____.
	The *n* may also be silent, as in _____ and _____.
	                              (solemn, rang) *(handle, tunnel)*
	The single letter *n* may also represent the /ng/, as in _____.
	                                                (banker, engine)

zipper *buzz*	**32.** The key symbol *z* represents the phoneme heard at the beginning of its key word _____. In general, it is fairly reliable. It may be silent; for example, one *z* is silent in _____. *(zigzag, buzz)*
s *azure* *size*	**33.** The *z* occasionally stands for the sound represented by the key symbol _____, as in *quartz,* and by the digraph *zh,* as in _____. Pronounce *size* *(size, azure)* and *azure* aloud. Which has the phoneme you hear in *zoo?* _____

Box 2.2

Why Z Comes Last

The letter *Z* has not always been the last letter of the alphabet. Thousands of years ago, *Z* was used by the Phoenician (tenth-century BC) and the Greek (eighth-century BC) alphabets (Ouaknin, 1999). When the Greeks passed their alphabet to the ancient Romans, the letter *Z* became the seventh letter in the Latin alphabet. Although the *Z* represented a speech sound in the Greek language, it served no real purpose in Latin because the Latin language did not use the sound represented by the letter. The *Z* might have stayed in the Latin alphabet had it not been for the fact that the letter *C* represented two Latin phonemes, the /k/ in *kite* and the voiced /g/ in *goat.* The Romans wanted to give the voiced /g/ its own letter, so they introduced a new letter, the letter *G.* To keep the order of the letters in the Latin alphabet intact, the Romans decided to delete the useless letter *Z* and to replace it with the newly created letter *G.* The letter *G* then became the seventh letter in the Latin alphabet, as it is in our own English alphabet. Eventually some Greek words entered the Latin language. When the Romans went to translate the Greek loan words into Latin, they found that they needed to add the letter *Z* to the Latin alphabet. Putting the letter *Z* into its old slot as the seventh letter would have changed the letter sequence, something the Romans did not want to do. The Romans solved their problem by adding the letter *Z* to the end of the alphabet, where it remains today in our own English alphabet.

	34. Check the words below in which the *z* stands for the phoneme heard at the beginning of the word *zipper*.
zero, prize	*zero* *waltz* *prize* *azure*

	35. We have noted that the consonants *d, f, j, n,* and *z* have irregularities. In the next two frames, select the word at the right that illustrates the irregularity described.
	The consonant may represent a phoneme other than that of its key symbol:
of *missed* *bank* *waltz* *azure*	*f* = /v/ *fish, of* *d* = /t/ *missed, list* *n* = /ng/ *bank, bone* *z* = /s/ *zoo, waltz* *z* = /zh/ *his, azure*

36.	**The key symbol may be represented by a different letter or digraph:**
phone *rough* *fudge*	*ph* = /f/ *phone, puff* *gh* = /f/ *bough, rough* *dg* = /j/ *jug, fudge*

Study Guide

Consonants d, f, j, n, z
Digraphs dg, gh, ph

Consonant	Key Symbol	Key Word
d	d	dog
f	f	fish
j	j	jeep
n	n	nut
z	z	zipper

Consonant	Key Symbol	Key Word
dg	j	jeep
gh	f, g, or silent	fish, goat (or no key word when silent)
ph	f	fish

Suffix	Key Symbol	Key Word
-ed	d	dog (fold_ed_)
-ed	t	table (hop_ed_)

Dd   may be silent (*ladder*) or may represent /t/ (*jumped*) when part of the -ed suffix.

Ff   is, in general, a reliable letter, with a notable exception in the word *of*, in which the letter *f* represents /v/.

Jj   is a very reliable letter (*jelly*). Occasionally a *d* or *di* represents /j/ (*graduation*, *soldier*).

Nn   may be silent when preceded by *m* (*autumn*). The single *n* may represent /ng/ (*thank*).

Zz   represents /z/ in the key word *zipper* and occasionally stands for /s/ (*waltz*) and /zh/ in *azure*.

dg   The *dg* digraph represents /j/ (*fudge, budget*).

gh   The *gh* digraph is usually silent when followed by *t* in a syllable (*night*). The *gh* is silent (*through*) or represents /f/ (*cough*) when it follows the vowel in a syllable. When *gh* occurs at the beginning of a word, the *h* is silent (*ghost*). There are only a handful of English words that begin with *gh*. They include *ghost, ghetto, ghastly,* and *ghoul*.

ph   The *ph* digraph represents /f/ and may occur at the beginning (*phone*) or end (*graph*) of a syllable (that is, before or after the vowel).

Review 5

1. Write the key symbols that represent the sounds of the consonant letters in each of these words:

   a. *bough* **b.** *tough* **c.** *hedge* **d.** *of* **e.** *phone* **f.** *tight*
   g. *ghastly* **h.** *rhyme* **i.** *zone* **j.** *huffed* **k.** *planned*
   l. *quilt* **m.** *zero* **n.** *sleigh* **o.** *column*

2. In which words do you hear the same phoneme as that represented by the underlined part of the first word?

a.	*dog*	*clapped*	*don't*	*ride*	*soldier*	*moved*
b.	*fish*	*fine*	*graph*	*of*	*photo*	*off*
c.	*jeep*	*wedge*	*soldier*	*gold*	*hallelujah*	*Roger*
d.	*nut*	*sling*	*hymn*	*knot*	*stranger*	*lank*
e.	*zipper*	*his*	*puzzle*	*does*	*seizure*	*waltz*

   See the Answers to the Reviews section for the answers to Review 5, page 231.

c, g, w, y

g *g* goat	**1.** Each of the four consonants *c, g, w,* and *y* is very irregular. However, each has a pattern of consistency within its inconsistencies. The *c* and *g* have some patterns in common, as do the *w* and *y*. *C* has been omitted in the table at the right because it has no phoneme of its own. Complete the table for each of the other three with the key symbol (2) and key word (3). Select the words from the following:
w *w* wagon	
y *y* yo-yo	

	1	2	3
g		_____	_____
w		_____	_____
y		_____	_____

   yo-yo   *jeep*   *wagon*   *why*   *goat*   *kite*   *van*   *city*

goat	**2.** *G* is the key symbol for the phoneme we hear at the beginning of its key word _____. Pronounce these words using /g/ whenever you see a *g*. Then pronounce them correctly. Check those in which you hear /g/.
guess, glass, go, begin	*guess* *huge* *page* *ginger* *glass*
	go *enough* *gnat* *begin* *sing*
	Does *g* always represent the sound we associate with the *g* in *goat*?
no	_____

guess *glass, go, begin* *huge* *page, ginger* *gnat* *enough, sing*	**3.** It is clear that *g* is a very unreliable letter. In the list of words in frame 2, *g* represents its hard sound (/g/, as in *goat*) in the words _____, _____, _____, and _____. G represents the soft phoneme, /j/, in the words _____, _____, and _____. G is silent when followed by *n,* as in _____. G is part of a digraph, representing a different sound from either of its components in _____ and _____.
j *j* *g*	**4.** *G* is the key symbol for the hard sound we hear at the beginning of *goat.* We have noted that the letter *g* often represents the *soft* sound we associate with the key symbol _____. Are these used interchangeably, or is there a pattern to the words that might give a clue as to whether the *g* represents the soft sound we associate with the key symbol _____ or the hard sound we identify with the key symbol _____? Let us examine some known words to see.

5. Study the numbered sets of words below. Add a word from the list at the bottom of the frame to each set. Choose a word in which the *g* represents the same phoneme as the other underlined letters in the set and has the same vowel following the underlined *g*.

1	2	3	4	5	6
g̲ain	g̲entle	g̲iraffe	g̲o	g̲ulp	g̲ypsy
a̲g̲ainst	ag̲e	en̲g̲ine	wag̲on	re̲g̲ular	ener̲g̲y
_____	_____	_____	_____	_____	_____
	gone	gem	gum	get	
	gym	gate	giant		

1. *gate*   2. *gem*
3. *giant*   4. *gone*
5. *gum*   6. *gym*

e, i, y	**6.** **The letter *g* *usually* represents the sound we associate with the key symbol *j* (the soft sound) when it is followed by the vowel _____, _____, or _____.** Carefully study the sets of words above before you answer.
get	**7.** The word *usually* in the generalization indicates that this is not always true. The word _____ in frame 5 does not follow this generalization. *(get, gentle)*

	8. We can make a generalization about the phoneme that we associate with the key symbol *g*:
	The letter *g* *usually* represents the sound we associate with the key symbol *g* when it is followed
a, o, u	**by the vowel_____, _____, or _____.**
	9. What happens when other letters follow *g*? Study the words below.
	great ghost pilgrim gleam egg
	The generalization will read:
	The *g* usually represents the soft sound when
e, i, y	**it is followed by _____, _____, or _____.**
	When it is followed by any other letter or when it appears at the end of a word, the *g* represents the
hard (or the one associated with *g*)	**_____ sound.**
	Memorize these sets:
	/j/—e i y /g/—a o u
	You may wish to compose a phrase to help you remember, such as "*an ornery ugly goat.*"
	10. Do not forget that there are exceptions. The generalization above, however, is a useful one. When you see a word you do not recognize that contains a *g*, try the generalization.
	Try the phoneme represented by the key symbol *j* when the *g* is followed by
e, i, y	_____, _____, or _____; otherwise, try the
g	hard sound, represented by the key symbol _____.
	11. Many words end in the letters *ge*. Pronounce the words below.
	huge sponge cage orange
	The key symbol that represents the final sound in each of these words is
j	_____.
yes	Does the generalization apply to words that end in the letters *ge*? _____
	12. Rewrite each of these words to show the pronunciation of the consonant letters. Omit each silent consonant and silent *e*. Copy the other vowels as they are.
guard, guilt, ej	*guard* _____ *guilt* _____ *edge* _____
gastly, naw, paj	*ghastly* _____ *gnaw* _____ *page* _____
	(It is interesting to note that an unnecessary *u* has been added to many words in which *g* represents the hard sound, thus eliminating many exceptions, for
guilt	example, _____ above.)

symbol, word	**13.** The letter *c* is also very irregular, but on top of that, it has no phoneme of its own and, therefore, no key _____ or key _____.
c *k* *s*	**14.** Study these words: *cute, city.* Both start with the letter _____. The first phoneme in *cute* represents the sound we associate with the key symbol _____. The first phoneme in *city* represents the sound we associate with the key symbol _____.
k, s	**15.** As a single-letter grapheme, the *c* not only represents no phoneme of its own but also commonly serves to represent two other phonemes, the _____ and the _____. There are some clues to guide us to the sounds the *c* represents in words we do not know.

16. Study the numbered sets of words below. For each set, choose a word from the words at the bottom of the frame in which the *c* represents the same phoneme as the other underlined letters in the set and has the same vowel following it.

	1	**2**	**3**	**4**	**5**	**6**
1. *cat* 2. *cent*	<u>c</u>ane	<u>c</u>ell	<u>c</u>ider	<u>c</u>ook	<u>c</u>urrent	<u>c</u>ymbal
3. *city* 4. *coat*	be<u>c</u>ame	mi<u>c</u>e	de<u>c</u>ide	ba<u>c</u>on	<u>c</u>ut	en<u>c</u>yclopedia
5. *cup* 6. *bicycle*	_____	_____	_____	_____	_____	_____
	coat	bicycle	city	cup	cent	cat

1, 4, 5 *a, o, u*	**17.** Which sets of words in frame 16 have a *c* that represents the hard sound, that of the /k/? _____ What vowels follow the *c* in each of these groups? _____

Box 2.3

Why Not K for Cat?

Alphabetically speaking, the letter *C* has a rather checkered past (Ouaknin, 1999). The Greeks referred to the letter *C* as *gamma* and used it to represent the voiced /g/ heard in *goat* (the hard g). The Etruscans, who inherited the alphabet from the Greeks, did not use the voiced /g/ in their spoken language. Rather than eliminating the letter *C* altogether, the Etruscans used it to represent the /k/ heard in *kite*. In changing the sound represented by the gamma from a /g/ to a /k/, the Etruscan alphabet came to represent /k/ with the letters *k, c,* and *q*. The Etruscan alphabet subsequently passed to the Latin alphabet and eventually to our own English alphabet. Today we continue the practice that was passed down from the Etruscans, using the same three letters to represent the /k/ in English words: *k, c,* and *q* (as in *antique*).

a, o, u	**18.** Complete the generalization:
	
	    The letter *c* usually represents the sound we associate with the
	
	    key symbol *k* when it is followed by _____, _____, or _____.

s
 	
e, i, y
	19. What about the soft sound?
	
	    The letter *c* usually represents the sound we associate
	
	    with the key symbol _____ when it is followed by
	
	    _____, _____, or _____.

The letter *g* usually represents the soft sound (*j*) when it is followed by *e, i,* or *y.*	**20.** What is the generalization about the phoneme we associate with the soft sound of *g?*

yes
 	
a, o, u
 	
e, i, y
 	
a, o, u
	21. Are there similarities between the generalizations concerning the sounds represented by *c* and *g?* _____
	
	The combined generalization might read:
	
	    The consonants *c* and *g* represent their hard sounds
	
	    when followed by _____, _____, and _____.
	    They usually represent their soft sounds when
	
	    followed by_____, _____, and _____.
	
	If you remembered the phrase *"an ornery ugly goat,"* you might relate it to *"an ornery ugly kid."* C generally represents the sound heard in *kid* when
	
	followed by _____, _____, or _____.

k *g,* hard hard	**22.** Study the words below. *regret glad crow magic climb big* What happens when other letters follow *c* and *g?* The *c* then represents the sound we associate with _____, and the *g* represents the sound we associate with _____. These are the _____ sounds. What happens when *c* or *g* is the *last* letter in the word? In that position, they also represent their _____ sounds.

hard	**23.** Let us summarize the generalizations:
	
	    The *c* and *g* usually represent their soft sounds when
	    they are followed by *e, i,* or *y.* When they are followed by any
	    other letter or when they appear at the end of the word, the *c*
	
	    and the *g* represent their _____ sounds.

cello, girl, gift, give	**24.** Now apply the generalizations to the words below. Check the words that **do not** follow the generalization. cube cello cotton cash receive giant girl guide gift give
siense, skool, sene skalp, skale, skold skreen, skum silent	**25.** There are many words in which s is followed by c. Examine the words below. Rewrite each word, using key symbols for the consonants. science _____ school _____ scene _____ scalp _____ scale _____ scold _____ screen _____ scum _____ Note that c can be a _____ letter, as in the scene.
ch k	**26.** You have learned that c, as a single letter, is unnecessary. Examine these words: <u>chair</u>, <u>child</u>, <u>check</u>. We have no substitute for the c in the digraph _____. We cannot get along without the c. We could get along without the q because _____ substitutes perfectly.
only one is sounded (Put another way, one consonant is silent.)	**27.** Complete the generalization you learned in frame 5, page 39: **When two like consonants appear together** **in a word, usually _____.**
k s	**28.** Does this hold for the c? This generalization does not hold when the consonants represent different sounds. In the word success, the first c represents the sound we associate with the key symbol _____, and the second c represents the sound we associate with the key symbol _____.
akses, stoping skil, aksident aksept, aksent	**29.** Examine the following words. Rewrite them, using key symbols for the consonants. Omit the silent letters. access _____ stopping _____ skill _____ accident _____ accept _____ accent _____
c n, k blok, duk blak, bak	**30.** In words containing ck, the _____ is usually silent. What consonants are sounded in knock? _____. Rewrite the words below to show pronunciation of the consonants. block _____ duck _____ black _____ back _____

sak, poket
 	
gimik, truk
	31. In frame 30, the *c* is part of the digraph *ck*. To discover a pattern for the placement of *ck* within a word, rewrite each word below, omitting the silent consonants.
	
	     sack _____ pocket _____
	
	     gimmick _____ truck _____

end *ck*	**32.** The *ck* is always found at the _____ of a word or syllable. The (beginning, end) vowels in the words above represent short sounds (such as in <u>a</u>pple and <u>i</u>gloo). When a word with a short vowel ends in /k/, the digraph _____ often represents the /k/.
a, o, u, end letter (consonant) digraph, *gh* silent	**33.** *C* and *g* generally represent their hard sounds when they are followed by _____, _____, or _____; come at the _____ of a word; or are followed by another _____. Both *c* and *g* are part of a _____ (*c* in *ch*, *g* in _____). Both *c* and *g* can be _____, as in the *ck* digraph in *ba<u>c</u>k* and the *g* followed by *n* in *<u>g</u>nome.*
y	**34.** Say *yo-yo* aloud. Listen to the first phoneme as you pronounce this key word again. The initial sound heard in *yo-yo* will be identified by the key symbol _____.
yo-yo *yellow, young, canyon* consonant	**35.** The *y* is very unreliable. You cannot assume that when you see *y* in a word, it will represent the sound you hear in its key word _____. Pronounce these words aloud, using /y/ for each *y* you see: *yellow* *sky* *rhyme* *young* *sadly* *play* *canyon* Check those in which the *y* represents the phoneme you hear in *yo-yo.* When *y* represents the phoneme heard in *yo-yo,* it is a _____.
beginning	**36.** Now pronounce the above words correctly. Listen to the sound represented by the *y* in each word. You will notice that when the *y* is at the _____ of a word or a syllable, it has the /y/ phoneme. (beginning, end)
vowel	**37.** You will notice also that each *y* within or at the end of a syllable has a _____ sound (see frame 35). (consonant, vowel)

consonant, /y/	**38.** The *y* is unreliable, but there is a distinct pattern to help us select those that are consonants. When the *y* appears at the beginning of a syllable, it is a _____ and has the sound we associate with _____. (another vowel, /y/) (Exception: some words borrowed from other languages, as *ytterbia* in chemistry.)
consonant yo-yo	**39.** As a consonant, *y* is very reliable. When we see a *y* at the beginning of a syllable, we can be sure it is a _____ and represents the sound heard in its key word _____.
w consonant	**40.** Say *wagon* aloud. Listen to the first phoneme as you pronounce this key word again. The initial sound heard will be identified by the key symbol _____. The *w* is very unreliable. Like the *y*, it serves as a vowel as well as a _____.
went, always	**41.** Use the words below for this and the following five frames (42–46) to illustrate the characteristics of the consonant *w*. <div align="center">once quilt went write who</div> <div align="center">snow dwell one queen always</div> *W*, as a consonant, always appears before the vowel in a syllable. (Note: *w* as a vowel always follows another vowel.) *W* is generally an initial consonant in a word or syllable, as in _____ and in _____. <div align="center">(select a one-syllable word) (select a two-syllable word)</div>
dwell (*quilt* and *queen* are okay, too!)	**42.** The phoneme represented by *w* may, however, be part of a blend of two consonants, as in _____.
quilt, queen	**43.** The *u*, when following *q*, often represents the consonant phoneme we associate with the key symbol *w*. We hear this when we say the words _____ and _____.
write	**44.** The *w* is silent before *r*, as in _____.
who (*hoo*)	**45.** Occasionally the letter *w* fools us. It appears to be a part of the digraph *wh* but is actually silent, as in _____. (This is a puzzle. Can you solve it?) Remember to refer to frame 41.
one once	**46.** We are familiar with the word *won*. But note the grapheme we use in the word that is pronounced the same but spelled _____. We use the same grapheme to represent the *w* in _____.

vowel before *way, wrap*	**47.** The *w* may be a consonant or a _____. As a consonant, it appears _____ the vowel in the syllable and represents the (before, after) phoneme heard in _____. It is sometimes silent, as in _____. (*way, blow*)(*wish, wrap*)
unreliable /g/, /j/ /ng/ /j/, silent	**48.** We have been studying four _____ consonants: *c, g, w,* and *y.* (reliable, unreliable) We have found that *g* may have the sound of / /, as in *goat,* or / /, as in *genius.* It may be part of a digraph that has the sound of / /, as in *sing,* or the sound of / /, as in *fudge.* G may be _____, as in *gnome.*
It has no key symbol of its own.	**49.** What is the distinctive key symbol for *c?*
/k/, /s/ digraph /k/, silent	**50.** *C* may represent the sound of / /, as in *corn,* or of / /, as in *nice.* It may, with the letter *h,* form a _____, as in *mu<u>ch</u>.* C, in combination with the letter *k,* may represent the sound of / /, as *bri<u>ck</u>.* It is _____ in *scissors.*
e, i y, /k/, a o, u, end of a word /j/, e, i y, /g/, a, o u, consonant, end of a word	**51.** *C* usually has its soft sound when followed by _____, _____, or _____. It usually has its hard sound, / /, when it is followed by _____, _____, _____, or any other consonant or when it comes at the _____. G usually represents its soft sound, / /, when it is followed by _____, _____, or _____ and its hard sound, / /, when it is followed by _____, _____, _____, or any other _____ or when it comes at the _____.
       wrote, two, who	**52.** **The consonants *w* and *y* are positioned before the vowel in a syllable. The consonant *y* is never silent. The consonant *w* may be silent.** In the list below, check the words that have a silent *w.* quit wrote wing two who W may be a part of a diagraph, as in <u>*white.*</u>

Review 6

1. What generalization helps you to determine the sound of /*g*/ in an unknown word?

2. Write the key symbols for the consonants in each of these words:

   a. *giant*   **b.** *bank*   **c.** *girl*   **d.** *big*   **e.** *circus*   **f.** *cook*   **g.** *who*

   h. *match*   **i.** *yellow*   **j.** *way*   **k.** *quick*   **l.** *write*   **m.** *yet*   **n.** *knack*

3. Which of the above contains an exception to the hard/soft *g* generalization?

4. What generalization helps you to determine the sound of a *c* in an unknown word?

5. What generalization helps you to determine whether *w* represents /*w*/ and *y* represents /*y*/?

6. What key symbol indicates the pronunciation of the last phoneme in each of the following words?

   a. *beg*   **b.** *cage*   **c.** *judge*   **d.** *quack*   **e.** *knowledge*

   f. *back*   **g.** *cough*   **h.** *unique*   **i.** *critic*   **j.** *rough*

7. The key symbol for the initial grapheme in *night* is _____, key word _____. The *n* may represent / /, as in *finger*.

See the Answers to the Reviews section for the answers to Review 6, page 232.

s, t, x

s	s	*sun*		
t	t	*table*		

1. The three consonants *s, t,* and *x* are unreliable. You cannot assume that when you see one of them in a word, you will hear the same phoneme as that in its key word. Complete the table, adding key symbols (2) and key words (3). Select key words from this set:

	1	2	3
s	_____	_____	
t	_____	_____	

   city   sun   chin   she   table   zipper   ax   thin

2. Why is there no *x* in the table above? The letter *x* has no key symbol because it has no distinctive sound of its own. It represents sounds we associate with other key symbols. Pronounce *box* aloud.

boks

Try to write *box* using other letters: _____

egzakt (or egzact) box	**3.** Pronounce *exact*. Rewrite it using other key symbols: _____ The letter *x* represents the sounds we associate with *ks* as in _____ *(box, exam)*
gz Either is correct.	and _____ as in *exact*. And we often interchange them! How do you pronounce *exit*? _____ We are more apt to use /gz/ when *x* *(egzit, eksit)* appears between two vowel phonemes.
/ks/, /gz/	**4.** We have seen that *x* may represent the phoneme / / or / /. This may sound confusing, but it presents no problem to an English-speaking person, who will automatically use the acceptable phoneme.
z eks	**5.** Then consider the word *xylophone*. At the beginning of a word, *x* consistently represents the sound we associate with the key symbol _____. Of course, at times we use *x* as a letter, such as *X-ray*. In this instance, _____ could be used as the grapheme to represent the *x*.
siks, zylofone, egzample boks, zeroks, egzist	**6.** **The *x* could be omitted from our alphabet by using the letters *gz*, *ks*, and *z*.** Spell the words below, substituting the proper graphemes for the letter *x* in each one. six _____ xylophone _____ example _____ box _____ Xerox _____ exist _____
k gz, ks, z ch s, k	**7.** The phonemes represented by *c, q,* and *x* need no key symbols. In our one-to-one correspondence, they are already represented. We could omit the letter *q* entirely by substituting the _____. We could omit the letter *x* by substituting _____, _____, or _____. We do use the *c* as part of the digraph _____, but as a single letter, the _____ (*city*) and _____ (*coat*) could adequately take its place.
s sun yes, no, no no, no is not cannot	**8.** The phoneme represented by *s* (key symbol _____) is heard in its key word _____. Does it represent the sound heard in *list*? _____ *has*? _____ *she*? _____ *was*? _____ *surely*? _____ The letter *s* _____ very reliable. When you see the letter *s* in a word you *(is, is not)* _____ be sure you will hear /s/ when it is pronounced. *(can, cannot)*

s, s, z	**9.** Say each of the words below aloud. Listen very carefully to the underlined part. Which key symbol represents each part? Write it in the space following the word. this _____ history _____ his _____
see, ask rose, his sure, sugar television, treasure	**10.** The grapheme s is used to represent different phonemes. Study the words below. see ask rose his sure sugar television treasure The single consonant s represents the sound we usually associate with: (1) s in the words _____ and _____ (2) z in the words _____ and _____ (3) with sh in the words _____ and _____ (4) with zh in the words _____ and _____
z /z/ z, z, z, s, s	**11.** Pronounce his and has aloud. The key symbol that represents the final sound in these words is _____. There are many words in which the grapheme s represents the / /. Write the key symbol for each of the plural endings of the words below. If you have trouble, try both the /s/ and the /z/. You must say them aloud. toys _____ dogs _____ beds _____ cats _____ hops _____
sizorz, zylofon, fuzy us, uz, fuz miks, klas, sak	**12.** Rewrite the words below using the key symbol that represents the sound of each consonant. Copy the vowels as they are but omit each silent e. scissors _____ xylophone _____ fuzzy _____ us _____ use _____ fuse _____ mix _____ class _____ sack _____
rugz, iz, doez peaz, some, pleazhure roze, so, shurely	**13.** **The consonant s is unreliable: It often represents the phonemes we associate with z, sh, and zh, as well as its key symbol s.** Rewrite each of the following words using s, z, sh, or zh to indicate the sound the s represents. Copy the vowels as they are, pronouncing them as they sound in the real words. rugs _____ is _____ does _____ peas _____ some _____ pleasure _____ rose _____ so _____ surely _____

s, sun *miss*	**14.** When we see an *s* in an unknown word, we have few clues to tell us which phoneme it represents. We might note the following: (1) The letter *s* usually represents the sound we associate with the key symbol _____. It is the sound heard in _____. (sun, sure) (2) Except for certain foreign names (as *Saar*), the *s* at the beginning of a word stands for the sound heard in _____. (miss, rose) (3) Except when acting as a plural, the *s* at the end of a word represents /s/ or /z/ with about equal frequency. (4) We tend to use the phoneme represented by the *z*, the voiced counterpart of /s/, when the preceding phoneme is voiced. (English-speaking people use the correct ending automatically; thus, we have not studied voice–voiceless phonemes in this edition.)
table *th*	**15.** The letter *t* as a single consonant (as heard in its key word _____) is fairly reliable. However, we must distinguish between *t* as a single letter and *t* as part of a digraph. Pronounce these words: *this, think, with*. We do not hear /t/ in the two-letter digraph _____. We will study this digraph later.
/t/ *h*	**16.** But then pronounce these words: *Thomas, thyme.* (Exceptions! Exceptions!) The *th* in each of these words does represent the phoneme / /. Or we could say that the _____ is silent.
no shun	**17.** One of the common "endings" in our language is found in these words: *motion, convention, station.* Pronounce them. Do you hear /t/? _____ This ending could be spelled _____. <div align="center">(shun, ton)</div>
/ch/, /ch/, /t/ /ch/, /sh/	**18.** Examine the words below. Pronounce them, paying special attention to the underlined parts. What phoneme does each part represent? Work carefully. <div align="center">righ<u>te</u>ous / / ques<u>ti</u>on / / moun<u>tai</u>n / /</div> <div align="center">na<u>tur</u>al / / ac<u>ti</u>on / /</div>
beginning	**19.** It is clear there are many word "parts" (never at the _____ (beginning, ending) of the word) in which the *t*, in combination with a vowel, represents a phoneme other than /t/.
silent	**20.** Pronounce these words: *bouquet, beret, debut.* There are several common words derived from the French language in which the *t* is _____.

t *often, soften, glisten* *listen, fasten, moisten*	**21.** When *t* follows *f* or *s,* the _____ is sometimes silent. These words are written without the silent consonants; write them correctly. ofen _____ sofen _____ glisen _____ lisen _____ fasen _____ moisen _____
match, watch, hatch	**22.** The *t* is also silent in the *tch* combination. Pronounce the words below saying the /ch/ as in *chair*. Spell them correctly. mach _____ wach _____ hach _____
   soften *s, listen* *ch, catch* *letter* *ballet* *future, lotion* *father*	**23.** **The *t* may be silent and often loses the /t/ phoneme** **when combined with other letters.** Let us review patterns that indicate that *t* represents a phoneme other than that in the key word *table*. The words below will aid you in filling in the blanks in the following paragraph. catch father soften letter listen future lotion ballet The *t* may be *silent* as when it follows *f* (as in _____) or _____ (as in _____) and when it precedes _____ (as in _____). Only one *t* is sounded in such words as _____. It may also be silent in words adopted from the French as in _____. In connection with a vowel, the *t* may represent /ch/ as in _____ or /sh/ as in _____. It is often a part of a consonant digraph as in _____, in which case the /t/ is not heard.
     ng z t, z, t s *s n t, z n z* *s r k l, z l f n*	**24.** We have noted that several different graphemes may represent the initial sound heard in *sun,* as well as the initial sound heard in *zipper*. To illustrate, write the key symbol that indicates the pronunciation of each of the consonants in the words below. (If you get these, you are really thinking!) anxiety _____ is _____ its _____ scent _____ zones _____ circle _____ xylophone _____
   sugar, pleasure, hose	**25.** We have also noted that the grapheme *s* may represent sounds other than that heard in *sun* and that the grapheme *z* occasionally represents sounds other than that heard in *zipper*. Check the words below in which the *s* stands for a phoneme other than that heard at the beginning of *sun*. sugar this pleasure whisp hose
ks *gz, z*	**26.** We called *x* an unnecessary letter because it can be replaced by _____ in *ax,* by _____ in *example,* and by _____ in *xylophone*.

Study Guide

Consonants c, g, s, t, w, x, y

Consonant	Key Symbol	Key Word
c	no key symbol	no key word
g	g	goat
s	s	sun
t	t	table
w	w	wagon
x	no key symbol	no key word
y	y	yo-yo

Cc   does not have a key symbol. *C* usually represents /s/ (the soft sound) when it is followed by *e* (*cent*), *i* (*city*), or *y* (*cycle*). *C* usually represents /k/ (the hard sound) when it is followed by *a* (*cat*), *o* (*coat*), or *u* (*cut*); when it appears at the end of a word (*comic*); and when it is followed by any other letter (*cloud*). *C* can be silent when it follows *s* (*scene*).

Gg   may represent /j/ (the soft sound) when it is followed by the vowel *e* (*gerbil*), *i* (*giant*), or *y* (*gypsy*), although with exceptions. *G* usually represents /g/ (the hard sound) when it is followed by *a* (*gate*), *o* (*go*), or *u* (*gum*); when it appears at the end of a word (*leg*); and when it is followed by any other letter (*glass*).

Ss,   except when acting as a plural at the end of words, represents /s/ (*miss*) or /z/ (*whose*) with about equal frequency. *S* also represents /zh/ (*television*) and occasionally stands for /sh/ (*sugar*).

Tt   may be silent when it follows the letter *s* (*listen*) or *f* (*soften*) and when it precedes *ch* (*catch*). In connection with a vowel, *t* may represent /ch/ (*future*) or /sh/ (*station*). When part of a digraph (*th*), the *t* is not heard (*father*). *T* may also be silent in words adopted from the French language (*ballet*).

Ww   serves as a consonant and a vowel. As a consonant, *w* precedes the vowel (*wagon*). As a vowel, *w* follows the vowel (*snow*). The *w* is silent before *r* (*write*). *W* may also be part of a blend (*dwell*) or a diagraph (*what*). Occasionally the letter *w* fools us. It appears to be part of the digraph *wh* but is actually silent (*who*).

Xx   does not have a key symbol. It may represent /ks/ (*six*), /gz/ (*exam*), or /z/ (*xylophone*). We are more apt to use /gz/ when *x* appears between two vowel phonemes (*exempt*).

Yy   serves as a consonant and as a vowel. The *y* at the beginning of a syllable acts as a consonant and represents /y/ (*yellow*). *Y* within a syllable or at the end of a syllable acts as a vowel and may be silent (*play*) or may represent a vowel sound (*rhyme*).

Review 7

1. There are three consonants that, as single letters, represent no distinctive phonemes:

   a. The *c* usually represents the sound we associate with *s* when followed

   by_____, _____, or _____. The *c* usually

   represents the sound we associate with _____ when followed

   by the vowel _____, _____, or _____ or
   by most other consonants or when appearing at the end of a word.

   b. The *q* represents the sound we associate with _____.

   c. The *x* can adequately be represented by the consonants

   _____, _____, and _____.

2. There are other letters that represent two or more sounds, one of which is the sound we commonly associate with that particular letter (key symbol).

   a. The *g* represents "its own sound," /g/ (the _____
                                                    (hard, soft)

   sound), when followed by the vowel _____, _____,

   or _____ or by another consonant or when it appears at the
   end of a word.

   b. The *g* usually represents its _____ sound, that which we
                                         (hard, soft)

   ordinarily associate with the letter _____, when followed by

   _____, _____, or _____.

3. The two most common sounds represented by the single letter *s* are:

   a. The sound we ordinarily associate with the letter *s,* as in

   _____.
      (some, sugar)

   b. The sound we ordinarily associate with the letter _____, as in
   his.

4. The letter *d* may represent the sound we associate with _____ or the

   sound we associate with _____ when it appears in the suffix *-ed.*

5. *F* occasionally represents the sound we associate with _____, as in *of.*

6. *T* in combination with a vowel may represent different sounds, as

   _____ in *question* and _____ in *patient.*

7. Generalizations:

   a. Consonant letters may represent more than one sound.

The *s* represents the sound of _____ (as the key symbol indicates), of _____ (*sure*), of _____ (*has*), and of _____ (*treasure*).

The *z* represents the sound of _____ (as the key symbol indicates), of _____ (*quartz*), and of _____ (*azure*).

b. Consonant sounds may be represented by more than one letter. The sound we hear at the beginning of the word *say* is often represented by *s*, by _____ (*cent*), or by _____ (*chintz*).

The sound we hear at the beginning of the word *zipper* is sometimes represented by the letters _____ and _____.

c. Consonant letters may represent no sound. The three consonant letters that represent no sound in *knight* are _____, _____, and _____. We call them _____ letters. The letter _____ is _____ in *soften*, *ballet*, and *latch*.

8. Reread the generalizations in question 7. Be sure you determine the differences among them. These generalizations would carry more precise meanings if the words *phoneme* and *grapheme* were used. Then they would read:

a. Consonant _____ may represent more than one _____.

b. Consonant _____ may be represented by more than one _____.

c. Consonant letters may represent no _____.

See the Answers to the Reviews section for the answers to Review 7, page 232.

References

National Governors Association Center for Best Practices & Council of Chief State School Officers. (2010). *Common Core State Standards for English Language Arts & History/ Social Studies, Science, and Technical Subjects: Reading Standards: Foundational Skills—Phonological Awareness, Phonics and Word Recognition*. Washington, DC: Authors. Retrieved May 15, 2012, from http://www.corestandards.org/assets/CCSSI _ELA%20Standards.pdf

Ouaknin, M. C. (1999). *Mysteries of the alphabet: The origins of writing* (J. Bacon, Trans.). New York, NY: Abbeville Press.

Part Three

Consonant Digraphs and Consonant Blends

Common Core State Standards for English Language Arts
Reading Standards: Foundational Skills—Phonics and Word Recognition
Standard 3 *Know and apply grade-level phonics and word analysis skills in decoding words.*

FIRST GRADE
a. Know the spelling–sound correspondences for common consonant digraphs.
b. Decode regularly spelled one-syllable words.

The most common digraphs in English words are *th*, *sh*, *ch*, *ph* and *wh*. Schools are likely to select these digraphs to be among the learning expectations for first grade. Expectations are also likely to include common consonant blends and, perhaps, other consonant digraphs such as *ng* and *gh*. These standards require that children remember (3a) and apply (3b) the sounds that consonant digraphs represent. Application (3b)—decoding one-syllable words—is more difficult than learning letter-sound correspondences (3a). In decoding one-syllable words, first graders must use their knowledge of consonant digraphs along with other code-related knowledge and skills. For example, in order to sound out the one-syllable word *crash*, first graders need, at a minimum, (a) phonemic awareness, (b) knowledge of consonant digraphs and consonant blends, and (c) some understanding of vowel letter-sounds. While we consider only those portions of the standards that pertain to our study of the code as we progress through this book, we should remember that using phonics to read and spell new words calls for applying many different sources and types of information.

Consonant Digraphs

	1. We have been relating each of the consonant phonemes to its respective letter.
26	There are _____ letters in the alphabet.
vowels, 21	Five are _____, so there are _____ consonant letters.
Three	_____ of these have no distinctive phonemes of their own.
18	This leaves _____ single-letter consonant graphemes, each of which has been assigned a key symbol so as to build up a one-to-one correspondence between symbol and phoneme.

seven grapheme	**2.** Eighteen symbols but 25 consonant sounds! Where do we find the _____ remaining symbols? We gain seven additional phonemes through the use of the two-letter _____. (grapheme, phoneme)
consonant digraph	**3.** Note the spelling of digraph: _di_ for two, _graph_ referring to writing. We will use **consonant digraph** to identify the two consonant letters that represent a single phoneme. The two-letter combination _sh_, as in _shoe_, is called a _____. **The consonant digraphs stand for the seven phonemes not represented by single-letter graphemes.**
not	**4.** The _ch_ is one of the two-letter consonant digraphs we will study. Pronounce _chair_ as though <u>each</u> consonant was sounded. You said either /_s-hair_/ or /_k-hair_/. Now pronounce _chair_ as it should be pronounced. Note that you hear neither the sound represented by the _c_ nor the one represented by the _h_. The combination _ch_ represents a phoneme _____ represented by a (already, not) single consonant letter. It functions like another letter of the alphabet.
c h	**5.** **A digraph is a two-letter combination that represents a single phoneme.** The consonant digraph _ch_ does not represent the sound of the _____ or the sound of the _____ with which it is spelled.

_ch_ _ch_ _chair_ _sh_ _sh_ _ship_ _th_ _th_ _thumb_ _th_ _t̶h̶_ _that_ _wh_ _wh_ _whale_ _zh_ _treasure_ _ng_ _ng_ _king_	**6.** The key symbols that represent the seven missing phonemes are listed at the right. Fill in the missing items in the table: consonant digraphs (1) and key words (3). Select the key words from these: _ship, whale, king, thumb, chair, treasure_. Pronounce aloud the word and phoneme each represents. Notice that each is a distinctive consonant sound not represented by any single letter in our alphabet.	

6. (table at right)

1	2	3
_____	_ch_	_____
_____	_sh_	_____
_____	_th_	_____
_____	_t̶h̶_	_that_
_____	_wh_	_____
	_zh_	_____
_____	_ng_	_____

ng	**7.** Some dictionaries use key symbols other than those shown in column 2 of the previous frame to indicate pronunciation. Some join each set of letters to show one sound, as c͡h, s͡h, n͡g. Some use č to represent the initial phoneme heard in _chair_. The symbol η is often used to represent _____ as heard in _king_. Look up _chair, ship,_ and _king_ in your dictionary to see how the pronunciations are indicated.

8. There are other consonant digraphs, such as *ph* and *gh*. However, they are not listed in frame 6 because they are already represented. The key symbol

f

_____ indicates the sounds of the *ph* and the *gh*.

Review 8

Check yourself: Are you writing every answer and finishing each frame before moving the mask down? Are you getting almost every answer correct? Do you study more carefully when you miss one? Do you analyze your errors? Can you give yourself 100 on each review?

1. A grapheme composed of two letters that represent a single sound is called

   a(an) _____.

2. Indicate the pronunciation of the underlined part or parts of each of the following words by using key symbols:

qui*ck*	w*ho*	mea*s*ure	w*hy*	w*h*ich	bo*th*
*th*ick	no*ti*on	*s*u*g*ar	*wi*sh	vi*si*on	stro*ng*

3. In each of the following words, underline all the consonant digraphs that serve as key symbols and cannot be replaced by a single letter from our alphabet:

weather	enough	whom	which	bring
wrist	wish	both	through	condemn

4. There are 25 consonant sounds in the American-English language. We

   identify 18 of them with single _____ symbols. We should have

   _____ more consonant letters in the alphabet. Since we do not, we

   use two-letter combinations called _____ to serve as key symbols for

   these phonemes. Write the seven two-letter symbols. _____

5. Our sound–symbol system is complicated by the use of other consonant digraphs standing for phonemes already represented in the system. Select three examples of such digraphs from these words:

   tough   chalk   sheath   short-sighted   luck   phoneme

6. These three consonant digraphs are already represented by (use key

   symbols) _____, _____, and _____.

7. Rewrite these words using the appropriate key symbols for the consonants. Copy the vowels as they are.

   sunk   squash   know   graphic   pheasant   cough

See the Answers to the Reviews section for the answers to Review 8, page 233.

ch, sh, zh

ch	**1.** We have no single letter in the alphabet to represent the first phoneme we hear in the key word *chair*. We will use the logical two-letter combination, the _____, to identify this phoneme. Study the consonant digraphs in these sets of words:

<table>
<tr><th>1</th><th>2</th><th>3</th></tr>
<tr><td>chair</td><td>character</td><td>chiffon</td></tr>
<tr><td>chalk</td><td>chord</td><td>machine</td></tr>
<tr><td>churn</td><td>chaos</td><td>chute</td></tr>
</table>

no *no*	Each word contains the grapheme *ch*. Does each grapheme represent the phoneme we associate with the key symbol *ch*? _____ Try pronouncing each one using the first phoneme in *chair* for each consonant digraph. Is the digraph *ch* reliable? _____
ch *k* If you guessed *sh*, you are right!	**2.** The consonant digraph in each of the words in set 1 represents the phoneme we associate with the key symbol _____. The digraphs in set 2 represent the phoneme we associate with the key symbol _____. Can you guess what key symbol represents the consonant digraphs in set 3? _____
no *ch, k* *sh*	**3.** Is the consonant digraph *ch* reliable as to the phoneme it represents? _____ If we do not know the word, we cannot tell which key symbol to identify with it. It might be _____ or _____ or _____. (However, if you are an expert on language derivation, you will have clues.)
ship	**4.** The sound heard at the beginning of *ship* is very common, but there is no letter in the alphabet to represent it. We shall use the key symbol *sh* to represent the phoneme, as heard in the key word _____. (ship, clip)
one *no*	**5.** When *s* and *h* appear together in this order in a syllable, we expect them to represent _____ phoneme(s). Can you hear the separate phonemes (How many?) represented by *s* and *h* in *shut*? _____ If you could, you would hear the word *hut* in *shut*.

/sh/	**6.** *Sh* is very reliable in that when we see *sh,* we can be sure we will hear / /. However, the phoneme we represent by *sh* has a variety of graphemes; that is, it is spelled in a variety of ways. Examine the words below. Look at the underlined parts. Rewrite the words, using *sh* to represent the underlined graphemes.
shure, shoe, moshon	*sure* _____ *shoe* _____ *motion* _____
shugar, mashine, speshal	*sugar* _____ *machine* _____ *special* _____
s, sh, ti	**7.** The graphemes that we associate with the key symbol *sh* are:
	_____ in *sure* _____ in *shoe* _____ in *motion*
s, ch, ci	_____ in *sugar* _____ in *machine* _____ in *special*
no	**8.** Now listen for the middle consonant sound as you say *treasure.* Is there a letter in the alphabet to represent this sound? _____
zh	**9.** We shall use the consonant digraph *zh* as the key symbol to represent the phoneme heard in the key word *treasure,* although it is never represented in a word with the grapheme _____ .
pleazhure, vizhon, sabotazhe	**10.** Rewrite the words below to indicate, by using the key symbols, the sounds of the underlined letters. Copy the vowels as they are.
	pleasure _____ *vision* _____ *sabotage* _____
azhure, pich	*azure* _____ *pitch* _____
seizure	**11.** The *z* occasionally stands for the /zh/ as in _____ .
	(seizure, dozen)
	Pronounce *seizure* and *dozen* aloud. Which has the phoneme you hear in
dozen	*zipper?* _____
leisure, regime	**12.** The *s* and *g* are two other graphemes that occasionally represent the /zh/ as in _____ and _____ . The *s* in the key word
	(leisure, base) (regime, age)
treasure, do not	_____ represents the /zh/ phoneme. We _____ have a
	(treasure, sun) (do, do not)
	grapheme to represent the /zh/ phoneme.
decision, seizure, beige, collage, measure	**13.** Check the words below in which the underlined graphemes represent the /zh/. If you identify all of the words in which the /zh/ phoneme occurs, you are really thinking!
	deci̱sion *sei̱zure* *bei̱ge* *colla̱ge* *peṟson* *mea̱sure*

Box 3.1

Too Many English Sounds, Too Few English Letters: The French Solution

History books tell us that the French-speaking Normans ruled England from 1066 to roughly 1500. French became the language of the government, and hordes of French-speaking scribes were moved to England to keep the official records. The Norman French scribes were relatively unfamiliar with the English language. When the scribes realized that there were not enough English letters to represent the sounds in English words, they turned to the French writing system for a solution, introducing the *ch, sh, wh,* and *th* consonant digraphs to represent the /ch/, /sh/, /wh/, voiced /th/, and unvoiced /th/. Let us consider why the Norman French scribes chose these particular two-letter combinations.

In Old French, the letter *h* was occasionally used to signal when the preceding consonant had an atypical pronunciation. When the French-speaking scribes wanted to represent the English /ch/, they used the *h* in English just as it had been used in Old French—to mark the unexpected pronunciation of the consonant letter. This is the reason the *ch* digraph is spelled with a *c + h*. Following the same line of reasoning, the scribes used the letter *h* to alert the reader to the unexpected pronunciation of *s* when the /sh/ phoneme occurs in English words. The *sh* digraph reliably represents /sh/, except in French loan words, in which the Norman scribes used the *ch* digraph to represent /sh/ (*machine, chivalry, chef, sachet*).

In Old English spelling, the *wh* in <u>when</u> was written as *hw.* The French-speaking scribes reversed the letters, thereby introducing the *wh* digraph. Say *when.* Do you hear /hw/? The Old English *hw* letter sequence is a more accurate description of English pronunciation. Modern dictionaries use the Old English letter sequence—*hw*—to record the pronunciation of the *wh* digraph in words such as *hwen, hwite,* and *hwisper.*

Old English used two letters, the *thorn* and the *edh,* to record the voiced *th* (*this*) and the unvoiced *th* (*thumb*). These two Old English letters were used interchangeably, so the reader did not know whether to use the voiced or unvoiced pronunciation. The Norman French scribes preferred the *th* digraph and used it to represent both the voiced and the unvoiced phonemes. Eventually, both the *thorn* and the *edh* disappeared from the English alphabet. In the Middle English period, after the Old English *thorn* had dropped from the alphabet, the letter *y* was occasionally used to represent /th/ in the initial position. How would you pronounce "Ye Olde Malt Shoppe" in modern English? (If you said, "The Old Malt Shop," you are right! In the word *ye,* the letter *y* represents the /th/!)

s, g	**14.** What letter represents the sound we associate with *zh* in *measure?* _____ In *rouge?* _____
never	**15.** *Zh* _____ appears in a word, so it is not appropriate to make (never, seldom) a statement regarding reliability.

Review 9

1. Use the key symbol to indicate the sound of each consonant in each of the following words. Underline the consonant digraphs that represent distinctive phonemes.

   a. *shiver* **b.** *eggs*   **c.** *sure*   **d.** *share*   **e.** *treasure* **f.** *character*

   g. *leisure* **h.** *thought* **i.** *schools* **j.** *ghosts*   **k.** *charge*   **l.** *chute*

   m. *quack* **n.** *lotion*   **o.** *division* **p.** *Chicago* **q.** *magic*

2. How does the *zh* differ from the other consonant digraphs?

See the Answers to the Reviews section for the answers to Review 9, page 233.

th, ŧh, wh

no, no	**1.** Listen to the first phoneme while you pronounce *that* aloud. Compare it with the first phoneme in *thumb.* Do you hear the /t/ in either phoneme? _____ The /h/? _____
voiced	**2.** The /th/ heard in *thumb* is a whispered sound, a voiceless sound. However, we use our vocal cords when we say the first phoneme in *that.* We call it a _____ phoneme. (voiced, voiceless)
	3. You have learned that the *th* digraph represents two phonemes. One phoneme is the **voiced ŧh** (*that*); the other phoneme is the **voiceless th** (*thumb*). A **voiced phoneme** is produced when the vocal cords vibrate. A **voiceless phoneme** is produced when the vocal cords do not vibrate. Pronounce the words below. Write the words in which the *th* is voiced in Column 1 below. Write the words in which the *th* is voiceless in Column 2.
	think there thick these those thing this thank
there think these thick those thing this thank	**Column 1: Voiced** **Column 2: Voiceless** _____ _____ _____ _____ _____ _____ _____ _____
thorn	**4.** You must say the words in frame 3 aloud or you will not hear the voiced quality. Note that the voiceless phoneme has a whispered sound even when you say it aloud. The *th* in _____ has a whispered or voiceless sound. Our vocal cords (this, thorn) do not vibrate.

	5. Many people do not realize that *th* is a grapheme that represents two sounds that are just as different as the sounds represented by *p* and *b* or *s* and *z*. They automatically use the correct sound for the words they have heard before.
	Check the words below in which the *th* represents the voiceless phoneme. You will not be able to tell the difference if you do not say them out loud!
fourth, thought, thin,	*fourth* *the* *though* *thought* *them*
through, length, both	*they* *thin* *through* *length* *both*
	6. Repeat all the words in the previous frame in which the *th* represents the voiceless phoneme. Then say all the words in which the *th* represents the voiced phoneme.
	We shall use *t̶h* as the key symbol to represent the voiced sound. We shall use *th* as the key symbol to represent the voiceless sound.
	Rewrite the following words; underline the consonant digraphs that represent the voiceless phonemes and put a slash through the digraphs that represent the voiced phoneme.
toge̶t̶h̶er, thorn, throw	*together* _____ *thorn* _____ *throw* _____
phoneme	**7.** When we see an unknown word in our reading that contains the digraph *th,* we have no way of knowing which _____ it represents. We can use the dictionary. Some dictionaries may use the slash to indicate that the **t̶h**
voiced, *their*	represents the _____ phoneme as in _____. (*their, worth*)
	Dictionaries may also underline the voiced *t̲h̲* or print the voiced *th* in italics. Check your dictionary to see how it indicates the voiced **t̶h**.
the, bath	**8.** The *th* is not a reliable consonant digraph. It may represent the voiced sound heard in _____, the voiceless sound heard in _____,
/t/	(*the, third*) (*bath, bathe*) or, in rare instances, the / / as in *Thomas.*
wh	**9.** Another phoneme represented by two letters is _____ as heard in
what	*whale.* It is also heard in _____. (*who, what*)
	10. The phoneme /*wh*/ may give you some trouble because it is rapidly disappearing from our language. If you pronounce *weather* and *whether* exactly the same, you are following the trend in the United States.
	Many people make the phoneme represented by the key symbol *wh* sound
w You are correct, whatever your response.	like that represented by the single letter _____. What do you do? Pronounce *whistle* and *white*. Do they sound like *wistle* and *wite?* _____

Box 3.2

A Demonstration of Voiced and Voiceless Phonemes and Insight into Invented Spelling

You have learned that your vocal cords vibrate when pronouncing voiced phonemes and do not vibrate when pronouncing voiceless phonemes. However, sometimes it is difficult to determine from listening alone whether a particular phoneme is voiced or voiceless. To identify a voiced phoneme, you must find your voice. Here is a quick and easy way to do this:

1. Lightly place your hand over the lower part of your throat.

2. Pronounce each pair of words below:

   <u>z</u>ap <u>s</u>ap   <u>b</u>an <u>p</u>an   <u>d</u>en <u>t</u>en   <u>g</u>in <u>k</u>in   <u>v</u>an <u>f</u>an

3. Now pronounce each pair again, only this time draw out the phoneme that is represented by the underlined grapheme. When exaggerating the pronunciation of the phoneme, pay special attention to the vibration of your vocal cords. When you feel your vocal cords vibrate, you have found your voice, and you have also identified a voiced phoneme! Which phoneme in each word pair is voiced? Which is voiceless? (See answers below.)

4. To put this into a useful context for the teaching of reading, pronounce each pair once again, this time paying special attention to the way in which you form (articulate) each voiced and voiceless phoneme. Concentrate on your tongue, teeth, and lips. What do you notice about the way in which you articulate each voiced and voiceless phoneme pair? If you noticed that the phonemes in each pair represent the same articulation and differ only in the presence or the absence of breath, you are very observant!

Understanding the voiced and voiceless phoneme pairs will help you to interpret children's misspellings. Sometimes, as children spell, they confuse phonemes that have the same articulation but differ in voicing. Suppose a child writes *bumkin* for *pumpkin*. This misspelling might be due to having insufficient phonics knowledge or to misperceiving the letters *b* and *p*.

There is, however, another explanation: Perhaps the child, when thinking about the sounds of the English language, confused the /b/ and /p/ phonemes. After all, these phonemes are articulated in the same manner and differ only in their voiced and voiceless qualities. Understanding the voiced and voiceless phonemes helps you, the teacher, recognize the many ways in which children combine their knowledge of the phonemes of the English language with their knowledge of phonics in order to spell words when writing.

Answer to step 3: If you said that the voiced phonemes are /z/, /b/, /d/, /g/, and /v/, you are right!

wh *while*	**11.** Most dictionaries note this trend but continue to indicate the pronunciations of words beginning with *wh* as *hw*. We will use the key symbol _____ to represent the sound of the digraph, although it actually is better represented by *hw*. *Wh* represents the phoneme heard in _____. (Pronounce *whom* and (*whom, while*) *while* carefully so that you will hear the distinction.)
beginning	**12.** The *wh*, like the consonant *w*, appears at the _____ of a word or syllable and is followed by a vowel.

Review 10

1. We have identified each of the seven graphemes that serve as additions to our alphabet. Six of them are contained in the words below. Write the key symbol following the word in which each of six graphemes is found.

   swing _____   *whale* _____   *measure* _____

   mother _____   *flash* _____   *porch* _____

2. One grapheme is missing from the group of consonant digraphs above. It is

   found in _____.
         (*breath, breathe*)

3. We have identified all 18 single-letter consonant phonemes. They are heard in the initial position in each of the following words: *boat, dog, fish, goat, hat, jeep, kite, lion, moon, nut, pig, ring, sun, table, van, wagon, yo-yo, zipper.* Select key words from those above to illustrate phonemes represented by the underlined graphemes in the following words. Those that have no key word may be left blank.

   (1) *cou<u>l</u>d* _____

   (2) *<u>y</u>onder* _____

   (3) *<u>c</u>ircle* _____

   (4) *jumpe<u>d</u>* _____

   (5) *<u>g</u>ist* _____

   (6) *bom<u>b</u>* _____

   (7) *<u>ph</u>one* _____

   (8) *<u>g</u>hetto* _____

   (9) *o<u>f</u>* _____

   (10) *<u>g</u>et* _____

   (11) *<u>h</u>onor* _____

   (12) *tai<u>l</u>* _____

   (13) *m<u>y</u>* _____

   (14) *<u>w</u>rong* _____

   (15) *<u>l</u>ittle* _____

   (16) *li<u>k</u>e* _____

4. The word *gem* _____ a key word because the *g* _____
   (is, is not)   (does, does not)

   represent the phoneme we associate with the key symbol *g*.

5. The word *try* is not a key word for the *y* phoneme because the *y* is not at the

   beginning of the syllable; it is, therefore, not a _____ letter.
                                                      (consonant, vowel)

6. From the following words, select those that contain the /th/ phoneme:

path	*thorn*	*write*	*wheel*
white	*theme*	*this*	*author*
father	*whip*	*mouth*	*cloth*
wrong	*feather*	*them*	*whistle*

7. Which of the words in question 6 contain the /wh/ phoneme?

8. What do the consonants *w* and *y* have in common?

See the Answers to the Reviews section for the answers to Review 10, page 233.

ng

beginning follows	1. The phoneme /ng/ is different from the others represented by consonant digraphs in that it is never heard at the _____ of a syllable, or, to put (beginning, ending) it another way, it always _____ the vowel. (precedes, follows) Some dictionaries use the symbol η to indicate pronunciation. We will use *ng* in our study. You may use η, if you choose.
bang, ranjer, stung hinj, hunggry, junggle yes no	2. Say the words below aloud. Rewrite the words to show pronunciation of the consonants. (Copy the vowels, omitting silent *e*). bang _____ ranger _____ stung _____ hinge _____ hungry _____ jungle _____ Does each contain the letters *ng*? _____ Does each contain the digraph *ng*? _____
/ng/ sing, pingk, blangk, fingger jinjer, singk, trianggle, lingk	3. Recall that *n* generally represents / / when followed by *g* or *k*. Rewrite the following words, indicating pronunciation of the consonants. Use *ng* (but underline it) to represent the consonant digraph. Work carefully. This takes a keen ear. sing _____ pink _____ blank _____ finger _____ ginger _____ sink _____ triangle _____ link _____
finger, triangle	4. In which words from the preceding frame do you hear hard *g*, /g/, as well as /ng/?

Study Guide

Consonant Digraphs ch, sh, th, wh, ng

Consonant Digraph	Key Symbol	Key Word
ch	ch	chair
sh	sh	ship
th	th	thumb
th	t͟h	that
wh	wh	whale
	zh	treasure
ng	ng	king

The consonant digraphs are two-letter combinations that represent unique phonemes. The phonemes that the digraphs represent are different from the sounds associated with either of the two consonant letters when they occur alone in words.

ch   The digraph *ch* is not reliable. *Ch* may represent the /ch/ (*chair*), the /k/ (*character*), or the /sh/ (*machine*).

sh   The /sh/ is a common sound in the English language. The *sh* (*ship*) is very reliable.

Voiceless th   The digraph *th* represents two distinct phonemes, one voiceless and one voiced. The /th/ in the key word *thumb* is a whispered sound, which we call the voiceless *th* (*thorn*, *thick*).

Voiced t͟h   We use our vocal cords to pronounce the /t͟h/ phoneme in the key word *that*, which we refer to as the voiced *t͟h* (*there*, *father*). Dictionaries may use a slash, a line, an underline, or italics to indicate the voiced digraph *t͟h* (*th̶*, *th*, *th*). We will use the slash (*t͟h*) as the key symbol.

wh   The digraph *wh* represents /hw/ (*why*, *white*). *Wh* occurs in the beginning of syllables and is followed by a vowel.

zh   While /zh/ occurs in English words (*measure*, *vision*), it is never represented in a word with the grapheme *zh*. The /zh/ may be represented by the *s* (*pleasure*, *vision*), the *g* (*collage*), or the *z* (*seizure*).

ng   The digraph *ng* is never heard at the beginning of a syllable and always follows a vowel. The letters *ng* may represent /ng/ (*sing*, *among*). The letter *n* may also represent /ng/ when it is followed by the letter *g* (*finger—fing-ger*) or the letter *k* (*pink—pingk*). Your dictionary may use the symbol η to represent /ng/.

kang ga roo
 	
sing gle
	5. Which set of symbols below indicates the pronunciation of *kangaroo?* Of *single?*
	
	  kan ga roo *kang ga roo* _____
	
	  sin gle *sing le* *sing gle* _____

consonant digraph (If you said digraph, you are also correct.) *gingham*	**6.** The letters *n* and *g* together in a word are most commonly a _____, that is, a two-letter combination representing a single phoneme, as in _____. *(gingham, orange)*
ungrateful, two	**7.** However, the *n* and *g* may represent *two* separate phonemes, as in _____. The *n* and *g* represent _____ phonemes when *(ungrateful, among)* *(How many?)* they are in separate syllables (*un grate ful*).

consonant digraphs
 	
chair
 	
sh
 	
zh
 	
th
 	
that
 	
whale
 	
ng
	8. We have identified the seven _____ that represent distinct phonemes not represented by the single letters in the alphabet. They are as follows:
	
	    1. *ch* as in _____
	                (chair, choir)
	
	    2. _____ as in *ship*
	
	    3. _____ sounded like the *s* in *treasure*
	
	    4. _____ as in *thumb*
	
	    5. *th* as in _____
	                (that, thrill)
	
	    6. *wh* as in _____
	                (whole, whale)
	
	    7. _____ as in *king*

/f/, /j/ /f/, *light*	**9.** The digraphs *ph, dg,* and *gh* may represent single phonemes. These consonant digraphs are not among the seven digraphs in frame 6 (page 72) because they represent sounds that already have key symbols. The *ph* represents / / as in *graph*. The *dg* represents / / as in *dodge*. The *gh* represents / / in *cough* or may be silent, as in _____. *(light, laugh)*

Review 11

1. Rewrite these words, showing consonant pronunciation. (This calls for acute hearing.) Underline the consonant digraphs. Pronounce as you would in the actual word.

   a. *mango, mangle, mangy*
   b. *pin, ping, pink, ping-pong*
   c. *ban, bang, bank, banking*
   d. *ran, rang, rank, ranking*

2. There are 25 consonant sounds in the American-English language.

   a. We identify 18 of them with single-letter symbols. Write the 18 consonant letters.

   b. We use _____ to identify the seven additional phonemes. Write the seven consonant digraphs.

3. C was not included in question 2a because _____.

4. What other consonant letters were not included? _____

5. The digraph *ph* was not included in question 2b because _____.

6. Rewrite the following words using appropriate key symbols for the consonants. Omit silent consonants. Copy vowels as they are.

whole	_____	*high*	_____
quick	_____	*gopher*	_____
wholly	_____	*phone*	_____
thatch	_____	*that*	_____
taught	_____	*comb*	_____
glistening	_____	*etch*	_____
rustle	_____	*doubt*	_____
knot	_____	*budget*	_____
wrap	_____	*thinking*	_____

See the Answers to the Reviews section for the answers to Review 11, page 234.

Consonant Clusters and Blends

letters consonant digraphs two /b/, /l/	**1.** We have identified each of the 25 consonant phonemes of the American-English language: 18 of these are represented by single _____; 7 are represented by _____. Now let us turn our attention to consonants that are blended together when pronounced. Pronounce the word *blue.* How many consonant phonemes does *blue* contain? _____ What are they? _____
one blends	**2.** A consonant **digraph** is a two-letter grapheme that represents _____ speech sound. The word *blue* does **not** contain a consonant digraph. Neither the *b* nor the *l* loses its identity. Both are sounded, but they are blended together. We call such combinations of consonant letters **consonant clusters** and the sounds they represent consonant _____. We need to study the **consonant blends** because, in many ways, they act as one phoneme.
bl, cl, fl, dr ft *sk, fr, spr, spl* *Sh* is a consonant digraph. *k*	**3.** **A consonant cluster is composed of two or more consonants that blend together when sounded to form a consonant blend.** The letters do not form a consonant digraph. The phonemes in the blend retain their individual identities. Pronounce the words below. For each, fill in the blank with the letters that form the consonant cluster. black _____ clown _____ flying _____ draft _____ desk _____ fry _____ spray _____ splash _____ Why did you omit the *sh* in *splash?* _____ The *ck* in *black* represents the single consonant _____, not a blend.
s *p, l,* blends	**4.** Some teachers' manuals and curriculum guides use the term **cluster** to describe these consonant combinations; other manuals and guides use the term blend. When consonant blend is used, **blend** refers to both letters and sounds. In the word *splash,* for example, the letters _____, _____, and _____, as well as /spl/, are called _____. Recognizing that blend is a common term for consonant clusters, you may use either term in your answers. Consistent with the trend to use blend when the intention is to refer to the consonant clusters that are blended when pronounced, we will use these terms interchangeably.

r, l, s

5. Pronounce the words in each set below. Each set has one of the common "blenders." Write the letter common to each consonant cluster in the set.

1	2	3
brown	flame	skate
street	claim	snow
great	split	street
_____	_____	_____

r

l, s

6. The common blenders are represented by the letters _____,

_____, and _____. However, there are clusters that do not contain these letters.

blend or cluster

digraph

sh, ch, th

7. We distinguish a _____ from a consonant digraph by the fact that it

represents two or more phonemes blended together. The _____ represents a single sound. Check those combinations in the following list that do **not** represent consonant blends.

bl	cr	qu	tr	scr
cl	dr	tw	sh	spr
gl	sk	ch	sm	spl
sl	pr	th	mp	str

w

equal, quart, queen, quick

8. It may seem strange to classify *qu* as a consonant blend (or cluster) when *u* is a vowel.

The *u* in this case, however, takes the sound of the consonant _____. So this combination is actually a /kw/ **blend**. Select the words with the /kw/ blend from the following:

equal   quart   unique   queen   opaque   quick

tree, twin, great, splash, quit
please, street, slow, pretty, grasp
(**Not** sh or ch!)

9. Underline the consonant blends (clusters) in these words:

tree	twin	great	splash	chair	quit
please	she	street	slow	pretty	grasp

s, h

10. The *sh* in *splash* and the *sh* in *she* cannot be blends because the sounds

represented by the _____ and the _____ are not heard.

field, lamp, bent, task

fast, hand, belt, draft

11. Many consonant clusters represent phonemes that are "blended" together in the final position in English words or syllables. Read the words below. Underline the consonant blends (clusters) that occur at the end of the words.

field	dish	lamp	bent	task
fast	hand	church	belt	draft

train *ta<u>sk</u>*	**12.** As you have seen, consonant blends may appear at the beginning of a word or syllable, as in *train,* or at the end of a word or syllable, as in *task.* Underline the appropriate blend (cluster) in each of these examples: *train, task.*

13. Arrange the words below in two columns: those with clusters representing phonemes that are blended in pronunciation and those with digraphs. Some words may be used in both columns. Underline to indicate the part in each word that qualifies it to be in the particular column.

			Blends	Digraphs
<u>sp</u>eech	<u>sp</u>ee<u>ch</u>		_____	_____
<u>r</u>e<u>st</u>	<u>ch</u>ur<u>ch</u>		_____	_____
di<u>gr</u>aph	di<u>gr</u>a<u>ph</u>	speech rest church digraph shield	_____	_____
<u>sh</u>iel<u>d</u>	<u>sh</u>iel<u>d</u>		_____	_____

t, h, r *th*	**14.** There are many words in which a consonant digraph is a part of a consonant blend. Examine the word *throw.* The first three letters, _____, _____, and _____, compose a cluster. Within the cluster is the consonant digraph _____. All blend together: /*thr*/.

<u>thr</u>, <u>shr</u>, <u>chr</u>, <u>phr</u> *ch (chrome), ph (phrase)*	**15.** Draw a single line under the consonant digraph and another line under the entire cluster in each of these words: through shrimp chrome phrase Which of the consonant digraphs in the above words are not among the seven key symbols needed to complete the phonemes of our language? _____ _____

squ, str, str ngth, *bl st, sm, thr ft*	**16.** All consonant clusters (written) represent blends (spoken). Write the consonants that represent blends in these words: squash strap strength blast small thrift

strength, /ng/, /th/	**17.** Which word in frame 16 has a cluster composed of two digraphs? _____ The two digraphs that blend together are / / and / /.

Blends	**Digraphs**	**18.** Now arrange the words below in two columns: those containing clusters that represent blends and those containing digraphs. Some of these words, too, may be used in both columns, so underline to indicate the part of each word that places it in a column. toast shelter grapheme three clanging strike altogether father	**Blends Digraphs**
toa<u>st</u> *<u>gr</u>apheme* *<u>thr</u>ee* *<u>cl</u>anging* *<u>str</u>ike*	*<u>sh</u>elter* *grap<u>h</u>eme* *<u>th</u>ree* *clan<u>g</u>ing* *altoge<u>th</u>er* *fa<u>th</u>er*		

phoneme	**19.** We have studied the single-consonant phonemes (Part Two), the consonant digraphs, and the consonant clusters that are blended together when pronounced. We include the clusters because, in many ways, one blend, when pronounced, acts as though it were one _____.

Study Guide
Consonant Blends

Consonant Blends (Clusters)

A *consonant blend* is a *cluster* or group of two or more consonants that *blend* together when pronounced (*clown*, *spray*). Each consonant letter represents a sound. Some teachers' manuals and guides use the term *cluster*. Other manuals and guides use the term *blend*. When manuals and guides use consonant blend, the term *blend* refers to both letters (the *st* in *stop*) and sounds (/*st*/ in /*stop*/). We will use the more common term, *blend,* in this study guide. You may wish to substitute *cluster* if this term is used in your teachers' manual or curriculum guide.

Beginning Consonant Blends

The most common blends that occur at the beginning of a word or syllable include one of the letters *r, l,* or *s.*

r Blends		*l* Blends		*s* Blends			
br	bright	bl	black	sc	scout	scr	scrap
cr	crayon	cl	class	sk	sky	spl	splash
dr	dress	fl	flower	sl	slip	spr	spring
fr	free	gl	glad	sm	small	squ	square
gr	green	pl	plan	sn	snow	str	string
pr	pretty			sp	spot		
tr	train			st	stop		
				sw	swim		

tw and dw   The *tw* (*twin*) and *dw* (*dwell*) blends are less common in English than the blends that include one of the letters *r, l,* or *s.*

qu   *Qu* is a consonant blend when it represents /kw/ as in *quick* and *quiet.*

Consonant blends are taught as units, rather than as single graphemes (e.g., *st* as representing two blended phonemes, rather than as an isolated /s/ and an isolated /t/).

Consonant Digraphs and Consonant Blends

Blends that occur at the beginning of a syllable may include a consonant digraph and a consonant blend, such as in *shr* (*shrimp*) and *thr* (*throw*).

Final Position Blends

Many consonant blends occur in the final position of an English syllable. Some of the more common final blends include these:

ld	old	nd	end	st	most	mp	amp	lt	salt
lk	milk	nt	went	sk	desk	ft	lift		

In teaching, vowels may be combined with consonant blends to create sequences called **rimes**. You will learn about rimes in Part VI of this book. Examples of vowel and consonant blend rimes include *old* (*told*); *ild* (*wild*); *ilk* (*milk*); *alt* (*salt*); *end* (*mend*); *ent* (*went*); *ost* (*most*); *esk* (*desk*); *amp* (*lamp*); and *ift* (*lift*).

Review 12

1. A blend (or cluster) differs from a consonant digraph in that _____.

2. Why were no key symbols given to represent the blends?

3. Seven specific digraphs, together with 18 single letters, supply us with the consonant sounds of our language. Which of the seven digraphs appear in the following paragraph? List them in the order in which they make their *first* appearance.

   > *It started as a pleasure trip. The driver, nearing the exit leading through the city, changed lanes. He jerked the wheel too quickly and landed on the shoulder.*

4. There are three unnecessary single letters in our alphabet. Illustrations are in the above paragraph. Rewrite these words to show how other letters could be substituted.

5. What consonant blends are heard at the *beginning* of the words in the above paragraph?

See the Answers to the Reviews section for the answers to Review 12, page 234.

For a helpful summary and review of the phonemes, turn to page 143. Work through the consonant section, using a separate sheet of paper. Then you will be able to have a complete review after you have studied the vowels.

Recap I

25 phonemes word	1. In our study of consonants, we identified _____ consonant _____ (the smallest units of sound that distinguish one _____ from another).
symbol b, d, f, g, h, j, k, l, m, n, p r, s, t, v, w, y, z digraphs ch, sh, th, t̶h̶, wh, zh, ng	2. To know exactly to which sound we are referring, we assigned each phoneme a key _____ and a key word. As you go through the alphabet, write the 18 consonant letters that symbolize specific phonemes: ____ ____ ____ ____ ____ ____ ____ ____ ____ ____ ____ ____ ____ ____ ____ ____ ____. But we need 25 symbols. We use _____ to complete our representation of the consonant phonemes: ____ ____ ____ ____ ____ ____ ____.

phoneme	**3.** Although consonants are fairly reliable (there is a high relationship between grapheme and _____), there are irregularities.
phoneme	A letter (or grapheme) may represent more than one _____. For example:
/k/, /s/	the *c* represents / / in *camp* and / / in *ace*
/d/, /t/	the *d* represents / / in *date* and / / in *jumped*
/j/, /g/	the *g* represents / / in *age* and / / in *go*
/n/, /ng/	the *n* represents / / in *ran* and / / in *rank*
/s/, /sh/, /z/, /zh/	the *s* represents / / in *soap*, / / in *surely*, / / in *runs*, and / / in *measure*
/s/, /z/, /zh/	the *z* represents / / in *waltz*, / / in *quiz*, and / / in *azure*

	4. A phoneme may be represented by more than one grapheme. Write the phoneme that is represented in each set of words. Then rewrite the words, using the key symbols for the consonants.
/f/, fase, lauf, fone	/ / as in *face* _____, *laugh* _____, *phone* _____
/j/, paje, joke	/ / *page* _____, *joke* _____,
fuje, grajual	*fudge* _____, *gradual* _____
/k/, ankor, antikue	/ / *anchor* _____, *antique* _____,
kue	*cue* _____
/z/, uze, frozen	/ / *use* _____, *frozen* _____,
zylofone	*xylophone* _____

silent	**5.** A letter may represent no phoneme: It may be _____. Some common silent letter patterns include the following:
t	(1) The second of two like consonants, as the _____ in *letters* and
s	the _____ in *dress*
b	(2) _____ following *m*, as in *bomb,* or followed by *t*, as in *doubt*
k	(3) _____ followed by *n*, as in *know*
h	(4) _____ following *g*, as in *ghost*
	Did you feel there were any words that did not belong in this and the last three frames, words you would pronounce differently? Check your dictionary to verify.

	6. Repeat the generalization regarding the hard and soft sounds of *c* and *g*. Check each of the following words that do not follow the generalization.							
girl, give	*epic*	*gem*	*ghost*	*girl*	*cake*	*gate*	*cycle*	*give*

before	**7.** The consonants *w* and *y* are found _____ the vowel in a word.
	(before, after)
no	Is the consonant *y* often a silent letter? _____
k	**8.** The key symbol for *q* is _____.

Did you get all the exercises in this recap correct? What a sense of satisfaction you must have. Congratulations! We have been studying the consonants, the most regular of all the phonemes. But the consonants cannot get along without the vowels. We will now proceed with a study of the vowels and their relationships with the consonants.

Reference

National Governors Association Center for Best Practices & Council of Chief State School Officers. (2010). *Common Core State Standards for English language arts & history/social studies, science, and technical subjects: Reading: Foundational Skills—Phonological Awareness, Phonics and Word Recognition.* Washington, DC: Authors. Retrieved May 15, 2012, from http://www.corestandards.org/CCSSI_ELA%20Standards.pdf

Part Four

Vowels

Children learn phonics during the first three years they are in school; that is, kindergarten, first and second grade. Vowel letter-sound learning begins in kindergarten when children are expected to learn the most common spelling-sound correspondences for the short and long sounds of *a, e, i, o* and *u* (kindergarten standard 3b). Vowels are often found in the middle of one-syllable words or syllables; that is, preceding the consonant, as in *l<u>u</u>nch* or, in the silent *e* pattern, both before and after the final consonant, as in *m<u>ade</u>*. Therefore, children need to be aware of the middle sounds in spoken words and, of course, must be able to segment and blend. It is logical, then, for the teacher of reading to call attention to the middle sounds in spoken words that are represented by the vowel letters in written words. While kindergarten standard 3d does not specifically mention knowledge of vowel letter-sounds, this standard would apply to vowels when similarly spelled words differ in the sounds that vowel letters represent.

Building on the foundation developed in kindergarten, first graders are expected to decode one-syllable words that sound like they are spelled, such as *free* (3b), identify words with the final-e long vowel pattern, as in *brave* (3c) and read words with other vowel patterns, such as *trail* (3c). Second graders continue to increase and refine their knowledge of vowel spelling-sound correspondences. By the end of the second grade, children are sensitive to long and short vowels in words (3a), know additional vowel patterns (3b) and decode two-syllable words that are spelled with long vowels (3c). While there are no standards that specifically pertain to vowels beyond the second grade, children in the third through fifth grades are expected to decode multisyllable words. This expectation has bearing on vowel knowledge. Each written syllable contains one vowel spelling-sound pattern. Therefore, knowledge of vowels is necessary for decoding short, one-syllable words, as well as long, multisyllable words. You will learn the important vowel patterns as you complete the frames in this part.

A reminder: Do not pull the mask down until you have written your response to the entire frame.

Introduction

vowels	**1.** The 26 letters of the alphabet are divided into two major categories: consonants and _____.
phonemes phonemes, 19 phonemes	**2.** Although there are many variations due to dialect, individual speech patterns, and so forth, for all practical purposes in the task of teaching reading, we can consider the American-English language to contain 44 separate and distinctive _____. We have noted that 25 of these are consonant _____. Therefore, there are _____ vowel _____.
vowels	**3.** The letters *a, e, i, o, u,* and sometimes *w* and *y* are classified as _____.
yo-yo	**4.** How can you tell when *y* is a consonant and when it is a vowel? You have learned that the key symbol *y* (consonant) represents the phoneme heard in _____. *Y* functions as a consonant **only** when it represents the (yo-yo, say) phoneme heard in *yo-yo*.
initial	**5.** The consonant *y* is always the _____ letter in a word or syllable. (initial, final) It is always found before the vowel.
<u>y</u>ellow, <u>y</u>et, be<u>y</u>ond consonant vowel	**6.** Study the words below. Underline each *y* that is a consonant. *they yellow yet may very beyond* The _____ *y* is never a silent letter. (consonant, vowel) The _____ *y* is often a silent letter. (consonant, vowel)
vowel	**7.** *Y* does not serve as a key symbol for a vowel phoneme. **Y represents no *vowel* sound of its own. When *y* is a** **_____, its pronunciation is shown by the key symbols we** **associate with the *i* or the *e*.**
y̆ear, gy̆m, my̆, ready̆, cany̆on	**8.** Study the function of the *y* in the words below. Place a <u>c</u> or a <u>v</u> above each *y* to identify *y* as a consonant or as a vowel. Check each *y* consonant to see that it represents the same sound as the initial phoneme in *yo-yo*. *year gym my ready canyon*
canyon	In which word is the *y* the first letter in the second syllable? _____

wagon	**9.** Now let us examine the *w*. You have learned that *w* as a consonant represents the phoneme heard in _____. (*wagon, snow*)

symbol	**10.** **As a vowel, the *w* represents no
	                    distinct phoneme of its own.**
	
	Therefore, it cannot be represented by a key _____.
	
	  ***W* is always used in combination with another
	vowel, as in *few, cow,* and *grow.***

thaw, threw
 	
follows
	11. Underline the *w*s that function as vowels in the following words:
	
	  water which thaw threw dwarf
	
	(Be sure that they do not represent the phoneme you hear at the beginning of *wagon.*)
	
	The vowel *w* always _____ another vowel.
	  (*precedes, follows*)

w, y	**12.** Two of the seven vowels are not identified by distinctive key symbols because they do not represent sounds of their own. These are the vowels _____ and _____.
a, e, i, o *u*	**13.** Now let us turn our attention to the vowels that do represent phonemes and can be assigned key symbols to distinguish them from each other. The vowel phonemes are represented by five letters. They are _____, _____, _____, _____, and _____.
cannot be	**14.** These five vowels, alone and in combination with another vowel, represent the 19 vowel phonemes of our language. Therefore, there _____ a one-to-one correspondence between phoneme and letter. (is, cannot be)
a, five	**15.** Study the words below. Pronounce the sound represented by the underlined vowel. *same dare can arm about* We can see that one vowel, the _____, represents at least _____ different phonemes.
phoneme vowels	**16.** Each vowel letter represents more than one _____. If we meet an unfamiliar word, how will we know which sounds its vowels represent? There are some patterns (with exceptions, of course) that will give us some help in determining the sounds represented by the _____ in unknown words.

phonemes vowel	**17.** Our task, then, is twofold: (1) to identify the vowel _____ of the American-English language and assign each a key symbol and (2) to become acquainted with the generalizations that will aid us in associating the correct phonemes with the _____ letters in unknown words.
     letters	**18.** For our study, we shall divide the vowel phonemes into two major groups: (1) those represented by single vowel letters and (2) those represented by combinations of vowel letters. Each of the single letters (as in group 1) and each of the combinations of _____ represent **one** phoneme.
letter	**19.** We shall begin our study of the vowel phonemes with group 1: those represented by a single vowel _____. <div align="center">(letter, phoneme)</div>

Review 13

1. The vowel letters are _____, _____, _____, _____, _____, and sometimes _____ and _____.

2. We need not select key symbols to represent the sounds of _____ and _____ because they duplicate the sounds of other vowels.

3. Indicate whether the *w* and the *y* in these words are consonants or vowels by writing C̲ or V̲ following each word:

   yet _____   *type* _____   *play* _____

   wide _____   *draw* _____   *when* _____

4. The *w* in *white* is part of a _____ _____.
   (consonant, vowel)   (blend, digraph)

5. There are _____ vowel phonemes than there are vowel letters.
   (fewer, more)

6. How many vowel phonemes will we need to identify?

See the Answers to the Reviews section for the answers to Review 13, page 234.

Short Vowel Sounds

a	ǎ	ǎpple	
e	ě	ědge	
i	ǐ	ǐgloo	
o	ǒ	ǒx	
u	ǔ	ǔmbrella	

ǎ (apple)   ě (edge)   ǐ (igloo)   ǒ (ox)   ǔ (umbrella)

1. Pronounce the words above. Listen to the initial phoneme. One set of phonemes represented by single vowel letters includes those that stand for "short" vowel sounds. The **breve** (˘) is a diacritical mark used to indicate the specific pronunciation of each vowel in this group. Its linguistic relationship to "short" can be noted in such words as *abbreviate* and *brevity*. It is the custom, in phonics, to call the vowel sound whose key symbol contains a breve a **short vowel** sound.

1	**2**	**3**
a	ǎ	apple
e	ě	edge
i	ǐ	igloo
o	ǒ	ox
u	ǔ	umbrella

short

breve

The vowels in column 3 at the right represent the _____ sounds. Each key symbol (2) consists of the vowel marked with a _____. Mark the initial vowel in each key word.

ǐ, ǒ, ǔ

phonemes

2. The key symbols that identify the vowels when they represent their short sounds are ǎ, ě, _____, _____, and _____. Reading would be easier if five additional characters representing these _____
(letters, phonemes)
were added to our alphabet.

---

ox

map

3. It is important to note that various dictionaries indicate pronunciation in different ways. We must study the pronunciation key of the particular dictionary we use. For example, some dictionaries use the ä to represent the short o (ǒ), key word _____. Other dictionaries may use the symbol ə to represent the short u (ǔ). These dictionaries use bəs to represent the pronunciation of *bus*. You may find that your dictionary indicates the pronunciation of short vowel sounds with the letter and no diacritical mark. In this case, the pronunciation of *map* is written _____.

---

m

a, consonant

p

apple

4. Pronounce the word *map*. Listen for three phonemes: the consonant phoneme represented by _____, the vowel phoneme represented by _____, and the _____ phoneme represented by _____. Pronounce the vowel sound alone. The same vowel sound is heard in _____.
(apple, far)

---

mǎp

ran, grab, back

5. Pronounce the vowel phoneme in *map*. Rewrite *map* using key symbols.

_____

Now pronounce the words below. Check those words in which the vowel phoneme is the same as that heard in *map*.

ran   all   car   above   grab   back   paw

three hĕn	**6.** There are _____ phonemes in *hen*. Listen for the vowel phoneme as you say *hen* aloud. Rewrite *hen* using key symbols to indicate its pronunciation. _____
mĕt, hĕm, ĕnd	**7.** Mark with a breve each of the vowels in the words below that represents the same vowel phoneme heard in the key word *edge*. *feed met her hem end reward* If you find this difficult, pronounce the first vowel phoneme heard in *edge*. Then pronounce each word, substituting that sound for each vowel phoneme.
three rĕd	**8.** Read this sentence aloud: *I read a book yesterday.* How many phonemes do you hear when you say *read* in the sentence above? _____ Rewrite *read* using a key symbol to indicate each phoneme. _____ You have written in code. Anyone who knows the code can pronounce *read* correctly without a sentence to clarify it.
pĭn, drĭp, lĭft, thĭk	**9.** Pronounce *igloo.* Now say the first vowel phoneme. Rewrite the following words using key symbols to code each phoneme: *pin* _____ *drip* _____ *lift* _____ *thick* _____

three
 	
ox
	10. Pronounce *hot.* It contains _____ phonemes.
	        (How many?)
	The vowel phoneme sounds the same as that in _____.
	                                  (boy, ox)

lĭp, tŏp, pŏp, lăp, glăd, pŏd key symbols	**11.** Use a breve to indicate the short vowel in each word that contains a short vowel phoneme. *lip top note pop lap glad pod home* The vowel letters with the marks you placed above them are the _____ for the phonemes they represent.
breve or ŭ jŭmp, ŭs, dŭk, cŭp, tŭb	**12.** Pronounce *umbrella.* We use a _____ to indicate that the *u* represents a short sound. Now pronounce the vowel sound alone. Rewrite the following words to show pronunciation. Place the correct diacritical marks above all the vowels in these words that represent the same sound as the first vowel phoneme in the key word *umbrella.* *jump use us duck cup house tub*

vowel short, *i* (or *ĭ*)	**13.** We have noted the sounds represented by *a, e, i, o,* and *u.* How about the *y?* *gym sys tem sym bol* Study the words above. Each contains a _____ *y* <u>within</u> the (consonant, vowel) syllable. The *y* represents the _____ sound of the letter _____. (long, short)
yes *Dăn kĕpt hĭs pŏp gŭn*	**14.** The key words given at the beginning of this section will help us remember the phoneme for each vowel. A sentence that contains each of the short vowel phonemes may be easier to remember. Would the sentence below furnish a key word for each of the short vowel phonemes? _____ (Check each word with the set at the beginning of this section.) Mark the vowels with breves. *Dan kept his pop gun.*
4 *Năn's pĕt ĭs nŏt fŭn.* *Săm's nĕt ĭs nŏt cŭt.* *Săd Tĕd ĭn hŏt hŭt.* *All mĕn ĭn hŏt bŭs.*	**15.** Look at the groups of words below. In each group, mark the vowels that represent the short sound. Number _____ is not a good key phrase. (1) *Nan's pet is not fun.* (2) *Sam's net is not cut.* (3) *Sad Ted in hot hut.* (4) *All men in hot bus.*
short *fĕnce, dŭg*	**16.** Pronounce the vowel phoneme represented by the vowel letter in each of the words below. *an fed pin hot cup* Each vowel represents its _____ phoneme. Now pronounce the vowel phoneme in each of the following words. Place a breve above each vowel in this set of words that represents its short sound. Check carefully. *car fence pine cow dug*
hĕd, sĕd *sĕnts, ĕnd*	**17.** Say the words below. Listen carefully for the vowel phonemes. Rewrite each word, using the key symbols that indicate the sounds we associate with the vowel and consonant phonemes. *head* _____ *said* _____ *cents* _____ *end* _____
vowel consonant	**18.** **The most common vowel-consonant pattern is that of VC (vowel-consonant), in which the V (vowel) represents its short sound.** There are many one-syllable words and many syllables in multisyllable words that follow this pattern. These words and syllables consist of a _____ followed by a _____.

short breve	**19.** **The VC pattern gives clues to the pronunciation of unknown words. We would expect the vowel to represent** the _____ sound. To indicate the pronunciation of the vowel, we place a _____ above it. Your teachers' manual or curriculum guide may use CVC to identify the short vowel pattern. The CVC pattern indicates that a consonant precedes the vowel. You may use either VC or CVC in your answers.
shop, brick, rab bit, thrift	**20.** The C (consonant) in the VC pattern may represent a digraph or a blend. Check the syllables (or one-syllable words) that are spelled with the VC pattern. shop brick rab bit be side rain thrift

CCVC, CVC, CCVC
 	
CVCC, CCVCC, VC
	21. Show the vowel-consonant pattern of the words below. Use a C to represent *each* consonant and a *V* for each vowel.
	
	    shop _____ hat _____ chat _____
	
	    fast _____ trust _____ in _____

yes no lăst, sĕt, lŏt	**22.** Do all the words below have the VC pattern? _____ Do all the vowels represent the short sound? _____ Examine the words below. Mark the vowels that represent the short sounds with breves. Work carefully. far last set lot her

one
 	
one
 	
two
 	
two
 	
phoneme
	23. To obtain a better understanding of the short vowels, we will consider them as they usually occur within the English syllable. A **syllable** is the smallest unit of speech that has one vowel phoneme.
	
	When you say the word *mat,* you hear _____ vowel phoneme(s).
	                              (How many?)
	
	The word *mat* consists of _____ syllable(s). When you pronounce
	                         (How many?)
	
	mattress, you hear _____ vowel phoneme(s). *Mattress* has
	                        (How many?)
	
	_____ syllable(s). A syllable in the English language has only one
	(How many?)
	
	vowel _____.

chim   can   wish
 	
men   sun   win   gin
	24. We often find the vowel phoneme in a closed syllable to be short.
	
	   A closed syllable ends with a consonant <u>phoneme</u>.
	
	Pronounce the words below. Check the closed syllables, including closed one-syllable words.
	
	       chim ney tree can wish
	
	         men sun win dow begin

short	**25.** One vowel in a closed syllable (or in a closed one-syllable word) usually represents its _____ sound. With your key sentence in mind (frame 14), check the vowel phonemes in the following words. Which words do *not* have the short vowel phoneme?
don't, bird	clap don't skin sick trust fed bend bird
closed	**26.** Syllables with the VC pattern (such as *ant*) are _____ syllables; those (closed, open)
closed	with the CVC pattern (such as *chant*) are _____ syllables. (closed, open)
	27. *chick en* *pen cil*
two	*Chicken* and *pencil* are _____ -syllable words. Is each syllable a (How many?)
yes	closed syllable? _____ Write the closed syllables here:
chick en, pen cil	_____ _____ _____ _____
yes	Is there a single vowel in each syllable? _____
	28. The **accented syllable** in a multisyllable word receives greater stress than other syllables. Say *chicken* and *pencil*. Listen for the syllable that receives the greater emphasis. If you do not "hear" the accented syllable, pronounce each word twice. Emphasize the first syllable and then the last syllable: *CHICK en* or
first	*chick EN; PEN cil* or *pen CIL.* The _____ syllable receives the greater stress. (first, second)
	The vowel phoneme in an accented syllable is easier to hear. Your dictionary may use ' to indicate the accented syllable. We can show the syllable and accent
pen'cil	for chicken: *chick'* en. Show the syllable and accent for *pencil.* _____
	29. We might expect that we can properly indicate the pronunciation of each of the vowels in *chicken* and *pencil* with a breve. If you pronounce the words too carefully—that is, artificially—you might indicate their pronunciations that way.
	Say a sentence aloud containing the word *chicken* and then one with *pencil*.
unaccented	You will notice that the vowel in the _____ syllable represents (accented, unaccented) more of an "uh" sound and not the phonemes you hear in the words *edge* and *igloo.*
	30. The generalization for the short vowel phoneme is most useful when it is stated as follows:
	A single vowel in a closed accented syllable usually represents the short sound of the vowel.
	Indicate the pronunciation of the syllables that follow this generalization:
lĕm băn hŏp	re pay lem on ban jo hop per

(Any errors? Recheck the sound!) wĕt, păn, pĕg, trŭck, fĭt, stŏp	**31.** Let us review the short sounds of the vowels. Check the words below against the key words you have learned. Place a breve above each of the vowels that represents the short sound of that vowel. date wet pan peg truck fit stop cute
short	**32.** We can expect that single vowels in closed accented syllables will usually represent _____ sounds. Remember that all one-syllable words are considered accented syllables.
short shelve, glance, fence, rinse	**33.** There are many words in which the vowel is followed by two consonants and a final *e* (VCCe). Note that in words ending with a vowel that is followed by two consonants and a final *e,* the first vowel phoneme is usually _____. <div align="right">(short, long)</div>Which words have the VCCe pattern? shelve glance fence ride rinse smile
e consonants, short silent	**34.** Study the words below. dance wedge rinse fence bronze lapse bridge smudge We can make a generalization concerning these words. **When a word (or a syllable) has two vowels, one of which is a final** **_____, and the two vowels are separated by two** **_____, the first vowel often represents its _____** **sound and the final *e* is _____.**
VCCe	**35.** The generalization is applied to words that have the ending pattern of VCCe (with exceptions, of course!). The word *lapse* is an example of the VCCe pattern: vowel–consonant–consonant–final *e.* **When a word (or a syllable) has two vowels, one of which is a final *e,*** **and the two vowels are separated by two consonants,** **the first vowel often represents its short sound and the final *e*** **is silent.** *Since* and *judge* end with the _____ pattern.
chance, ridge, since sense, prince	**36.** Check the words below that end with the VCCe pattern. chance ridge telephone since could shape tree sense toy prince

Study Guide

Short Vowels

Short Vowel	Key Symbol	Key Word
a	ă	apple
e	ě	edge
i	ǐ	igloo
o	ǒ	ox
u	ŭ	umbrella

Breve (˘) The breve (˘) is the diacritical mark used to indicate the pronunciation of the short vowels. Some dictionaries indicate pronunciation in different ways. Your dictionary may indicate the pronunciation of short vowel sounds with the letter and no diacritical mark. You may also find that your dictionary uses the ə to represent the short /u/ or that the symbol ä is used to represent the short o. Note that in these dictionaries, əm brel ə represents the pronunciation of the key word *umbrella* and äks represents the pronunciation of the key word *ox*.

VC Pattern The most common vowel–consonant pattern is that of the VC (vowel-consonant), in which the V (vowel) represents its short sound (*ant, etch, itch, odd, up*). Some teachers' manuals and curriculum guides use CVC to represent the short vowel pattern.

VCCe Pattern When a one-syllable word or a syllable has two vowels, one of which is a final *e*, and the two vowels are separated by two consonants, the first vowel often represents the short sound, and the final *e* is silent (*dance, fence, since, dodge, fudge*).

Closed Syllable A closed syllable ends with a consonant phoneme (*at*). A single vowel in a closed accented syllable usually represents the short sound of the vowel.

Ww as a Vowel As a vowel, the *w* represents no distinct phoneme of its own. The vowel *w* always follows another vowel in English words and is used in combination with the other vowel (*new, cow, saw*).

Yy as a Vowel Within a Syllable As a vowel, *y* represents no distinct phoneme of its own. *Y* within a syllable (VC pattern) often represents the sound of short *i* (ǐ), as in *symbol* and *gym*.

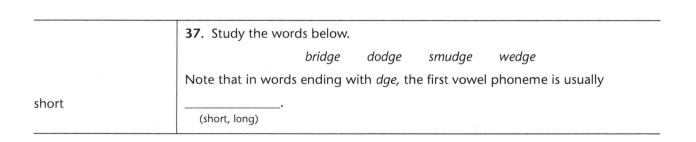

37. Study the words below.

   bridge   dodge   smudge   wedge

Note that in words ending with *dge,* the first vowel phoneme is usually

short   _____.
   (short, long)

no	**38.** Now consider the following words. *fence* *range* *paste* *hinge* *prance* Is the VCCe pattern completely reliable? _____ The VC and VCCe patterns give clues to pronunciation. These patterns are helpful, but they do not apply to all words (and syllables) spelled with the VC and VCCe patterns.
ă, ĕ, ĭ ŏ, ŭ ăpple, ĕdge, ĭgloo, ŏx ŭmbrella	**39.** Write the key symbols we are using in this text to represent the short vowel phonemes. _____, _____, _____, _____, _____ Write the key word for each short vowel. Mark the initial vowel in each key word. _____, _____, _____, _____, _____ Pronounce the short vowel phonemes. Can you say them rapidly? Practice them. Since they are so common, you should be familiar with them.

Review 14

1. What are the major generalizations concerning short vowel sounds?

    a. Write the generalization that applies to the words *pet* and *in*.

    b. Write the generalization that applies to the vowel–consonant ending pattern in the words *since* and *dance*.

2. We are studying the vowel phonemes that are represented by single letters. We have learned to associate 5 of the 19 vowel phonemes with their key pronunciation symbols. Mark the vowels to indicate their pronunciations.

    bed   *next*   *lot*   *cat*   *trip*   *skin*   *mop*   *us*   *send*   *bug*

3. Write the vowel-consonant pattern for each of the following words. Use a *V* to indicate each vowel and a *C* to indicate each consonant.

        up   *hat*   *lapse*   *tub*   *ad*   *rinse*

4. Examine the words in question 3. These six words represent two patterns that indicate vowel pronunciation. Write the two patterns.

5. We expect the single letter *g* to represent its hard sound *except* when it is

    followed by _____, _____, or _____.

See the Answers to the Reviews section for the answers to Review 14, page 235.

Long Vowel Sounds

a	ā	apron
e	ē	eraser
i	ī	ice
o	ō	overalls
u	ū	unicorn

name

ā (apron)   ē (eraser)   ī (ice)   ō (overalls)   ū (unicorn)

1. Another set of phonemes represented by single vowel letters is those that "say their own names." The key symbol for these vowel phonemes is a **macron** (-). Pronounce the first word at the right. Make the sound represented by the <u>underlined</u> vowel; then say the name of the underlined vowel.

1	2	3
a	ā	apron
___	___	eras<u>e</u>r
___	___	<u>i</u>ce
___	___	<u>o</u>veralls
___	___	<u>u</u>nicorn

The sound represented by the vowel is the same as the _____ of the vowel. Pronounce the rest of the key words (3), vowel phonemes (key symbols) (2), and letter names (1) the same way. Complete the table.

(Many dictionaries are now using an equivalent symbol, the yo͞o, to indicate the ū. Check your dictionary.)

ē, ī, ō, ū

2. The key symbol, as found in the dictionary, for the a in apron is ā. What would the key symbol be for each of the other underlined vowels in frame 1?

_____   _____   _____   _____

---

pine

3. "Macron" contains the word element *macro*, which means "long" or "great." It has been the custom, in phonics, to call the vowel sound whose key symbol is a macron over the vowel letter a **long vowel** sound.

Therefore, we would say the *i* in _____ represents a long vowel sound.
(pin, pine)

---

tāke, gō, fīne, bē, sāme

(If you had any incorrect, study them carefully. Does the *a* in *many* "say its own name"?)

4. Place a macron above each of the vowels that represents a long sound in these words. Be sure the vowel "says its own name."

take   go   many   fine   once   all   be   same

---

5. Though we will use ū, we will briefly consider the use of the yo͞o and the o͞o to indicate the long ū. Some teachers' manuals use the yo͞o to indicate the pronunciation of the long ū in *cube* and the o͞o to indicate the pronunciation of the long ū in *tune*.

Say *cube* and *tune*. Listen carefully. You may hear different pronunciations of the long u in *cube* and *tune*.

yōō

is not

ōō

A /y/ phoneme precedes the /oo/ phoneme in *cube*. This long vowel sound is, therefore, represented by _____. The sound that the *u* represents in
(yōō, ōō)

tune _____ preceded by /y/.
(is, is not)

We would expect this sound to be represented by a(n) _____.
(yōō, ōō)

(Consult your teachers' manual for the symbols that are used to represent the long *ū*.)

---

6. The five long vowel phonemes are represented by the key symbols *ā, ē, ī, ō,* and *ū*. Pronounce each word below. Now select a word from the list that illustrates each.

cake, be, time

home, huge

ā _____   ē _____   ī_____

ō _____   ū _____

be   up   cake   home   huge   time   run

---

7. Study the words below. Indicate those vowels that represent their long sounds by placing macrons above them. Put a diagonal line (/) through each vowel that is silent.

nāmȩ, thēsȩ, cūtȩ, bōnȩ,
tōȩ, pīnȩ

name   these   cute   bone   toe   pine

---

8. There are many one-syllable words with two vowels in which *e* is the second vowel, as well as the final letter of the word. We can make a generalization concerning these words. Study the words *name* and *pine;* then complete this generalization:

When a one-syllable word has two vowels, one of which is a final

e, e

long

_____ , the _____ is silent and the first vowel *usually*

represents its _____ sound.

---

9. This generalization most often applies to words that have the ending pattern of VCe. The word *use* is an example of VCe: vowel–consonant–final vowel *e*.

VCe

yes

Time and *plate* have the ending pattern of _____. Does this

generalization apply to them? _____

When a one-syllable word has two vowels, one of which is the final *e*,
the *e* is silent and the first vowel *usually* represents its long sound.

VCe	**10.** The C in the VCe pattern may signify a single consonant letter or a consonant digraph but only *one* consonant phoneme. Since *ph* represents a single–consonant phoneme, the nonsense word *sophe* has an ending pattern _____.
dīnȼ, hōpȼ, fācȼ, rīdȼ, cūbȼ, hōmȼ VCe	**11.** Mark each vowel in the following words with the proper diacritical mark. Put a slash (/) through each silent letter. dine hope face ride cube home All of the above have the vowel–consonant ending pattern _____.
When a one-syllable word has two vowels, one of which is the final *e*, the *e* is silent and the first vowel usually represents its long sound.	**12.** Write the generalization concerning vowel sounds illustrated by these words: ate game ice
come, some, there (The digraph *th* represents one phoneme.)	**13.** It is well to remember that the generalization is very helpful but not infallible. Check the words in the following set that **do not** follow the generalization. (Is the final *e* silent? Does the first vowel "say its own name"?) come place these some there late clothe same
dance *pāste* *fence* VCCe VCCe VCCe *wāste* *rinse* VCCe VCCe	**14.** This generalization is of little value in helping to determine the vowel sounds in words ending with the vowel–consonant pattern of VCCe, even when such words are of one syllable. Study the words below. Indicate the vowels that represent the long sound by using the macron. Write the ending pattern (begin with the vowel) under each of the words. *dance* *paste* *fence* *waste* *rinse* _____ _____ _____ _____ _____

dăns, rīd, sāf
brĭj, kāk, fĕns
 	
long
 	
short
 	
silent
	15. Write each word below to show pronunciation, using the key symbols we associate with each vowel and consonant letter. Omit each silent letter.
	
	  dance _____ ride _____ safe _____
	  bridge _____ cake _____ fence _____
	
	We can see that in one-syllable words that end with the pattern of VCe, the first vowel is usually _____; in one-syllable words that end with the pattern of VCCe, the first vowel is usually _____. The final *e* in both patterns (VCe and VCCe) is usually _____.

cīse

tāke

tǐve

pōse

pēde

mǐre

16. Study the two-syllable words below in column 1. The syllable division and accent placement for each word is shown in column 2. Mark the vowel in the last syllable in each word to show pronunciation.

1	**2**
concise	con cise'
mistake	mis take'
native	na' tive
compose	com pose'
stampede	stam pede'
admire	ad mire'

With these words in mind, our generalization might be extended to read:

When a word or an accented syllable has two vowels, one of which is the final *e*, the *e* is silent and the first vowel usually represents the long sound.

Follow	**Do Not Follow**
stove	come
cone	one
throne	none
globe	some

17. Let us consider an exception. Say the words below. Listen carefully to the sound that the vowel *o* represents.

stove	cone	come	one
throne	none	globe	some

Arrange the words in two columns: (1) those in which the ending pattern VCe is of value in determining the pronunciation of the vowel and (2) those in which the ending pattern VCe does not help in determining the pronunciation of the vowel.

Words do not follow the generalization when the vowel letter *o* is pronounced like the sound of "uh" as in the word *done*.

---

long

rōle, māke

scēne, prīce, cūbe

18. We have identified five vowel phonemes that represent the _____ sounds of the letters.

We have also learned one generalization that gives a clue to that sound. Select one word for each of the five vowels to illustrate this generalization. Place a macron above the vowels selected.

rattle	one	role	piece	make
scene	come	price	cube	dance

---

consonant

long

VCe

19. We have noted that when we see a word or an accented syllable with the pattern of a single vowel followed by a single _____ and final *e*, the single vowel is likely to represent its _____ sound. The vowel–consonant ending pattern we expect to see is _____.

---

short

20. All the vowels in the words below represent the _____ sound. Check each one to make sure.

Then add a silent *e* to the end of each word to see what happens. To show the new pronunciation, mark the first vowel in each of the new words you've made with the appropriate diacritical mark.

pīne, rāte, kīte, hāte	pin rat kit hat
cūte, strīpe, pāle, āte	cut strip pal at
long	The vowels now represent their _____ sounds.
e pronunciation (or sound)	**21.** We can see from words such as *cut* and *cute* that the silent _____ at the end of a word has a purpose. It changes the meaning of the word, as well as the _____ of the word.
	22. Another situation in which we often find the vowel to be long is that of the open syllable. **An open syllable ends with a vowel <u>phoneme</u>.** Study the words below. Underline the open syllables, including open one-syllable words.
<u>go</u>, <u>so</u> lo, <u>me</u> <u>fe</u> ver, <u>ti</u> ger, <u>pa</u> per	go so lo pine me con vene fe ver ti ger pa per

Box 4.1

Final E Solves Four Spelling Problems

Before spelling was finalized in the 17th century, early writers used the final *e* to solve several tricky spelling problems. We will consider four ways in which the final *e* came to the rescue:

1. English words ending with a /v/ or a /z/ phoneme presented a sticky spelling problem for early writers. Although English words can end with a /v/ or /z/ phoneme (*groove, breeze*), spelling conventions did not provide for a single *v* or *z* to be the final letter (*groov, breez*). The inventive writers added a final *e* to avoid ending words with a final *v* or *z* grapheme (e.g., *starve, swerve, bronze, snooze*).

2. Early writers needed a way to indicate when the *th* is voiced (*teethe*) and when it is unvoiced (*teeth*). In solving their problem, the inventive writers once again used the final *e,* adding it to words such as *teethe* and *clothe* so as to avoid confusion with words such as *teeth* and *cloth*.

3. The final *e* also came in handy when spelling words that end in /s/. Sometimes the /s/ is part of the word (*dense*); sometimes it is part of a suffix (*dens*). In using the final *e,* the writers of yesteryear generously provided the reader with a helpful visual cue for sorting out when the final letter *s* is part of a base word (*tens + e = tense, brows + e = browse*) and when the final letter *s* is part of a suffix (*horse + s = horses; lapse + s = lapses*).

4. Thanks to the final *e,* it is clear when to use the soft *c* (key word: *sun*) and *g* (key word: *jeep*) in words such as *choice* and *damage*. Without the final *e,* the reader might be tempted to pronounce *choic* (*choice*) as /choik/ and *damag* (*damage*) as /damag/.

English is a dynamic and evolving language in which spelling changes occur over relatively long periods of time. Will the final *e* eventually drop away from words in which the *e* neither contributes to pronunciation nor gives the reader an important visual clue? No one knows—but we might speculate. Generally speaking, American spelling changes make words simpler, such as dropping the *u* from the British *colour* and substituting the trendy *nite* for *night*. So perhaps the writers in some future century will spell *groove* and *breeze* as *groov* and *breez*.

	23. This generalization most often applies to words and accented syllables that have the vowel–consonant pattern of CV. Study the words and the underlined syllables below.
	<div align="center">me <u>be</u> long <u>ma</u> ple so</div>
	The words and the underlined syllables have the vowel–consonant pattern of
CV	_____. Each of the above words and underlined syllables is a(n)
open	_____ syllable.
	(open, closed)
consonant	**24.** The first syllable of *convene* ends with a _____ phoneme. The second syllable of *convene* is not an open syllable because it does not end with
phoneme, silent	a vowel _____. The last letter is a vowel, but it is _____.
	(letter, phoneme)
yes	**25.** Is the first syllable of *fe ver* an open syllable? _____ What key
ē	symbol represents the final phoneme of the first syllable? _____ The
CV	first syllable in *fe ver* has the vowel–consonant pattern of _____. Is the
no	second syllable an open syllable? _____ What key symbol represents
r	the final phoneme? _____
	26. Study these words:
	<div align="center">hel <u>lo</u> <u>be</u> <u>me</u> ter <u>pi</u> lot</div>
long	The underlined vowels represent their _____ sounds.
	(long, short)
	27. In the words below, place a macron above each vowel (*a, e, i, o, u*) that represents its long sound.
fā vor, hē, sī lent, tō tal,	<div align="center">fa vor he si lent to tal hu man</div>
hū man	We might generalize:
open	**A single vowel in an _____ accented syllable often**
long	**represents its _____ sound. The vowel–consonant**
CV	**pattern for an open syllable is _____.**
	28. Study the words below. Draw lines under the single vowels in the open syllables. Place macrons above those vowels you underlined that represent long sounds. Work carefully. You may find exceptions.
shē, bē long, dī graph,	<div align="center">she be long di graph ha lo hel lo do</div>
hā lō, hel lō, do	

Box 4.2

The Extra E

Exception words such as *gone* and *done,* which we expect to be pronounced with a long *o,* are a consequence of the quirky way in which the English spelling system developed. Before the 14th century, the final *e* represented an "uh" that was pronounced at the end of words. To get a sense of how contemporary words would sound with a final "uh," say *gone* and *done,* and then add an extra "uh" to the end—"gonuh" and "donuh." Sometime around the 14th century, the "uh" was dropped from pronunciation, and the final *e* became the silent letter in words spelled with the VCe pattern.

Then something curious happened. For some unknown reason, the early writers began to attach a final *e* to short vowel words that ended in a consonant letter. The writers usually doubled the final consonant, suggesting that they knew that the final *e* in the VCe pattern signaled that the preceding vowel is long. Put into a contemporary context, the word *pit* might be spelled *pitte* and *pin* as *pinne.*

For some time, English spelling was cluttered with extra consonants and final *es.* Spelling was eventually untangled in the 17th century when the practice of adding an extra *e* to the end of short vowel words was discontinued. However, some of the words from this earlier period still continue to be spelled with the unnecessary final *e,* which is the reason we have words such as *gone* and *done* in our English language dictionary today.

a open	**29.** Although the *a* in *about* (*a bout*) and the _____ in *soda* are single vowel letters in _____ syllables, they do not represent (closed, open) long sounds. <div align="center">**We tend to shorten the vowel sounds in unaccented syllables.**</div>
long	**30.** The generalization has more application when we limit it to accented syllables: **A single vowel in an open accented syllable** **usually represents its _____ sound.** We will study this more fully later.
lō *lō*	**31.** We should note, however, that sometimes single vowel letters in open unaccented syllables do represent the long sounds. Consider these words: *so′ lo ha′ lo* Two syllables from these words that illustrate this are _____ from *solo* and _____ from *halo.* Mark the vowels in these unaccented syllables.

32. We should also note that not all vowels in open accented syllables represent long sounds. (Exceptions, exceptions!) Recall that all one-syllable words are accented. In the words below, underline the syllables that are exceptions to the generalization:

> **Single vowel letters in open accented syllables usually represent their long sounds.**

la, to

no   la′ va   to   she

---

33. We will now consider long vowel exceptions to the closed-syllable generalization. We expect that single vowels in closed syllables—the VC

short

pattern—will usually represent _____ sounds.
(long, short)

no

Do the words below follow the closed-syllable generalization? _____

sight   high   right   sigh

> **An exception to the closed-syllable generalization is found in words in which the *i* is followed by *gh*.**

long, silent

The *i* represents the _____ sound and the *gh* is _____ in such words.
(long, short)

---

34. The words below represent another exception to the closed-syllable generalization.

child   wild   mild   sold   told   hold

We can summarize:

ld

> **When *i* or *o* is followed by _____, the vowel usually represents the long sound.**

---

closed

35. Let us review. Syllables with the VC pattern (such as *ant*) are _____
(closed, open)

open

syllables. Syllables that have the CV pattern (such as *be*) are _____
(closed, open)

phoneme

syllables. An open syllable ends with a vowel _____.
(phoneme, letter)

---

36. The previous frames in this section contain examples of the five vowels,

a, e, i, o

_____, _____, _____, _____, and

u

_____, in which they represent their long sounds.

---

vowel

37. We have learned that the vowel *w* always appears with another _____ letter. Therefore, there would be no instances in which we could apply the single-vowel open-syllable generalization to the *w*.

bī, mī, whī, flī, krī *ī* CV	**38.** Let us examine the generalization with respect to the vowel *y*. Look at the words below. Rewrite these words. Use the key symbol we associate with each vowel and consonant phoneme. by my why fly cry In each instance, the *y* represents the phoneme we associate with the key symbol _____. The vowel–consonant pattern for these words is _____.
long, *e*	**39.** Study the words below, and then complete the generalization: **When *y* is the final letter of a two-syllable word, it represents the** _____ **sound of** _____. *happy lucky baby windy*
bī pas, sī pres, pī thon	**40.** *Y* is not always the final letter in a word. Study the words below. Rewrite them to show the pronunciations of the consonants and of the vowels representing the long sounds. by pass _____ cy press _____ py thon _____

cry
 	
lucky
	41. *happy tiny candy empty*
	
	If *y* represents the long sound of the *e* when it is the final and only vowel in the last syllable of a multisyllable word, then the open-syllable generalization we have been studying applies to *a, e, i, o, u,* and *y*.
	
	The *y* would represent the sound of the long *i* in _____ and the
	                                                                                              (*cry, happy*)
	
	long *e* in _____.
	              (*my, lucky*)

A single vowel in an open accented syllable often represents its long sound.	**42.** State the generalization that concerns a single vowel in an open accented syllable.

Study Guide

Long Vowels

Long Vowel	Key Symbol	Key Word
a	*ā*	*apron*
e	*ē*	*eraser*
i	*ī*	*ice*
o	*ō*	*overalls*
u	*ū*	*unicorn*

Macron (-)   The macron (-) is the diacritical mark used to indicate the specific pronunciations of the long vowels.

Long ū   Some dictionaries are now using the (y)$\overline{oo}$ to indicate the *ū*. Some teachers' manuals use two symbols to indicate the *ū*—y$\overline{oo}$ for the *ū* in *unicorn* and *cube* and $\overline{oo}$ for the *ū* in *tune* and *true*.

VCe Pattern   When a word or an accented syllable has two vowels, one of which is a final *e*, the *e* is silent and the first vowel usually represents the long sound (*ape, hope*).

O Pronounced as "uh" Exception to the VCe Pattern   Words do not follow the VCe generalization when the vowel letter *o* is pronounced like the "uh" in the words *done* and *come*.

Open Syllable   An open syllable ends with a vowel phoneme (*be, try*). Single vowel letters in open accented syllables usually represent their long sounds (*she*).

Unaccented Syllables   We tend to shorten vowel sounds in unaccented syllables (*a bout'*).

CV Pattern   The CV pattern is an open syllable that ends in a vowel phoneme. In open syllables, represented by CV, the vowel usually represents its long sound (*be, tree*).

Yy as a Vowel   *Y* as the final letter in a one-syllable word (*my*) usually represents the sound we associate with long *i* (key word: *ice*). *Y* as the final letter in a two-syllable word (*happy*) usually represents the long sound of *e* (key word: *eraser*). *Y*, when preceded by the letter *a*, may form the long vowel digraph *ay*, as in *play* and *crayon*. *Y*, when preceded by the letter *e*, may form a long vowel digraph, as in *key*.

igh Exception to the Closed-Syllable Generalization   When the *i* is followed by *gh* in a word or a syllable, the *i* usually represents the long sound, and the *gh* is silent (*light*).

i or o Followed by ld Exception to the Closed-Syllable Generalization   When *i* or *o* is followed by *ld*, the vowel usually represents the long sound (*wild, fold*).

Review 15

1. We have been studying five phonemes that represent the long sounds of the vowels: ā, _____, _____, _____, and _____.
   We can show the pronunciation of each vowel by placing a(an) _____
   (name of diacritical mark)
   over it.

2. *Y* can represent a long sound and a short sound, but it does not have a key symbol: It is a duplication of either the long _____ (as in *cry*) or the long _____ (as in *lucky*).

3. We have learned to recognize two patterns that may give clues as to the vowel sound in an unknown word. One is the vowel–consonant–silent _____ pattern (VCe). State the generalization: _____.

4. The other is a single-vowel, open-syllable pattern: The single vowel in an open _____ syllable is often _____.

5. We can state the same generalization in another way: When the only vowel in a word or accented syllable comes at the _____ of the syllable, that vowel usually represents its _____ sound.

6. The long sounds of the vowels are easiest to recognize in known words because the name of each vowel is the same as the _____ it represents.

7. Pronounce each of the words below.

dine	*tack*	*way*	*watch*
table	*go*	*tight*	*enough*

   a. Place a *C* after each word that ends with a consonant phoneme.

   b. Place a *V* after each word that ends with a vowel phoneme.

   c. Indicate the pronunciation of the final phoneme by writing the key symbol. If the word ends with a consonant blend, use only the symbol that represents the final phoneme in the blend.

   d. Underline the words in which the final syllable is an open syllable.

8. We are studying the vowel phonemes that are represented by single letters. We have learned to associate 10 of the 19 vowel phonemes with their key pronunciation symbols. Mark the following vowel graphemes to indicate their pronunciations. Use a slash to indicate silent letters.

   bite   bit   can   cane   pet   Pete   cut   cute   mop   mope

See the Answers to the Reviews section for the answers to Review 15, page 235.

Schwa (ə)

a	*ə*	*comma*	**1.** Say the words at the right aloud. Listen to the phoneme represented by the underlined letter. When you say the words slowly and distinctly (and artificially), they may sound quite different from one another, but when these words are used in ordinary speech, the underlined part represents a very soft "uh."

1. Say the words at the right aloud. Listen to the phoneme represented by the underlined letter. When you say the words slowly and distinctly (and artificially), they may sound quite different from one another, but when these words are used in ordinary speech, the underlined part represents a very soft "uh."

			1	**2**	**3**
a	*ə*	*comma*	_____	*ə*	*comm__a__*
e	*ə*	*chicken*	_____	*ə*	*chick__e__n*
i	*ə*	*family*	_____	*ə*	*fam__i__ly*
o	*ə*	*melon*	_____	*ə*	*mel__o__n*
u	*ə*	*circus*	_____	*ə*	*circ__u__s*
a, e, i			The letters that represent the "uh" sound in the words at the right are _____, _____, _____,
o, u			_____, and _____. Place them properly in column 1.

---

2. Dictionaries usually indicate the soft vowel sound found in unaccented syllables with a **schwa** (ə).

ə   The pronunciation is shown by the sign _____ (an inverted *e*).

---

3. How is the word *schwa* pronounced? The *sch* grapheme in *schwa* represents the phoneme we associate with the key symbol *sh*.

blend   The *sh* and the consonant *w* form a _____. The *a* represents an "ah"
                                                                (digraph, blend)

sound.

---

4. Rewrite each of the words below to show the pronunciation of the vowel in the **unaccented syllable.**

commə, chickən, gerbəl   com' ma _____   chick' en _____   ger' bil_____

melən, circəs   mel' on _____   cir' cus _____

Without the schwa, each of these vowels would need a separate diacritical mark.

---

5.   **The schwa is used to indicate the
pronunciation of the vowel phoneme in
many unaccented syllables.**

Study the word below. Rewrite it, indicating the sound of each letter.

bā' kən   ba' con _____

---

6. Say the words below in a natural manner. Rewrite them, using key symbols to indicate each of the phonemes.

kăk təs, lī̄ən, sĕk ənd,   cactus   lion   second   pilot
pī̄ lət

Check the vowels that can represent the schwa phoneme:

a, e, i, o, u   a   e   i   o   u

unaccented	**7.** The use of the schwa for each vowel that represents the short "uh" sound, along with the frequent use of the short *i* (ĭ), has simplified pronunciation keys greatly. Almost all vowels in _____ syllables represent one of these two short, (accented, unaccented) soft sounds.
ə *i*	**8.** Let us examine the words *distant* and *village.* The dictionary may indicate the pronunciations as *dĭs' tənt* and *vĭl' ĭj.* The _____ and the _____ indicate the two soft phonemes, regardless of spelling.
manage, sicken *banquet, melon*	**9.** The following words are written to show their pronunciations. What are the words? *măn' ĭj* _____ *sĭk' ən* _____ *băng' kwĭt* _____ *mĕl' ən* _____
vegetable, postage	**10.** Examine the words below. They are written the way they might appear in your dictionary. What are the words? *vĕj' tə bəl* _____ *pōs' tĭj* _____ Note that we pronounce the syllable *ble* as though a very short vowel precedes the *l: bəl.*
stā' bəl, mī' nəs *bal' ət, rŏk' ĭt*	**11.** Rewrite the words below to show pronunciation. Omit the silent letters. *sta' ble* _____ *mi' nus* _____ *bal' lot* _____ *rock' et* _____
sō' fə, klŏz' ət *kwĭv' ər, frē' kwənt* *kō' kō, də mĕn' chən*	**12.** Rewrite the words below to show pronunciation. They should be written as they might appear in parentheses following the boldface entry word in the dictionary. To avoid artificial pronunciation, check each one by saying it in a sentence. *so' fa* _____ *clos' et* _____ *quiv' er* _____ *fre' quent* _____ *co' coa* _____ *di men' sion* _____
sĭn' ə nĭm, lej' ə bəl *dĭl' ə jəns, ăn tēk'*	**13.** Are you ready to code some more difficult words? Rewrite these words to show pronunciation. *syn' o nym* _____ *leg' i ble* _____ *dil' i gence* _____ *an tique'* _____

Study Guide
Schwa

Vowel in an Unaccented Syllable	Key Symbol	Key Word
a	ə	*comm<u>a</u>* (soft "uh")
e	ə	*chick<u>e</u>n* (soft "uh")
i	ə	*fam<u>i</u>ly* (soft "uh")
o	ə	*mel<u>o</u>n* (soft "uh")
u	ə	*circ<u>u</u>s* (soft "uh")

Vowels in Unaccented Syllables   The vowels in unaccented syllables can reasonably be expected to represent a soft "uh" or the sound we associate with a short ĭ.

Schwa   The dictionary uses a schwa (ə) to indicate the soft "uh" sound found in many unaccented syllables. Without the schwa (ə), the vowels that represent the soft "uh" in unaccented syllables would each need a separate diacritical mark to indicate pronunciation.

Short ĭ   The vowels in unaccented syllables may also represent the short ĭ, such as in *manage* (*măn' ĭj*). The vowels in unaccented syllables represent the soft "uh," the schwa, more often than the short ĭ.

short *i*	**14.** The first vowel in *decay* represents the _____ phoneme. This use represents the trend toward simplification. It is not *e*. Try it in a sentence to check this. Now try it using *i* as a guide in pronouncing the first syllable.
	15. It is necessary to note that various dictionaries indicate pronunciation in different ways. We must study the pronunciation key of the particular dictionary we use. For example, many dictionaries indicate the pronunciations of all short sounds with the letter and no diacritical mark.
hap' ən	The pronunciation of *happen* is written in these dictionaries as _____.
	16. Let us review. We have learned that a vowel grapheme in an unaccented syllable could reasonably be expected to represent the sound we associate with the short *i* (ĭ) or with the sound represented by the schwa (ə).
	The *i* would identify the vowel phonemes in the last syllable of
village, pilot	_____. The ə would identify the last syllable of _____.
	(*candy, program, village, hotel*) (*pilot, locate, liquid, railroad*)

Review 16

1. The key symbol used to represent many of the vowel phonemes in unaccented syllables is called a _____ (ə).

2. This symbol is very useful because _____.

3. The words below are written to show their pronunciations. How are they correctly spelled?

rē′ gəl   hănd mād′   sĕl′ ə brāt   ĕp′ ə sōd   dăm′ĭj

4. Almost all vowels in unaccented syllables represent one of two short, soft vowels. These symbols are the ə and the _____.

See the Answers to the Reviews section for the answers to Review 16, page 235.

Other Single Vowels

five	**1.** Thus far we have identified 11 vowel phonemes using only _____ (How many?)
schwa, phoneme	vowel letters and a _____. We can readily tell which _____ (letter, phoneme) is represented when diacritical marks are used, as in a dictionary, glossary, or other pronunciation guides.
short	**2.** We also have examined patterns common to the English language so that we can make a reasonable guess as to the sound of certain vowels. For example, we expect the vowel letter in the pattern VC to represent its _____ sound.
apple	**3.** If the vowel in the VC pattern is *a*, then we would expect *a* to represent the same sound as the vowel phoneme heard in _____. (*said, car, ball, apple, date, saw*)
long, silent	**4.** We expect the first vowel grapheme in the ending pattern VCe to represent its _____ sound and the final *e* to be _____.

sew			**5.** If the first vowel grapheme in the VCe pattern is an *o*, then we would expect *o* to represent the same vowel phoneme as that heard in _____. *(done, gone, boy, sew)*

schwa *sofa*			**6.** A vowel in an unaccented syllable could reasonably be expected to represent the sound we associate with the short *i* or with the _____. The ə would identify the vowel phoneme in the last syllable of _____ . *(sofa, remit, require, insect)*

7. There are still other single-vowel phonemes, as shown in the words at the right. Some are influenced by the consonant following the vowel. We will identify these vowel phonemes and suggest a key word by which each can be remembered.

a	*ä*	*father*
a	*ô*	*ball*
a	*â*	*care*
u	*û*	*fur*

	1	**2**	**3**
	a	_____	*father (fǟthər)*
	a	_____	*ball (bôl)*
	a	_____	*care (câre)*
	u	_____	*fur (fûr)*

However, we commonly use the pronunciation key given in the pronunciation guide of our dictionary for these more difficult phonemes. Each of these phonemes is represented by a variety of spellings—in other words, by a

graphemes

variety of _____.

(phonemes, graphemes)

Complete the table by filling in the key symbols (2).

We have noted that various dictionaries use different ways to indicate pronunciation. Check the pronunciation guide in your dictionary for key symbols.

graphemes (or spellings)	**8.** Let us begin with the *ä* phoneme. The phoneme that we will identify with the key symbol *ä* and the key word *father* may be confusing because of regional differences in pronunciation. It is represented by many different letters and combinations of letters. Dictionaries reveal anywhere from 3 to 11 different _____ that represent this phoneme.

ä	**9.** Pronounce the words below. If you do not hear the same vowel phoneme as in *father*, your pronunciation reflects a regional difference. You are not wrong. arm calm hearth sergeant bazaar Now pronounce each word so you can hear the phoneme we represent by the key symbol _____ in each one.

a, al, ea, e, aa	**10.** In the words below, underline the graphemes that represent the phoneme we identify with the key symbol *ä*. Include the silent letters that could be considered a part of the grapheme. arm calm hearth sergeant bazaar

fär, täkō, pläzə *käm, gärd, därk*	**11.** If you cannot agree with the pronunciation for each word, use your dictionary. Your pronunciation may reflect that of your region. Use the key symbols to show the pronunciations of these words: far _____ taco _____ plaza _____ calm _____ guard _____ dark _____
r *guard, dark* *är*	**12.** Study the vowel phoneme in the word *far.* We can barely separate it from the following consonant phoneme, so we call it a(n) _____-controlled (r, l, w) vowel. Which words in frame 11, in addition to *far,* include an *r*-controlled vowel? _____ Write the r-controlled vowel (*ar*) to show pronunciation. _____
raw, caught, walk, broad *fought, tall, coffee*	**13.** Pronounce *ball.* Listen to the vowel phoneme. We will represent this phoneme with the key symbol ô. Say the words below. Check those in which you hear the phoneme heard in *ball.* raw caught walk broad bead fought tall coffee Some of the answers here may also be affected by regional variations in pronunciation. Check your dictionary.
aw, au, al, oa *ou, a, o*	**14.** What graphemes in the frame above represent the vowel phoneme heard in *ball?* _____ _____ _____ _____ _____ _____ _____
rô, kôt, wôk, brôd *bēd, fôt, tôl, kôfē*	**15.** Rewrite the words in frame 13, using key symbols to indicate pronunciation. _____ _____ _____ _____ _____ _____ _____ _____
ball *sô, kôl*	**16.** Pronounce *saw.* The *a* represents the vowel phoneme in _____. (ball, sat) When *a* is followed by an *l* or *w* in the same syllable, the *a* may represent the sound we associate with the key symbol ô. Rewrite the words below to show pronunciation. saw_____ call _____
shawl, small *false, drawn*	**17.** These words are written to show their pronunciations. What are the words? shôl _____ smôl _____ fôls _____ drôn _____

	18. Now let us consider the *r*-controlled *ô*. Say the words below. Check those in which you hear the *r*-controlled *ô* (*ôr*).
short, port, torn	*short shot pot port spot torn*
o	The *r*-controlled vowel in these words consists of the letter _____
r	followed by the letter _____ (*or*). Write *or* to show pronunciation.
ôr	_____
	19. Write the words below to show pronunciation.
kôrəs, skôr, shärk	*chorus* _____ *score* _____ *shark* _____
pôrch, bôrdər, krangk	*porch* _____ *border* _____ *crank* _____
	20. The word in frame 19 that does not contain an *r*-controlled vowel is
crank	_____.
	21. Now let's examine the vowel phoneme in *chair*, key word *care*. The key symbol we use to represent this phoneme is *â*.
	Study the words below. Pronounce each word aloud. Is the vowel phoneme
yes	the same in each word? _____
	chair share their there bear prayer
	In these examples, one vowel phoneme is represented by _____
six	(How many?)
	graphemes.
	22. In each word below, underline the grapheme that represents the same vowel phoneme heard in *care*. The graphemes represent vowel phonemes, so do not underline the controlling consonants.
ai, a, ei, ea, ay	*chair share their bear prayer*
	You can see that our table in frame 7 is greatly oversimplified. Column 1 should show the six graphemes that, when followed by *r*, represent the vowel phoneme we hear in *care*.
	23. Rewrite the words below, using the key symbols to indicate the pronunciations of consonants and vowels. Omit silent letters.
kôr, whâr, fârē	*core* _____ *where* _____ *fairy* _____
shâr, hâr, bär	*share* _____ *hair* _____ *bar* _____

	24. The following words are written as they would appear in a dictionary to show pronunciation. Spell them correctly.
air, anchor, square	âr _____ ăng′ kər _____ skwâr _____
pile, scarce, chair	pīl _____ skârs _____ châr _____
race, civic, their or there	rās _____ sĭv′ ĭk _____ <s>t</s>hâr _____
	You can interpret the dictionary code!

r	**25.** Another *r*-controlled vowel phoneme is that heard in *fur*. In fact, it is impossible to separate the vowel phoneme from the _____.
	What graphemes represent the vowel phoneme heard in *fur* as shown by the words below? Underline each one, taking care to identify only the vowel.
i, e, ea, o, u, y	*thirst* *germ* *learn* *worm* *purple* *myrtle*

	26. Rewrite the words in frame 25, using the *û* to show pronunciation.
thûrst, jûrm, lûrn	_____ _____ _____
wûrm, pûrpəl, mûrtəl	_____ _____ _____

several different	**27.** The phoneme that we associate with the key symbol *û* may be represented by _____ grapheme(s). Its key word (only one, several different)
fur	is _____.

	28. Note that this phoneme is not the same as the phoneme heard in the unaccented syllable of a multisyllable word, as in *lemon* (*lĕm ən*), or the phoneme heard in a suffix, generally a separate syllable, as in *farmer* (*färm ər*) and *smaller* (*smôl ər*).
	Rewrite the following words to show pronunciation.
wûrkər, wûrkt, snâr	*worker* _____ *worked* _____ *snare* _____

	29. Although the word part *er* has only a touch of a vowel sound, the schwa is used with the *r* to indicate pronunciation. Thus, the key symbols for *tiger* are
tī gər	_____.
	(Check your dictionary to see how it represents the *er* in *tiger*.)

	30. Rewrite these words to show pronunciation.
kärnāshən, bärnyärd, bâr	carnation _____ barnyard _____ bear _____
pârənt, bāk, hûrt	parent _____ bake _____ hurt _____

31. There are two broad generalizations that may be of some help in determining the pronunciations of these single vowels in unknown words.

If the only vowel letter in a word or syllable is followed by *r*, the vowel will be affected by that *r*.

Say the words below.

> car   serve   curl   first   corn   hair

short

The vowel sounds are neither long nor _____. They are almost lost in

r

the consonant letter _____.

precedes

32. A vowel _____ the letter *r* in the words in frame 31. Some
(precedes, follows)
teachers' manuals use *Vr* (vowel-*r*) to represent this pattern and use the term
r-controlled vowel when referring to this sequence.

33. Your teachers' manual may indicate five *r*-controlled vowels: the *ar* as in

er, ir

farm, the _____ as in *her*, the _____ as in *stir*, the

or, ur

_____ as in *short*, and the _____ as in *fur*.

Write these words using key symbols to show pronunciation.

färm, hûr, stûr

        farm _____   her _____   stir _____

shôr, fûr

        shore _____   fur _____

three

The five *r*-controlled vowels represent only _____ pronunciations.
(How many?)

care

For our study, we acknowledge that *âr*, key word _____, is an
r-controlled vowel. Check your teachers' manual to determine the *r*-controlled
vowels it identifies for instruction.

34. Here is another helpful generalization:

If the only vowel in a word or syllable is followed by *l* or *w*, the vowel will be affected by that *l* or *w*.

Study the words below.

> draw   saw   late   fall   small   shawl

late

Which word does not belong in the list? _____

no

Do any of the others represent the long or short sound of *a*? _____

yes

Does the *a* followed by *l* represent the same sound as the *a* followed *w*? _____

Again, regional variations in the pronunciations of these words may cause you
some difficulty.

Study Guide
Other Single Vowels

Vowel Letter	Key Symbol	Key Word
a	*â*	*care*
u	*û*	*fur*
a	*ä*	*father*
a˙	*ô*	*ball*

R-Controlled Vowels When the only vowel letter in a one-syllable word or syllable is followed by *r*, the vowel will be affected by that *r*. When pronouncing a vowel followed by the *r*, the vowel phoneme is almost lost in the consonant.

R-Controlled ä(r) The *a*, when preceding the letter *r*, represents an *r*-controlled vowel. Examples of the *r*-controlled *a*, pronounced as /är/, may be heard in the words ar̲m, ya̲rd, a̲rch, and *large*. In the teaching of reading, the /är/ is often associated with the *ar* spelling in words such as *star, car, shark,* and *jar*.

ä The *ä*, (key word: *father*), does not always precede the letter *r* in English words. This phoneme may also be spelled with other letter combinations, as in he̲arth, t̲aco, s̲ergeant, c̲alm, and *baza̲ar*.

R-Controlled ô(r) The *o*, when preceding the letter *r*, represents an *r*-controlled vowel. Examples of the *r*-controlled *o*, pronounced as /ôr/, may be heard in the words mo̲re, po̲rch, and o̲rder. The teacher of reading may teach the child to associate /ôr/ with the *or* spelling in words such as in *corn, fork,* and *storm*.

ô The *ô*, (key word: *ball*), is heard in c̲aught and br̲oad. Several graphemes represent the *ô*, as in the words s̲aw, c̲aught, w̲alk, br̲oad, f̲ought, and c̲offee.

R-Controlled û(r) It is impossible to separate, in normal pronunciation, the /û/ from the /r/. Several graphemes represent the *û(r)*, as we see in the words fi̲rst, ge̲rm, le̲arn, wo̲rm, pu̲rple, and my̲rtle. In the teaching of reading, the teacher may present three ways to spell /ûr/: (1) the *er* in words such as *her* and *germ;* (2) the *ir* in words such as *first, stir,* and *bird;* and (3) the *ur* in words such as *turn, hurt,* and *curl*.

R-Controlled â(r) It is impossible to separate, in normal pronunciation, the /â/ from the /r/. Six graphemes represent the *â* when followed by *r:* c̲are, h̲air, h̲eir, w̲ear, pra̲yer and wh̲ere.

a Before l or w (ô) When the letter *a* is the only vowel in a one-syllable word or syllable and precedes the letter *l* or the letter *w*, the *a* is affected by the *l* or *w* and is pronounced /ô/. Notice the difference in the phonemes that the letter *a* represents in *bald* (bôld) and *bad* (băd) and in *jaw* (jô) and *jam* (jăm). Examples include *call, almost, talk, draw, awful,* and *shawl*.

Review 17

1. We have been studying the vowel phonemes that can be represented by single-vowel key symbols. The first group of five (example: _apple_) we labeled

   the _____ vowel phonemes. Write their key symbols: _____

2. The second group of five (example: _ice_) we labeled the _____ vowel

   phonemes. Write their key symbols: _____

3. The third (example: _comma_) was given a key symbol not in the alphabet,

   called the _____. This key symbol, _____, represents each

   of the vowels when it has the sound heard in _____.

(happy, agree)

   It is very useful because _____.

4. That left us with four additional single vowel phonemes. The key words for these vowel phonemes can be placed in the following sentences. (1) Fill in the blanks with the correct spelling, and (2) then write the words to show pronunciation.

   a. She hit the _____ over the fence.

   b. The kitten has soft, fluffy _____.

   c. Tom's _____ will take Tom on a fishing trip next Saturday.

   d. The mother dog takes good _____ of her puppies.

5. The four vowel phonemes we have been studying are influenced by the

   phoneme that _____ the vowel. We have learned that these

(follows, precedes)

   vowels are affected by the _____, _____, and _____.

See the Answers to the Reviews section for the answers to Review 17, page 235.

Diphthongs

	1. We have been studying the vowel phonemes that are represented by single-vowel letters. We will now turn our attention to those that are represented by combinations of letters.
	Say _oil._ The word _oil_ is composed of two phonemes: one vowel and one
consonant	_____.
_l_	They are represented by the graphemes _oi_ and _____.

	2. The *oi* functions as one phoneme called a **diphthong**.
	A diphthong is a single-vowel phoneme, represented by two letters, resembling a glide from one sound to another.
	A study of **phonetics** (the science of speech sounds) would show that many single-letter vowels are actually diphthongs. They represent more than a single
diphthongs	sound. We will call only the two-letter gliding combinations _____.
	3. In this study, we have made the arbitrary statement that there are 44 phonemes. It really is not that simple!
	Say *few*. Is the vowel phoneme equivalent to the phoneme heard at the beginning of *use*, or should we consider *ew* a separate diphthong, not a duplication of any single-vowel phoneme?
diphthong	Our decision is to consider that *few = fū*. So we will **not** call *ew* a _____.
	4. It seems most helpful to classify only two of the vowel phonemes as diphthongs. These are the vowel sounds heard in *oil* and *house*. The
oi, ou	_____ and the _____, then, represent 2 of the 44 speech sounds in our language. A diphthong begins with one vowel phoneme and then changes (glides) into another phoneme. For simplicity and for our purposes in the teaching of reading, we will consider the diphthongs to be
oi, ou	represented by the graphemes _____ as in *oil* and _____ in *house*.
	5. Examine the words below. Underline the grapheme in each word that represents the diphthong *oi*.
b<u>oi</u>l, b<u>oy</u>, c<u>oi</u>n	boil boy coin
enj<u>oy</u>, t<u>oy</u>	enjoy toy
oi	There are two spellings that represent this diphthong: _____ and
oy	_____.
	6. Rewrite the five words in frame 5 using the marks of pronunciation (the diacritical marks).
boil, boi, koin, ĕnjoi, toi	_____ _____ _____ _____ _____
oi	The key word for this diphthong is *oil*, and the key symbol is _____.
	7. The second diphthong is that heard in the key word *house*. The key symbol is *ou*. Read the words below. Underline the diphthongs.
h<u>ou</u>se, br<u>ow</u>n, c<u>ow</u>	house brown cow
m<u>ou</u>se, bl<u>ou</u>se, <u>ow</u>l	mouse blouse owl
ou	This diphthong is also represented by two spellings: the _____ and the
ow	_____.

	8. Complete the table at the right with the two spellings of each diphthong (1), key symbols (2), and key words (3).	1	2	3
oi, oy oi oil ou, ow ou house		oi, _____ _____, _____	oi	_____ house

ou kloun	9. The key symbol for the vowel phoneme heard in *clown* is _____. Rewrite *clown* to show its pronunciation. _____

two, two
 	
two
 	
zero, ou, oi
	10. We are recognizing _____ diphthongs. Each has _____ spellings.
	
	            (How many?) (How many?)
	
	The key symbol for each diphthong is composed of _____ letters
	
	                                      (How many?)
	
	with _____ diacritical marks. These letters will be either _____ or _____
	
	  (How many?) (ou, ow) (oi, oy)
	
	because they are the **key** symbols. We find them used in most dictionaries for pronunciation purposes.

	11. Study the words below. Rewrite them using key symbols to indicate the pronunciations of all the phonemes. Underline the diphthongs.
koi, noiz, broil snō, kou snow	coy _____ noise _____ broil _____ snow _____ cow _____ There is no diphthong in _____.

	12. Underline the diphthongs in the following words. Work with care. The *ou* and *ow* often represent other phonemes. Be sure you underline only those that have the vowel phonemes found in *oil* and *house*.
powder, proud, how, soil	powder proud course how soil courage gracious

short	13. The *ous* ending, as in *gracious,* is more likely to represent the phonemes we associate with the key symbols _____ *u* and *s* (or the schwa and *s*) (long, short) than with the diphthong *ou* and the *s*. If we do not have the word in our speaking vocabulary, however, it is difficult to determine whether the *ou* (*ow*) is a diphthong.

Review 18

1. Two of the 44 phonemes are classified as diphthongs. What are the key symbols of these two diphthongs? _____ _____

2. The diphthongs are _____ phonemes.
(vowel, consonant)

3. Copy each of the following words that contain a diphthong, and write the key symbol of the diphthong following it.

cough   owl   grow   cow   through   moist   oyster

4. Use key symbols to show the pronunciation of each of the following words; omit silent letters and underline diphthongs.

house   boy   ounce   enjoy   noise   brow

See the Answers to the Reviews section for the answers to Review 18, page 236.

Vowel Digraphs: oo

	ōo (food) ŏŏ (hook) **1.** The second category of phonemes represented by two-letter vowels is that
two one	of the **vowel digraph.** A digraph is a _____-letter grapheme that represents _____ phoneme(s).
two digraph	**2.** Listen to the vowel sound as you pronounce *food* aloud. Separate the phonemes as you pronounce *food* again: /f/ /oo/ /d/. Say the vowel phoneme aloud. The key symbol we use to identify the vowel sound heard in *food* is ōo. This is a _____-letter vowel grapheme representing a single phoneme. We call it a vowel _____.
 ōo, ōo, ō ōo, ŭ, ōo ō, ōə or ōĭ, ō	**3.** Write the key symbols to indicate the pronunciations of the vowels in each of the following words. Omit silent letters. Work carefully. school _____ broom _____ blow _____ soon _____ flood _____ through _____ so _____ poet _____ though _____

no no, *flood*	**4.** Does o͞o represent the same phoneme as ō? _____ When we see *oo* in a word, can we be sure that it has the sound heard in *food?* _____ The word _____ in frame 3 contains two *o*s but has the sound of a short *u*.
no *through*	**5.** Is the sound indicated by the key symbol o͞o always spelled with two *o*s? _____ Which word in frame 3 contains /o͞o/ but is not spelled with two *o*s? _____
ou, o͞o, o͞o ō, o͞o, o͞o o͞o, o͞o, oi ā, o͞o, o͞o	**6.** Examine the following words carefully. On the line following each word, write the key symbol that represents the vowel. *mouse* _____ *cool* _____ *kangaroo* _____ *dough* _____ *drew* _____ *due* _____ *glue* _____ *moon* _____ *coil* _____ *main* _____ *soup* _____ *cartoon* _____
yes no breve	**7.** A second digraph that cannot be represented by a single letter is found in the word *hook*. Pronounce *food* and then *hook*. Pronounce the vowel phoneme in each word. Are they spelled the same? _____ Do they sound alike? _____ Since the key symbol for the sound heard in *food* is two *o*s covered by an elongated macron (o͞o), it is logical to represent the short phoneme heard in *hook* with an elongated _____ over the two *o*s (o͝o).

8. **A vowel digraph is a two-letter grapheme that represents one vowel phoneme.**

	1	2	3
oo o͞o *food* oo o͝o *hook*	Complete the table at the right with the most common spelling of each of each digraph (1), key symbol (2), and key word (3) for each digraph. _____ _____	o͞o o͝o	_____ _____

fo͝ot, go͞ose, to͝ok, lo͝ok, so͞on, po͞ol, wo͝od, to͞oth, lo͞om	**9.** Using *food* and *hook* as key words to aid you, mark the words below to show pronunciation. *foot goose took look soon pool wood tooth loom*
digraph no o͞o, o͝o	**10.** When we see the vowel _____ *oo* in a word, can we be sure of the phoneme it represents? _____ The double-*o* usually represents the _____ in *food* or the _____ in *hook*. (o͞o, o͝o) (o͞o, o͝o)

goose	**11.** When you see a double-*o* in an unknown word, the only clue to pronunciation is that it most often represents the o͞o in _____. *(goose, book)* You may wish to choose other key words to help you remember the phonemes. *Hook* serves as a good key word for the phoneme we represent by o͝o if we see a resemblance between an elongated breve and a hook! A mental image of the flat surface of a stool may help you remember that the
o͞o	key symbol _____ represents the sound heard in *sto͞ol* (or a *plāte* of *fo͞od!*).
blŭd, sto͝od, zo͞o *flŭd, dro͞op, dôr*	**12.** Not all *oos* represent the sounds heard in *food* and *hook*. Rewrite the words below to show the correct pronunciation of each. blood _____ stood _____ zoo _____ flood _____ droop _____ door _____
phonemes consonant, vowel	**13.** The /o͞o/ and /o͝o/ represent 2 of the 44 _____ of the American-English language. We now have identified all of the phonemes: 25 _____ phonemes and 19 _____ phonemes! However, we must study still another category of vowel combinations.

Review 19

1. What is a digraph?

2. What are the key symbols that identify each of the vowel digraphs we have studied thus far?

3. When you see a double-*o* in an unknown word, how will you know what sound it represents?

4. Using key symbols, indicate the pronunciation of each of these words: *tooth, spoon, book, loose, stood, moo, shook.*

5. Show, through the use of key symbols, how you would expect this nonsense word to be pronounced: *clood.*

6. Write the symbols, consonants, and vowels to indicate the pronunciation of each of these words. Omit silent letters.

    boot, fudge, down, toy, shook, cocoa, night, fruit, throw, through, though, thought, quit, book, smooth, fool, breath, breathe, knight, coin

See the Answers to the Reviews section for the answers to Review 19, page 236.

Long Vowel Digraphs

grapheme phoneme /o͞o/ /o͝o/	**1.** A digraph is a _____ composed of two letters that represent one _____. The *oo* in *food* represents / /. The *oo* in *hook* represents / /.
diphthongs	**2.** We have a special name for the digraphs represented by a "gliding phoneme," as found in *mouse* and *toil.* They are called _____.
one ā, ē, ā ē, ō, ā	**3.** Now examine the following words. Each has two vowels that represent _____ phoneme(s). What phoneme does each vowel digraph represent? Be sure to use the diacritical mark to identify the phoneme. *rain* _____ *heat* _____ *fail* _____ *green* _____ *coat* _____ *say* _____
grapheme, phoneme long	**4.** Each of the words in frame 3 contains a long vowel digraph: Each has a two-letter _____ that represents one _____. Each of these vowel digraphs represents a sound already studied: the _____ *(long, short)* sound we associate with a single vowel letter. None of these pairs has a distinctive sound of its own. We will call them **long vowel digraphs** to distinguish them from the vowel digraphs that represent distinctive sounds: o͞o and o͝o. It is important to note, however, that some teachers' manuals and curriculum guides use **vowel digraph, vowel team** or **vowel pair** to identify two adjacent vowels that represent one long vowel phoneme, as in *feet, coal, nail,* and *leaf.* First grade standard 3c and second grade standard 3b, cited at the beginning of Part Four, refer to these vowels as vowel teams. Check your manual or curriculum guide. You may use long vowel digraph, vowel digraph, vowel team, or vowel pair in your responses.
rā/i/n three, r a (ā), n	**5.** We need to give further study to this large group of long vowel digraphs because they form one of the common patterns in the English language. First, examine the word *rain.* Underline the long vowel digraph. Indicate the silent vowel by drawing a slash through it. Mark the long vowel. _____ *Rain* has _____ phonemes, represented by _____, long *(How many?)* _____, and _____.

macron silent ta̅i̷l, sa̅y̷, se̅a̷t, fe̅e̷d, co̅a̷t	**6.** Study the words below. Underline the pair of vowels (VV) in each word. As you say each word, place a _____ over the first vowel. (macron, breve) Indicate that the second vowel is _____ by drawing a slash through it. *tail say seat feed coat*
long silent C V V C	**7.** **A syllable must have only one vowel phoneme.** Many syllables (and one-syllable words) have two vowel letters. Note the words below. *rain feed hue toe boat stay* In these cases, the first vowel represents its _____ sound, and the second vowel is _____. The logical representation of the pattern is C _____ C. Some teachers' manuals and curriculum guides use VV to represent this pattern. You may use either representation in your responses.

two
 	
long, silent
	8. We can make a generalization about the vowels that form long vowel digraphs in the words you have studied:
	
	  **When _____ vowels appear together in an accented
	  syllable (or a one-syllable word), the first usually represents its
	
	  _____ sound and the second is _____.**

be̅a̷ch, pla̅y̷, ma̅i̷l, e̅a̷ch, flo̅a̷t, ke̅y̷ *play, key* silent	**9.** Mark each vowel in these words to show the pronunciation. Underline the long vowel digraphs. Place a slash through silent letters. *beach play mail each float key* Indicate the words in which the *y* is part of a VV long vowel digraph. _____ _____ Note that the vowel that precedes the *y* represents a long sound and the *y* is _____.

CVVC (VV)
 	
 Col. 1 Col. 2
 	
  i   *e*
 	
  o   *e*
 	
  o   *a*
 	
  e   *e*
	10. Study the words below.
	The first two follow the pattern VCe, and the last two follow the pattern
	
	_____. Place the vowel that represents the long sound in the first column following the word and the silent letter in the second.
	
	    Column 1 **Column 2**
	
	pine _____ _____
	
	rose _____ _____
	
	boat _____ _____
	
	jeep _____ _____

long **silent**	**11.** If the long vowel digraphs were as regular as those represented by the VCe ending pattern, we could form a generalization to include both types: **When there are two vowel letters in a one-syllable word or accented syllable, the first usually represents its _____ sound and the second is _____.**
diphthong	**12.** The generalization does not apply to *boil* because *oi* is a _____. It has a distinctive sound of its own.
digraph br*oŏ*k	**13.** The generalization does not apply to *brook* because *oo* is a double-*o* _____ with a distinctive sound. Use the diacritical mark to show pronunciation. _____
sounded	**14.** If the only exceptions to the "first-vowel-long" generalization were the diphthongs and the double-*o* digraphs, we might consider them "phonemes represented by single letters" because in each case only one of the letters is _____. (silent, sounded)
no pail, toe, snow CVVC (VV)	**15.** Study the words below. Can we depend on the "first-vowel-long" generalization for all but vowel diphthongs and double-*o* digraphs? _____ Check the words that follow this generalization: **When two vowels appear together in a word or accented syllable, the first may represent the long sound and the second is usually silent.** pail said been toe piece snow broad The pattern is _____ (vowel–vowel).
grō, hou, slō, kou, nō VV, diphthong	**16.** Pronounce the words below. Now rewrite the words to show pronunciation: grow how slow cow know The *ow* may be part of a long vowel digraph, as in *grow, slow,* and *know.* The pattern is _____. However, the *ow* may also be a _____, as in *how, cow,* and *shower.*
yes silent	**17.** The letter *y,* when preceded by a vowel in a one-syllable word or accented syllable, forms the long vowel digraph *ay.* Pronounce the words below. play away may stay Is *y* a vowel in these words? _____ When we see *ay* in a one-syllable word or in an accented syllable, we expect the *a* (*ā*) to be long and the *y* to be _____.

ī̸e, ĭ̸e, ĭ̸e, ĕ̸ā silent long	**18.** Place diacritical marks on the long vowel digraphs in the words below. Place a slash through silent letters. field believe niece great In this set, the first vowel is _____ and the second represents the _____ sound.
ai, oa, ee *ea, ay*	**19.** Although it is true that more words fall under the "first-vowel-long" generalization than any other, there are many exceptions. It can be used only as a clue to the possible pronunciation of a word. However, there are some VV long vowel digraphs (also known as vowel teams or vowel pairs) that follow the generalization more consistently than others. Those that are most consistent appear in these words: *rain, boat, keep, each,* and *play.* The long vowel digraphs that follow the generalization a greater percentage of the time are _____, _____, _____, _____, and _____.
sĕd, hĕd	**20.** However, even these are not without exception. One of the most common sets (*ai*) appears in *said.* Another long vowel digraph, the *ea,* occurs in *head.* Rewrite *said* and *head* using diacritical marks to show pronunciation. said _____ head _____
nā bər, bâr *ôt, brĕd* *sô, pēs* *grōn, grōō* *lăf, oul* *fŏŏt, fēl*	**21.** Indicate the pronunciations of all the vowels and consonants in the words below by using the key symbols. A part of a dictionary key is given below to provide a bit of assistance. neighbor _____ bear _____ ought _____ bread _____ saw _____ peace _____ grown _____ grew _____ laugh _____ owl _____ foot _____ feel _____

Dictionary Key

â care	ä	father	ô	ball,	order	û	fur
	ōō	food	ŏŏ	hook			

no thrōō, t͡hō, bou rŭf, kôf	**22.** Examine the spellings of the words below. They look as though they should rhyme. Do they? _____ To show the inconsistencies in our language, indicate the pronunciations of all the graphemes in these words. through _____ though _____ bough _____ rough _____ cough _____
no brāk, brĕd, shōō frēk, bēd, tō	**23.** The words below seem to consist of rhyming couplets. Say the words aloud in set 1, in set 2, and in set 3. Do they rhyme? _____ Indicate the pronunciations of all the graphemes in these words. Work set by set. **1** **2** **3** break _____ bread _____ shoe _____ freak _____ bead _____ toe _____
no **1 2 3** kou, kōm, pād lō, tōōm, sĕd bŏm	**24.** Do these sets consist of rhyming words? _____ Show their pronunciations. **1** **2** **3** cow _____ comb _____ paid _____ low _____ tomb _____ said _____ bomb _____
22: *though* 23: *freak, bead, toe* 24: *paid, low*	**25.** List the words in the last **three** frames (22–24) that follow the "first-vowel-long" generalization.
diphthong, digraph dictionary listening	**26.** We have been working with words you know to help you to get a background. But in your reading, if you come across an unknown word with a two-vowel combination, you might first check for *ou, oi, oo,* and so forth to see if it might be a _____ or a double-*o* _____. Next try the "first-vowel-long" generalization, since the VV pattern is the most common. If that doesn't give you a clue, use your reference book, the _____. For phonics to be of help, the word must be in your _____ vocabulary. (writing, listening)

Study Guide
Diphthongs and Vowel Digraphs

Vowel Diphthongs

Diphthong	Key Symbol	Key Word
oi, oy	oi	oil
ou, ow	ou	house

A **diphthong** is a single vowel phoneme, represented by two letters, resembling a glide from one sound to another. Examples of vowel diphthongs include *coin, boy, mouse,* and *how.*

Vowel Digraphs: oo

Vowel Digraph	Key Symbol	Key Word
oo	o͞o	food
oo	o͝o	hook

A **vowel digraph** is a two-letter grapheme that represents one vowel phoneme. The key symbol o͞o represents the sound heard in *food* and *school,* while the key symbol o͝o represents the sound heard in *hook* and *book.*

Long Vowel Digraphs (Vowel Teams or Vowel Pairs)

Some teachers' manuals and curriculum guides refer to the long vowel digraphs as vowel teams; other manuals and guides use vowel pairs. You will want to use the term that is consistent with the materials you use in your classroom and with the curriculum followed in the educational setting in which you teach.

Long Vowel Digraph	Key Symbol	Key Word
ai (*rain*)	ā	apron
ay (*play*)	ā	apron
ea (*each*)	ē	eraser
ee (*keep*)	ē	eraser
oa (*boat*)	ō	overalls

When two vowels appear together in a one-syllable word or accented syllable, the first may represent the long sound and the second is usually silent. Some vowel pairs follow the generalization more consistently than others. Long vowel digraphs that are the most consistent appear in the words *rain, play, boat, each* and *keep. Ow* may act as a long vowel digraph, as in *snow,* or as a diphthong, as in *cow.*

Review 20

1. We have been studying vowel phonemes that are represented by two-letter combinations. Many of these two-letter vowel combinations follow a pattern: A diphthong has a gliding sound as _____ (key symbol) in *oil* and _____ (key symbol) in _____ (key word).

2. In the double-*o* digraphs, the *oo* represents the _____ (key symbol) in *food* and the _____ (key symbol) in _____ (key word).

3. Then there are pairs of long vowel digraphs that do not have distinguishing key symbols because they represent single vowels that already have key symbols—for example, *boat, lean,* and *chain.* These words contain vowel pairs that often follow this generalization: _____.

4. The vowels may be separated, as in the pattern VCe. What is the generalization?

5. A syllable may have more than one vowel _____ but only one vowel _____.

See the Answers to the Reviews section for the answers to Review 20, page 236.

Recap II

phonemes	1. We have been studying 44 _____ (sound units) of the American-English language. The consonants fall into two groups: the 18 represented by
digraphs, phonemes	single letters and the 7 _____. The 19 vowel _____ also fall into two groups: 15 represented by single vowel letters and 4 represented by two-letter combinations.

		Vowel phonemes represented by

short
 	
long
	2. We put our greatest emphasis on the five _____ sounds (as in *hop*) and the five _____ sounds (as in *hope*). (As you work through these frames, complete the outline at the right. Write the diacritical marks for the short vowels in I.A and the diacritical marks for the long vowels in I.B.)	I. Single letter symbols
		
		  A. Short
		    1. ă
		    2.
		    3.
		    4.
		    5.

ə unaccented schwa	**3.** We use a nonletter symbol (_____) to designate the soft sound heard in the _____ syllables of many multisyllable words. We call it the _____. (C.1.)	

r
 	
câre, ärm, ôt, hûrt
	4. There are four other single-letter phonemes that are often controlled by the letter following them, generally *l, w*, or _____. These phonemes represent a large variety of graphemes (e.g., *â* may represent *ai, a, ei, e, ea*, and *ay* in various words). Mark the four key symbols in this sentence: *Take care of your arm; you ought not hurt it.* (Fill in C.2–C.5.)	B. Long
		    1.
		    2. ē
		    3.
		    4.
		    5.
		
		  C. Other
		    1. ə
		    2.
		    3.

diphthongs, *oi*
 	
ou, house
	5. We also studied four vowel phonemes represented by two vowel letters. Two of these are gliding sounds called _____. They are represented by _____ in *oil* and _____ in _____. (Fill in II.A.)	4.
		    5.
		
		II. Double letter symbols
		
		  A. Diphthongs
		    1.
		    2.
		
		  B. Digraphs
		    1.
		    2.

digraphs o͞o, o͝o	**6.** The other two-letter combinations with distinctive sounds needed to complete the 19 vowel phonemes are called _____. They are found in _____ as in *food* and _____ as in *hook*. (Fill in II.B.) You have now completed the outline of the key symbols that represent the vowel phonemes. Turn to pages 150–155 in the Review of Phonemes (Part Five) to check your answers. You have mastered all the phonemes!	

symbols	**7.** Other vowel digraphs do not have distinguishing key _____ because they represent single vowels with their own phonemes—for example, *coat, fleet, dean, main,* and *stay.* What vowel phoneme is represented in each
ō, ē, ē, ā, ā	of these? _____ _____ _____ _____ Mark the vowels in *coat, fleet, dean, main,* and *stay,* and place a slash through silent letters.
cōat, flēet, dēan, māin, stāy	_____ _____ _____ _____ In general,
long	the first vowel represents its _____ sound and the second of the pair
silent	is _____.

	8. Vowel letters are not very reliable.
	A. A letter may represent more than one phoneme:
ō, ŏ	For example, an *o* may represent _____ as in *hope,* _____ as
ə, ô	in *hop,* _____ as in *mammoth,* _____ as in *ought,* or
û	_____ as in *worm.*
	B. A phoneme may be represented by more than one vowel letter:
y, ĭ	The ĭ may be represented by _____ in *myth* or _____ in *fin.*
silent	**C.** A letter may represent no phoneme. It may be _____ as the
a, e, e	_____ in *roam,* the _____ in *race,* or the _____ in *doe.*
	Although vowels are not very reliable, the use of certain generalizations will
listening	help us to identify words already in our _____ vocabulary. (reading, writing, listening)
	(Of course, there are exceptions to the generalizations, too!)

	9. Some of these generalizations have been referred to previously, and others follow.
	When a one-syllable word or accented syllable contains two vowels, one of which is the final *e,* the first vowel usually represents its
long, silent	_____ **sound, and the final *e* is _____ (the VCe pattern).**

phoneme	**10.** An open syllable ends with a vowel _____ (phoneme, letter) (the CV pattern). Check the words that end with an open syllable:
echo, say, though, be	echo open say though thought rate be once

consonant *open, thought, rate, once* hearing the final phoneme	A closed syllable ends with a _____ phoneme (the VC, CVC pattern). Which of the words above have closed syllables? _____ Whether a syllable is open or closed depends on _____. *(hearing the final phoneme, seeing the final letter)*
long *he, why* CV	**11.** A single vowel in an open accented syllable often represents its _____ sound. Which of the following words follow this generalization? *he why pen road do* The vowel–consonant pattern is _____.
short *pin, sent, cat* VC (or CVC)	**12.** A single vowel in a closed accented syllable usually represents its _____ sound. Which of the following words follow this generalization? *pin sent cat hope thought* The vowel–consonant pattern is _____.
phoneme, vowel	**13.** Although a syllable may have more than one letter, it has only one vowel _____. The _____ has the most influence on the syllable. *(vowel, consonant)*
accented ə (schwa)	**14.** Vowels behave differently in accented and unaccented syllables. The vowel is most clearly heard in a(an) _____ syllable. The vowel in most unaccented syllables represents the _____ or the ĭ.
mē lēpe, phā tŏg, rĕl nō, phō, ŏt, drāif, skōōs	**15.** The generalizations we have studied in connection with these vowel phonemes should aid in the pronunciation of words we do not recognize. The words below are nonsense words. Take a chance that the vowel phonemes follow the rules even in unaccented syllables or have their most common sound. Mark every vowel in these "words" to show pronunciation: <center>*me lepe pha tog rel no pho ot draif skoos*</center>

Reference

National Governors Association Center for Best Practices & Council of Chief State School Officers. (2010). *Common Core State Standards for English language arts & history/social studies, science, and technical subjects: Reading: Foundational Skills—Phonological Awareness, Phonics and Word Study*. Washington, DC: Authors. Retrieved May 15, 2012, from http://www.corestandards.org/assets/CCSSI_ELA%20Standards.pdf

Part Five

A Review of Phonemes

Review of Phonemes

phonemes (or sounds)	**1.** Our written language is not based on pictorial representations of objects or ideas. It is a phonetic language in that there is a relationship between the letters of the alphabet and the _____ of the spoken language.
consonants	**2.** In fact, many of the _____ are fairly reliable as to sound. <center>(consonants, vowels)</center>
phonemes (or sounds) letter	**3.** However, there are so many inconsistencies that the English language is not an easy one to learn to read. If it were a consistent, strictly phonetic language, then: (1) there would be one and only one letter to represent each of the _____ of the spoken language, and (2) there would be only one phoneme represented by each _____ of the alphabet.
26 phonemes (or sounds)	**4.** The truth of the matter is: **(1) A letter may represent more than one sound.** For example, each vowel represents several sounds. Our alphabet has _____ letters (and some of them are useless) to represent the 44 _____.

phonemes (or sounds)	**(2) The same sound may be represented by more than one letter.** The 44 _____ are represented by 251 different graphemes. For example, we spell the first consonant phoneme we hear in *chute* (key symbol:
sh	_____) in 14 different ways! **(3) A letter may represent no sound.**
silent	Almost any letter may, at some time or another, be _____.
spoken	**5.** We have identified the 44 phonemes that, for all practical purposes in the teaching of reading, make up the sounds of our _____ language. <div align="right">(spoken, written)</div>
symbol *j*	**6.** We have designated a key symbol for each of these phonemes to serve as our pronunciation guide. These key pronunciation symbols, then, provide us with a one-to-one correspondence between sound and _____. For example, we use the _____ to symbolize the sound heard in *jam,* even though it may be represented by *g* as in *gentle, d* as in *graduate,* or *dg* as in *judgment.*
symbol	**7.** Let us review, through the following outline, the 44 phonemes we have identified and the _____ we have designated for each. Study and make responses as indicated. When choices appear in parentheses, write the answer in the blank or underline the correct answer. For example, there are 44 (phonemes, graphemes).

Review Outline

	I. CONSONANT PHONEMES	Key
	A. Represented by a single consonant letter	Symbol
boat	*b* as in _____ (pages 39–40). <div align="center">(boat, comb)</div>	**1.** *b*
	Complete this generalization:`	
silent, *m*	*b* is usually _____ when it follows _____ (*comb*) or precedes	
t	_____ (*doubt*) in the same syllable.	
syllable	The *b* in *lumber* is not silent because it is not in the same _____.	

one	Say *rabbit* aloud. How many phonemes do these two like consonants represent? _____
	Complete this generalization:
consonants	Two like _____ appearing together in a word or accented syllable
one	generally represent _____ phoneme (pages 39, 42).
	<div align="center">(How many?)</div>
	Make a slash through the second like consonant in each word to depict the silent letter.
les⁄son, bet⁄ter, ham⁄her	*lesson* _____ *better* _____ *hammer* _____
hap⁄pen, pud⁄dle, puf⁄f	*happen* _____ *puddle* _____ *puff* _____
symbol, word	*c* has no key _____ or _____.
	c usually represents the sound we associate with the *k* when it is followed by
a, o, u	the vowel _____ (*cat*), _____ (*coat*), or _____ (*cut*) or when it
end, letter (Consonant	appears at the _____ (*comic*) of a word or when it is followed by any
is also correct.)	other _____ (*clasp*) (pages 56–57).
e, i	*c* usually represents /*s*/ when it is followed by _____ (*cent*), _____ (*city*),
y	or _____ (*cycle*) (pages 56–57).

		Hard c	Soft c
cabin cymbal	Use the words below to complete the table at the right by selecting words in which *c* represents the hard sound or the soft sound.	_____	_____
cube city		_____	_____
cot cell		_____	_____
close mice	*cymbal city cabin cube cell cot close mice*	_____	_____
s	*c* can be a silent letter when it follows _____ as in *scene*.		
ch	We could replace the letter *c* with *k* and *s* were it not for the _____ digraph.		

dog	*d* as in _____ is fairly dependable. **2. d**
	<div align="center">(key word)</div>
ladder, /t/	*d* may be silent as in _____ , or it may represent _____ when
	<div align="center">(*ladder, laden*) (/f/, /t/)</div>
	part of the *-ed* suffix.
dg	*d* also represents /*j*/ as part of the combinations _____ (*bridge*) and
ld	_____ (*soldier*) (pages 47–48).

	f as in *fish* is a fairly reliable letter, with the notable exception in the **3. f**
/v/	word *of,* in which the letter *f* represents _____ (page 45).
gh, ph	This phoneme is sometimes spelled _____ , as in *enough,* or _____ , as in *graph* (pages 45–46).

goat, hard	*g* as in _____ represents the _____ sound. 4. *g* (goat, giant) (hard, soft)
a	This sound is usually heard when *g* is followed by the vowel _____ (*game*),
o, u	_____ (*goat*), or _____ (*gum*) or when it is followed by any other
letter (Consonant is also correct.), end	_____ (*glad*) or when it appears at the _____ of a word (*drag*) (page 55).
soft	*g* usually represents a _____ sound when it is followed by the (hard, soft)
e, i, y	vowel _____ (*gem*), _____ (*giant*), or _____ (*gym*) (page 55).
gift	The word _____ does not follow this generalization. (gym, gift)
	Study the words below. For each set, choose a word from the six at the right in which *g* represents the same phoneme as the other underlined letters in the set and has the same vowel following it.

gypsy
good
gentle
guard
ginger
gate

1	2	3	4	5	6
game	*gent*	*giant*	*goal*	*gulp*	*gym*
gave	*germ*	*margin*	*gold*	*guess*	*gyrate*
_____	_____	_____	_____	_____	_____

1. gate   2. gentle
3. ginger   4. good
5. guard   6. gypsy

hat	*h* as in _____. 5. *h* (ghost, hat, honor)
end	*h* is never heard at the _____ (*oh*) of a word or syllable.
beginning	Sometimes *h* is silent (*honor*) at the _____ of a word.
g, k	The *h* is silent when it follows the consonant _____ (*ghost*), _____
r	(*khaki*), or _____ (*rhyme*) (pages 40–41).
vowel	*h* is also silent when it follows a _____ (*oh*) in a word or syllable.
Ȟonor, oȟ, hurraȟ, rȟyme	Put a slash through each silent *h*.
	honor _____ oh _____ hurrah _____ rhyme _____
habit, pooȟ, gȟost, kȟaki	habit _____ pooh _____ ghost _____ khaki _____

	j as in jeep. 6. *j*
e	The /j/ phoneme is often represented by a *g* when followed by the vowel _____
i, y	(*gem*), _____ (*giant*), or _____ (*gypsy*) (pages 54–55).
ld	The /j/ phoneme may also be represented by _____ (*soldier*) and
dg	_____ (*fudge*) (pages 47–48).

kite	*k* as in _____. **7.** *k* _____(key word)_
silent *n*	*k* is _____ (*knight*) at the beginning of a word or syllable when followed by _____ (page 41). Put a slash through each silent *k*.
K̸not, K̸now	knot key know keep
lion	*l* as in _____. **8.** *l* ____(*lion, calm*) The letter *l* is sometimes silent when followed, in the same syllable, by
m, k, d	_____ (*calm*), _____ (*chalk*), or _____ (*should*) (page 42).
moon, reliable	*m,* as in _____ , *m* is a _____ letter. **9.** *m* _____(key word)_ _(reliable, unreliable)_
nut	*n* as in _____. **10.** *n* ____(*nut, condemn*)
m	*n* can be silent when preceded by _____ (*autumn*) (page 50).
/ng/	*n* generally represents _____ when it is followed by *g* (*sing*) or *k* (*thank*).
	p as in *pig*. **11.** *p*
reliable	As a single letter, *p* is _____. _____(reliable, unreliable)_
s, t	When *p* is followed by _____ (*pseudo*), _____ (*pterodactyl*), or
n, silent	_____ (*pneumonia*), it is usually _____ (pages 42–43).
symbol	*q* has no key _____.
k	The dictionary uses a _____ to indicate its pronunciation. The *que* at the end of a word (*antique*) represents the phoneme we
k	associate with _____. The letter *q* is almost always followed by the letter ____(*k, s*)_
u, silent	_____. The *u* may be _____ or represent the sound we associate
w	with the key symbol _____ (pages 35–37).
plăk, kwēn, kwĭt	Rewrite *plaque, queen,* and *quit* to show pronunciation.
	r as in *ring*. **12.** *r*
reliable	*r* is very _____. When we see *r*, we can be sure that it represents ____(reliable, unreliable)_
r	the sound we associate with the key symbol _____ (page 35).

sun	**13.** s s as in _____ . *(his, sure, sun)* Except when acting as a plural at the end of a word, s represents the phonemes
/s/, /z/	we associate with _____ *(miss)* and _____ *(his)* with about equal frequency.
/sh/	s also represents the phoneme _____ *(sugar)* and occasionally stands for
/zh/	the _____ *(treasure)* (page 64).
table	**14.** t t as in _____ . *(table, than)*
s, f	t may be silent when it follows the letter _____ *(listen)* or _____
ch	*(soften)* and when it precedes _____ *(catch).*
ch	In connection with a vowel, t may represent _____ *(future)* or
sh, silent	_____ *(station)* (page 66). t may be _____ in words adopted from the French language *(ballet)*.
thin	t is often part of the consonant digraph th as in _____ , in which *(thin, fast)* case the /t/ is not heard.
van	**15.** v v as in _____ is very reliable (page 35). *(van, off)*
wagon	**16.** w w as in _____ (page 60). *(two, why, wagon, who)*
consonant	w serves as a _____ and as a vowel. As a consonant, it precedes
vowel, follows	the _____ *(was)*. As a vowel, w _____ the vowel *(precedes, follows)*
silent	*(snow)*. Sometimes w is _____ *(wrote)*. w may also be part of a
blend (or cluster), digraph	consonant _____ *(dwell)* or a consonant _____ *(which)*.
silent	Occasionally w appears to be part of a digraph *(wh)* but is _____ *(who)*.
	x has no phoneme of its own (page 63).
/ks/, /gz/, /z/	It represents the _____ in *six,* the _____ in *exam,* and the _____
/gz/	in *xylophone*. We are more apt to use _____ when x appears between two vowel phonemes *(exam)*.

yo-yo	y as in _____ (page 59). **17.** y
	(day, yo-yo)
vowel	y serves as a consonant and as a _____.
	y at the beginning of a word or syllable represents the sound we associate
/y/, yo-yo	with _____ , key word _____.
zipper	z as in _____ (page 50). **18.** z
	(quartz, zipper)
/s/, /zh/	Occasionally z represents _____ (waltz) or _____ (azure).

B. Represented by consonant digraphs

chair	ch as in _____. **19.** ch
	(choir, chair, machine)
is not, /ch/	ch _____ reliable. ch may represent the _____ phoneme in change, the
	(is, is not)
/k/, /sh/	_____ phoneme in choir, or the _____ phoneme in chiffon (page 74).
	dg represents no phoneme of its own. It often represents the key symbol
/j/	_____ (fudge) (page 47).
	gh represents no phoneme of its own.
silent	gh is usually _____ (bright) when it precedes t in a syllable.
/f/	gh is silent (through) or represents _____ (enough) when it follows the
	vowel in a word or syllable (page 46). When it appears at the beginning of a
h	word or syllable, the _____ (ghost) is silent.
king	ng as in _____ (page 81). **20.** ng
	(king, congest)
beginning	ng is never heard at the _____ of a syllable, and it always follows a
/ng/	vowel. The letter n may also represent _____ when it is followed by a g
thangk	or k (bring, blank). Write thank to show pronunciation.
	ph has no phoneme of its own (page 46).
f	The key symbol _____ commonly represents the sound, as in phone.
ship	sh as in _____ (page 74). **21.** sh
	(ship, division)
thumb	th as in _____ (page 72). **22.** th
	(that, thumb)
voiceless	The /th/ in thin is _____ (page 77).
	(voiceless, voiced)

that	*th* as in _____ (page 72). *(that, thumb)*
voiced	*th* is _____ (page 77). *(voiceless, voiced)* Pronounce the words at the right. Write the words in which the *th* is voiced in Column 1 below. Write the words in which the *th* is voiceless in Column 2.

23. th

thaw
their
thief
theme
these
this
thing
those

	Column 1 Voiced	Column 2 Voiceless
their *thaw*	_____	_____
these *thief*	_____	_____
this *theme*	_____	_____
those *thing*	_____	_____

---

whale

24. wh

wh as in _____ (page 78).
            (who, whale)

wh appears at the beginning of a word or syllable and is followed by a

vowel

_____ (*which*). The trend is to pronounce the *wh* as /w/. Your dictionary may use /hw/ and /w/ to represent pronunciation (*hwāl* or *wāl*).

whole

wh may represent /h/ as in _____.
                        (whole, white)

---

treasure

25. zh

zh as in _____ (page 75).
            (treasure, edge)

The /zh/ is never represented in a word with the grapheme *zh*.

s

The /zh/ may be represented by the _____ (*pleasure*), the

g, z

_____ (*collage*), or the _____ (*seizure*).

C. Represented by consonant blends (clusters)

Consonant clusters are two or more consonants that, when pronounced, blend together. The phonemes in the blend retain their individual identities. The most common blends include the letters *l, r,* and *s,* as in *bl, cr,* and *st.* There are blends that do not contain these letters (page 86).

Consonant blends may occur at the beginning (*stop*) or the end (*jump*) of a word or a syllable (page 87).

II. VOWEL PHONEMES

A. Represented by single vowel letters

a, e, i, o

The letters _____ , _____ , _____ , _____ ,

u, w, y

_____ , and sometimes _____ and _____ are classified as vowels (page 94).

sounds, *y* *w*	Two of the seven vowels are not represented by key symbols because they do not represent _____ of their own. These are the _____ and the _____ (pages 94–95).
i, e silent	*y* as a vowel represents no sound of its own. When *y* is a vowel, its pronunciation is shown by the key symbols we associate with the _____ or the _____ (page 94). In the long vowel digraph *ay* (*play*), the *y* is _____.
vowel	As a vowel, *w* is always used in combination with a preceding _____ (*threw*) (page 55).

1. Short sounds

apple	*a* as in _____ (page 97). (*date, apple, all*)	**26.** ă
edge	*e* as in _____ (page 97). (*edge, even*)	**27.** ĕ
igloo	*i* as in _____ (page 97). (*ice, igloo*)	**28.** ĭ
ox	*o* as in _____ (page 97). (*over, ox*)	**29.** ŏ
umbrella	*u* as in _____ (page 97). (*umbrella, use*)	**30.** ŭ

Breve

short *wĕt, kăt* *wet, kat*	The breve (˘) is the diacritical mark used to indicate the pronunciations of _____ vowels (page 97). Write *wet* and *cat* to show pronunciation. _____ and _____ Many dictionaries indicate the pronunciations of the short vowel sounds with the letter alone. How would the pronunciations of *wet* and *cat* be indicated in these dictionaries? _____ and _____

Closed syllable

consonant short *hid*	The closed syllable ends in a _____ phoneme (page 100). (*consonant, vowel*) The vowel in a closed syllable usually represents its _____ sound, (*long, short*) as in _____. (*hid, hide*)

VC	**VC pattern** The most common vowel–consonant pattern is that of the _____ (vowel–consonant), in which the V (vowel) represents its short sound (pages 99–100).
consonant	The VC (or CVC) syllable ends with a _____ phoneme. <center>(consonant, vowel)</center>
single short	Complete this generalization: A _____ vowel in a closed accented syllable usually represents the _____ sound of the vowel (page 101).
two first, short silent	**VCCe pattern** Complete this generalization: When a word or a syllable has _____ vowels, one of which is a final *e,* and the two vowels are separated by two consonants, the _____ vowel often represents its _____ sound and the final *e* is _____ (page 102).
apron *eraser* *ice* *overalls* *unicorn* ī ĭ, ē	**2. Long sounds** *a* as in _____ (page 105). **31.** ā (*apron, ant*) *e* as in _____ (page 105). **32.** ē (*every, eraser*) *i* as in _____ (page 105). **33.** ī (*ice, itch*) *o* as in _____ (page 105). **34.** ō (*overalls, oven*) *u* as in _____ (page 105). **35.** ū (*up, unicorn*) *y* has no vowel phoneme of its own. Its key symbol can be the _____ as in *my,* the _____ as in *myth,* and the _____ as in *happy* (page 113).
long yo͞o o͞o	We use a macron (ˉ) to indicate the pronunciation of _____ vowel sounds (page 105). Some dictionaries and teachers' manuals use the _____ to indicate the pronunciation of the long *u* in *cube* and the _____ to represent the pronunciation of the long *u* in *tune.*

vowel long, /bē/	**Open syllable** An open syllable ends in a _____ phoneme (page 109). <div align="center">(consonant, vowel)</div> We hear a _____ vowel phoneme, as in _____. <div align="center">(short, long)</div> <div align="center">(/bē/, /bet/)</div>
CV no	**CV pattern** The open-syllable generalization most often applies to words and accented syllables that have the _____ vowel–consonant pattern, as in _____ (page 110). <div align="center">(no, not)</div>
two long silent mīc¢, bōn¢, māk¢, hīd¢	**VCe pattern** Complete this generalization: When a one-syllable word or accented syllable contains _____ vowels, one of which is the final *e*, the first vowel usually represents its _____ sound, and the final *e* is _____ (page 106). Mark each vowel in the following words with the proper diacritical mark. Put a slash through each silent letter. <div align="center">mice bone make hide</div>
two long silent ai, oa, ee ea, ay	**CVVC (VV) long vowel digraph pattern** Complete this generalization: When _____ vowels appear together in a one-syllable word or an (How many?) accented syllable, the first usually represents its _____ sound and the second is _____ (page 133). The vowel pairs that follow the generalization a greater percentage of the time are _____ (*rain*), _____ (*boat*), _____ (*street*), _____ (*beach*), and _____ (*play*) (page 135).
a, e, i o, u	**3. Other vowel sounds** 36. ə The schwa, key symbol ə, represents the soft, unaccented sound of the vowel _____ in *comma*, _____ in *chicken*, _____ in *family*, _____ in *apron*, and _____ in *circus* (page 116).

care	*â* is the vowel phoneme we associate with the key word **37.** *â*
	_____ (page 120).
c<u>a</u>re, ch<u>ai</u>r, th<u>e</u>re	Underline the portion(s) of the words *care, chair,* and *there* that, when combined with *r,* represent this phoneme.
fur	*û* is the vowel phoneme we associate with the key word **38.** *û*
	_____ (page 120).
h<u>u</u>rt, t<u>e</u>rm, c<u>ou</u>rage	Underline the portion(s) of *hurt, term,* and *courage* that, when combined with *r,* represent this phoneme.
father	*ä* is the vowel phoneme we associate with the key **39.** *ä*
	word _____ (page 120).
h<u>ea</u>rt, t<u>a</u>co, pl<u>a</u>za c<u>a</u>r, ch<u>a</u>rge, f<u>a</u>rm	Underline the portion(s) of *heart, taco,* and *plaza* that represent this phoneme. Underline the portion(s) of *car, charge,* and *farm* that, when combined with *r,* represent this phoneme.
ball	*ô* is the vowel phoneme we associate with the key **40.** *ô*
	word _____ (page 120).
c<u>au</u>tion, t<u>a</u>ll, c<u>o</u>st	Underline the portion(s) of *caution, tall,* and *cost* that represent this phoneme.
sh<u>o</u>rt, c<u>o</u>re, <u>oa</u>r, f<u>ou</u>r	Underline the portion(s) of *short, core, oar,* and *four* that, when combined with *r,* represent this phoneme.
	Complete these generalizations:
vowel	If the only vowel in a word or syllable is followed by *r,* the _____ is affected by that *r,* as in *car, hurt,* and *orbit* (page 124).
	If the only vowel in a word or syllable is an *a* followed by *l* or *w,* the *a* is affected
l, w	by that _____ or _____ , as in *saw* and *fall* (page 124).
	B. Represented by vowel combinations
	1. Diphthongs
oil	*oi* as in _____ . This phoneme is also represented by the letters **41.** *oi*
	(*oil, house*)
oy	_____ (page 128).
house	*ou* as in _____ . This phoneme is also represented by **42.** *ou*
	(*oil, house*)
ow	the letters _____ (page 128).

2. Vowel digraphs
Vowel digraph: *oo*

food

$\overline{oo}$ as in _____ (page 130).   **43.** $\overline{oo}$

(food, flood)

hook

$\breve{oo}$ as in _____ (page 130).   **44.** $\breve{oo}$

(food, flood, hook)

Long vowel digraphs: *ai, ea, ee, oa, ay*

The key symbols for the long vowel digraphs have already been given.

Part Six

Onsets and Rimes

Onsets and Rimes

26, 44	**1.** Thus far we have been studying the _____ letters and _____ phonemes of the American-English language. We have learned that the
vowels, consonants	arrangement of _____ and _____ within the syllable affects the pronunciation.
	2. We will now turn our attention to the consonant(s) at the beginning of the syllable and the vowel and the consonant(s) that follow it at the end of the syllable.
consonant	The **onset** is the _____ letter(s) that precede(s) the vowel in a syllable. The dictionary defines an onset as a "beginning or commencement."
begins	Therefore, a syllable _____ with an onset. We will use one-syllable (begins, ends) words in our study of onsets and rimes.
	3. The onset may be a the single-letter consonant, consonant blend, or consonant digraph that begins a syllable. Study these words: _bat_, _street_, _thorn_.
single consonant	The onset in _bat_ is a _____. (single consonant, consonant blend)
blend	The onset in _street_ is a consonant _____. (blend, digraph)
digraph	The onset in _thorn_ is a consonant _____. (blend, digraph)

dog, phone, smile, splash, wish, three	**4.** Underline the onset in the one-syllable words below.
	dog _____ phone _____ smile _____ splash _____ wish _____ three _____
single-letter	We can see that an onset may consist of a _____ consonant (*dog, wish*),
blend (cluster), diagraph	a consonant _____ (*smile, splash*), a consonant _____ (*phone*), or a consonant digraph that combines with another consonant letter to form a
th	blend, as the _____ in *three*.

5. Complete the table by filling in the onset (1) and key symbol (2) for each one-syllable word (3).

	1	2	3
c, k, cat	_____	_____	cat
kn, n, knight	_____	_____	knight
bl, bl, black	_____	_____	black
gh, g, ghost	_____	_____	ghost
ph, f, phone	_____	_____	phone
wh, wh, white	_____	_____	white
sk, sk, skin	_____	_____	skin
p, p, pink	_____	_____	pink
consonant	An onset consists of one or more _____ letters.
	(vowel, consonant)

6. There are many one-syllable words in the English language that do not begin with an onset. Examine the word *at*. Does *at* begin with an

no   onset? _____

consonant   *At* does not begin with an onset because there is no _____ letter preceding the vowel. Does the one-syllable word *chat* begin with an onset?

yes   _____ The onset in the word *chat* is the consonant digraph

ch   _____.

7. We have noted that a one-syllable word may not always begin with an onset. Mark the one-syllable words below that **do not** begin with an onset.

it, up, elf   show   it   split   up   elf   queen

8. Let us review what we have learned about an onset. An onset is the

consonant, precedes   _____ letter(s) that begin(s) the syllable. An onset _____

(precedes, follows)

the vowel in a syllable. Do we expect *every* syllable to begin with an onset?

no   _____

vowel, consonant(s)	**9.** The **rime** consists of the vowel and the consonant(s) that follows the vowel at the end of the syllable. *Rime* is a variation in the spelling of the word *rhyme*. Rhyme is agreement among the vowel and consonant sounds at the end of words. Therefore, in the teaching of reading, we consider the rime to be the _____ and the final _____ in a syllable.
spend, beg, shut, drink, stop, flat one, one	**10.** Study the one-syllable words below. Underline the rime in each word. spend beg shut drink stop flat How many vowel phonemes do you hear in each one-syllable word? _____ We could say that one rime contains _____ vowel phoneme(s). (How many?)
2, 1, 2, 1, 3, 2 3, 3, 2, 1, 1, 3 rime	**11.** Use the numbers of the rimes below to indicate the rimes in the words at the bottom of the frame. **1.** *ug* **2.** *ant* **3.** *op* *plant* _____ *bug* _____ *slant* _____ *dug* _____ *top* _____ *grant* _____ *drop* _____ *hop* _____ *chant* _____ *plug* _____ *rug* _____ *mop* _____ You can see that our written language has many words that contain the same _____.
can, match, kept, tent, ham, salt, trust consonant	**12.** Study the rimes in the words below to see if each rime always consists of one consonant that follows the vowel. Underline the rime in each one-syllable word. can match kept tent ham salt trust A rime may have more than one _____ letter following the vowel.
amb one silent	**13.** The rime in the one-syllable word *lamb* is _____. This rime consists of one vowel, *a,* and two consonant letters, *m* and *b.* Say *lamb* out loud. How many consonant phonemes do you hear in this rime? _____ The last consonant letter is _____.
look, sleep, mouse, write, blame, train, ride no yes	**14.** Study the rimes in the words below. Underline the rime in each one-syllable word. look sleep mouse write blame train ride Does the rime always consist of one vowel letter? _____ Does each rime consist of one vowel phoneme? _____
boat, made, store seed, choice two one	**15.** There are many rimes in written English that have more than one vowel letter. Say the one-syllable words below. Underline the rime. boat made store seed choice The rimes in the words above consist of _____ vowel letters. (How many?) How many vowel phonemes do you hear in each rime? _____

consonant	**16.** We have noted that a rime consists of the vowel and the _____ letter(s) at the end of the syllable. Write the rimes in the one-syllable words below.
ent, aste, ain *ar, arve, oint*	cent _____ taste _____ rain _____ star _____ starve _____ point _____
syllable	**17.** You identified the rime in each one-syllable word in frame 16. We can conclude that onset–rime is a means of dividing a _____ into the initial consonant(s) and the vowel and consonant(s) that follow it.

	18. In the teaching of reading, a **word family** consists of words that are spelled with the same rime (*bell, fell, sell*) and that, when pronounced, rhyme; that is, they have the same vowel and ending consonant phonemes (/*bell*/, /*fell*/, /*sell*/).
	
	Group the words below into word families.
	
	               bed fat run
	               cat red led
	               sun fun rat

bed, red, led *fat, cat, rat* *run, sun, fun*	**Word Family 1** _____ _____ _____ **Word Family 2** _____ _____ _____ **Word Family 3** _____ _____ _____
ed, at, un	**19.** Each word family in the frame above consists of three one-syllable words that contain the same rime. Or we might say that there are three word families represented in frame 18. They are _____, _____, and _____.
rime *ill* *ill* *ill*	**20.** A word family consists of words that are spelled with the same _____. For example, *cat, hat,* and *fat* are words in the *at* word family. _____ is the common rime in *bill, pill,* and *fill*. Therefore, *bill, pill,* and *fill* belong in the _____ word family. Put another way, *bill, pill,* and *fill* contain the rime _____.
bell, tell, fell, sell *bold, told, fold, sold, mold* *ban, tan, fan, man* 13	**21.** Combine the onsets with the rimes below to form one-syllable words. Form only real words. Write the words on the lines. **Onsets** **Rimes** **Words** *b, t, f, s, m* *ell* _____ _____ _____ _____ *b, t, f, s, m* *old* _____ _____ _____ _____ *b, t, f, s, m* *an* _____ _____ _____ _____ How many different real words did you make? _____

three consistently	**22.** How many word families are represented in frame 21? _____The rime in each word family _____ represents the same sounds. (consistently, inconsistently) We must now ask ourselves these questions: How reliable is the rime? Can we always depend on a rime to represent the same sounds in different words?
rime yes yes yes yes no yes no no	**23.** _Cream_ and _dream_ contain the same _____. Do _cream_ and _dream_ rhyme? _____ Do _cream_ and _dream_ belong in the same word family?_____ Do _cat_ and _mat_ belong in the same word family? _____ Do _best_ and _test_ belong in the same word family? _____ Do _four_ and _more_ belong in the same word family? _____ Do /bed/ and /head/ rhyme? _____ Are _bed_ and _head_ spelled with the same rime? _____ Do _bed_ and _head_ belong in the same word family? _____

rhyme
 	
fish, wish
 	
need, seed
 	
yes
 	
_no_
	24. We have noted that when words contain the same rime, the words may also _____. There are exceptions (of course!). Now pronounce the sets of words below.
	
	      Set 1 **Set 2** **Set 3** **Set 4**
	       fish _joke_ _pail_ _need_
	       wish _oak_ _stale_ _seed_
	
	Do the words in sets 1 through 4 rhyme? _____
	
	Does each set of words contain the same rime? _____ Mark the sets that contain the same rime.

rhymes phonemes rime	**25.** Each set of words in frame 24 _____. That is, in each set there is agreement among the ending vowel and consonant sounds. We have learned that the same _____ may be represented by different graphemes. Therefore, words that rhyme may not always contain the same _____.

night, light, might
 	
cave, save
	26. Study the words below. Use your knowledge to mark the words in each group that include a common rime that represents the same rhyming sounds.
	
	     Group 1 _night_ _light_ _might_
	     Group 2 _cave_ _save_ _have_

yes	**27.** Pronounce the words in the previous frame. Do the words in Group 1 rhyme? _____ Are these words spelled with the same rime?
yes, *ight*	_____ Write the rime._____
	Let us turn to Group 2. Do these words contain the same rime?
yes, no	_____ Does the rime represent the same sounds? _____ The
ave	rime is _____. Indicate the word(s) in Group 2 that do(es) not belong
have	in the same word family. _____

	28. Rime can provide the beginning reader with a tool for reading and spelling unfamiliar words. This said, we must be aware of inconsistencies. Rewrite *cave, save,* and *have* to show pronunciation:
kāv, sāv, hăv	_____ _____ _____
	Rewrite *red, bed,* and *said* to show pronunciation:
rĕd, bĕd, sĕd	_____ _____ _____

29. Pronounce the one-syllable words below. Complete the table by filling in the onset (1) and the rime (2) for each word (3).

		1	2	3
r	*ight*	_____	_____	*right*
sh	*ould*	_____	_____	*should*
shr	*ank*	_____	_____	*shrank*
tr	*ade*	_____	_____	*trade*
th	*ump*	_____	_____	*thump*
tr	*eat*	_____	_____	*treat*
qu	*ick*	_____	_____	*quick*
gr	*een*	_____	_____	*green*

	30. Let us establish the connection between the onsets and rimes in written words and the awareness of rhyme in spoken words (Part One, page 20). You have learned that rhyme awareness is the ability to identify and think of words
rhyme	that _____.
	Awareness of rhyming sounds makes it possible for the child to associate the
hears	rhymes the child _____ in spoken words with the rimes the child
	(hears, sees)
sees	_____ in written words. Let us assume a child recognizes that /*mat*/
	(hears, sees)
	and /*sat*/ rhyme. Would you expect the child, with instruction, and with reading and writing experiences, to learn the association between the *at* in
yes	*mat* and *sat* and the /*at*/ the child hears in /*mat*/ and /*sat*/? _____

consonant	**31.** Let us review. We have studied onset and rime in one-syllable words. We have learned that onset–rime is one means of dividing the syllable. The onset is the _____ letter(s) at the beginning of the syllable (_sat_). The rime
vowel, consonant(s)	consists of the _____ and _____ that follow(s) it at the end of the syllable (_sat_). The consonant letter(s) in the onset represent(s) the
phoneme(s) or sound(s)	beginning _____ in a word (/s/ in /_sat_/). The rime consists of the vowel and consonant(s) letters that represent the vowel and final consonant
sounds (phonemes)	_____ in a spoken one-syllable word (/at/ in /_sat_/).

	32. Continuing our review, we have learned that a one-syllable word may not
onset	have an _____. (onset, rime)
rime	However, a one-syllable word must have a _____. (onset, rime)
vowel	The rime represents only one _____ phoneme, but may represent
consonant	more than one _____ phoneme.
word family	We consider a _____ to consist of words that have a common rime and the same rhyming sound.

Study Guide

Onsets and Rimes and 50 Common Rimes

Onset

The **onset** is the consonant that precedes the vowel in a syllable. The onset may have more than one consonant letter.

Rime

The **rime** consists of a vowel and the final consonant(s) in the syllable. The rime may have more than one vowel letter but only one vowel phoneme (*reach*).

Rhyme

Rhyme is the agreement among the ending vowel and consonant phonemes in spoken words (the /ĭt/ in /bĭt/, /sĭt/, and /hĭt/).

Word Family

Words that are spelled with the same rime and that also rhyme form a **word family.** In the teaching of reading, word families are often identified by the common rime (the *it* family, as in *sit, hit,* and *fit,* or the *op* family, as in *hop, top,* and *mop*).

Words that share a rime (*bit, sit, hit*) often rhyme (/bit/, /sit/, /hit/). However, words that rhyme may not always share the same rime (*head* /hĕd/, *bed* /bĕd/). Furthermore, words that are spelled with the same rime may not always share the same ending vowel and consonant sounds (*head* /hĕd/, *bead* /bēd/).

50 Common Rimes

Rime	Examples	Rime	Examples
ab	cab, grab, lab, tab	ell	bell, fell, sell, tell
ace	face, place, race, space	en	den, hen, men, pen
ack	back, black, sack, track	ent	bent, sent, tent, went
ad	bad, had, mad, sad	est	best, rest, test, west
ade	grade, made, shade, trade	et	bet, set, pet, wet
ag	bag, flag, rag, tag	ice	dice, mice, nice, twice
ail	fail, mail, sail, tail	ick	brick, lick, quick, trick
ain	gain, main, pain, train	ide	bride, side, tide, wide
air	chair, fair, pair, stair	ig	big, dig, pig, wig
ake	bake, make, take, wake	ight	fight, night, right, sight
all	ball, call, fall, tall	ill	bill, fill, hill, pill
am	clam, ham, ram, slam	in	fin, pin, thin, win
ame	came, game, name, same	ing	king, ring, sing, sting
amp	camp, damp, lamp, stamp	ink	link, pink, sink, wink
an	can, fan, man, tan	ip	dip, hip, ship, slip
and	band, hand, land, sand	it	hit, pit, sit, slit
ang	bang, hang, rang, sang	ock	block, rock, sock, stock
ank	blank, drank, rank, sank	og	dog, frog, hog, log
ap	cap, lap, map, nap	old	cold, fold, hold, told
at	cat, fat, hat, sat	op	hop, mop, pop, stop
ate	date, gate, late, rate	ot	dot, hot, got, lot
eam	beam, cream, dream, team	ug	bug, dug, hug, tug
eat	beat, meat, neat, seat	ump	bump, dump, hump, pump
ed	bed, fed, led, red	un	bun, fun, run, sun
eed	deed, feed, need, seed	ut	but, cut, nut, shut

Review 21

1. Write the onset for each of the one-syllable words below.

   wrong   could   shop   high   stay

   sun   bowl   school   stage   goat

2. Indicate the one-syllable words below that *do not* begin with an onset.

   ask   loss   fan   ouch   am

   blue   green   leave   old   if

3. The rime consists of one _____ phoneme and the _____ that follow(s) it in the syllable.

4. Write the rime for each of the one-syllable words below.

     train   *sent*   *mice*   *swamp*   *flour*

     child   *bought*   *since*   *house*   *trip*

5. Which of the one-syllable words above have rimes that include more than one vowel letter?

6. Write the rime for the words in each of the following sets:

Set a	Set b	Set c	Set d	Set e	Set f
stand	*light*	*mail*	*wink*	*sock*	*bake*
hand	*sight*	*tail*	*blink*	*rock*	*make*

7. Mark the words in each group that belong in the same word family.

a.	b.	c.
said	*light*	*snow*
red	*fight*	*cow*
head	*right*	*now*
bed	*kite*	*how*

8. The words in a word family are all spelled with the same _____ and _____ when pronounced. Which words in groups *a, b,* and *c* above do not meet these criteria?

See the Answers to the Reviews section for the answers to Review 21, page 236.

Part Seven

Syllable and Accent Patterns

Common Core State Standards for English Language Arts

Reading Standards: Foundational Skills—Phonics and Word Recognition

Standard 3   *Know and apply grade-level phonics and word analysis skills in decoding words.*

FIRST GRADE

d. Use knowledge that every syllable must have a vowel sound to determine the number of syllables in a printed word.

e. Decode two-syllable words following basic patterns by breaking the words into syllables.

SECOND GRADE

c. Decode regularly spelled two-syllable words with long vowels.

THIRD GRADE

c. Decode multisyllable words.

FOURTH GRADE

a. Use combined knowledge of all letter-sound correspondences, syllabication patterns, and morphology (e.g., roots and affixes) to read accurately unfamiliar multisyllabic words in context and out of context.

FIFTH GRADE

a. Use combined knowledge of all letter-sound correspondences, syllabication patterns, and morphology (e.g., roots and affixes) to read accurately unfamiliar multisyllabic words in context and out of context.

The standards that pertain to syllables range from counting the syllables in written words (first grade standard 3d) to decoding multisyllable words with and without context clues (fourth and fifth grade standards 3a). Children who meet these standards combine knowledge of syllable patterns, phonics and affixes to read unfamiliar words. First grade standard 3e and second grade standard 3c require children to decode two-syllable words. We would expect first and second grade children who meet this standard to have grade level knowledge of syllable patterns, phonics and common affixes. The Common Core State Standards are designed so that learning in one grade develops the knowledge and skills needed to support learning in the next higher grade. We are not surprised, then, to observe the second grade standard of decoding two-syllable words is raised to decoding multisyllable words in third grade (standard 3c). Third graders have the foundation they need to recognize and read increasingly complex words. The fourth and fifth grade standards are identical (fourth and fifth grade standards 3a). These standards set the goal even higher, requiring children to use several sources of information to decode multisyllable words with and without context clues. Children who meet fourth and fifth grade standards 3a are skilled at decoding. Fifth graders who meet standard 3a at the end of the year enter sixth grade with the ability to learn new words on their own and, just as important, with the skills they need to continue to increase their reading vocabularies as they progress through school.

Introduction

	1. **The syllable is the unit of pronunciation.**
pronunciation	It is convenient to use one-syllable words to illustrate the vowel and consonant phonemes because a one-syllable word is, in itself, one unit of _____.
syllable	**2.** The generalizations that apply to a one-syllable word may apply to each syllable of a multisyllable word and generally apply to the accented _____ of a word.
syllable	**3.** **There is one vowel phoneme in each unit of pronunciation,** that is, in each _____.
vowel two	**4.** Each syllable contains only one _____ phoneme. If you hear two vowel phonemes, you may be sure the word has _____ syllables.
phoneme _pine ī, boy oi, right ī,_ _pause ô_ (If you missed _pause ô_, reread the frame.)	**5.** Each syllable may have more than one vowel letter but only one vowel _____. The word _cause_ (kôz) has one vowel phoneme: ô. Underline the vowel letters in the words below. Write the key symbol that represents the vowel phoneme in the space following each word; mark it to show pronunciation. pine _____ boy _____ right _____ pause _____

syllables	**6.** How many units of pronunciation (or _____) are there in each of these words? What is the vowel phoneme in each syllable? Mark the vowel(s) in the space at the right to show pronunciation.		
		No. of Syllables	**Vowel Phoneme(s)**
1 ě	_red_	_____	_____
1 ŭ	_jumped_	_____	_____
2 ō, ĭ (or ə)	_broken_	_____	_____
2 ā, ĭ	_raining_	_____	_____
1 ou	_house_	_____	_____

	7. **One syllable in a multisyllable word receives more emphasis,** **or greater stress, than the other syllables.**
syllable	We identify this accented _____ by placing an accent mark (') at the end of the accented syllable. The accent (or stress) given to a syllable in a word of two or more syllables affects the vowel phoneme.

accent (or stress)	**8.** **In multisyllabic words, more than one syllable may be stressed.** There will be one primary _____ (shown by ') and one or more secondary accents. The secondary accent is shown by '. Check your dictionary to see how it indicates the accented syllable(s) in multisyllable words.
vowel	**9.** We have already noted that the accent, or stress point, affects _____ sounds. (vowel, consonant)
accented	**10.** **The vowel phoneme is the most prominent part of the syllable. Vowels behave differently in accented and unaccented syllables.** The vowel is most clearly heard in the _____ syllable.
schwa	**11.** Many syllables, when pronounced carefully in isolation, appear to follow the generalizations we have noted. In normal speech, however, we have a tendency to give most vowels in the unaccented syllables the soft, short, indistinct _____ sound or, less frequently, the short *i* (*ĭ*).
ŏ ə	**12.** We can clearly see this behavior of vowels in accented and unaccented syllables in words that are spelled alike but accented differently. Read these sentences: *Your <u>conduct</u> is exemplary. (k _____ n' dukt)* *I will <u>conduct</u> you through the factory. (k _____ n dukt')* Show the pronunciation of the vowel in each of the first syllables above.
kŏn' kən kəm kŏm'	**13.** Write the first syllable of each of the underlined words to show its pronunciation. If the first syllable is the stressed syllable, include the accent mark. *I signed the <u>contract</u>.* _____ *"Can't" is a <u>contraction</u>.* _____ *The work is <u>complete</u>.* _____ *You are <u>competent</u>!* _____
phoneme letter	**14.** Each syllable has only one vowel _____. It may have more (phoneme, letter) than one vowel _____. (phoneme, letter)
accent	**15.** To decode a word not known at sight, we need to have some idea of where to place the accent. There are some clues to where the _____ may be found in unknown words.

Clues to Placement of Accents

accent	**1.** Obviously it is necessary to have some understanding of where to expect to find the accented syllable. <div align="center">**First, we consider one-syllable words to have a primary _____.**</div>
yes (They are one-syllable words; therefore, they are the accented syllable.)	**2.** The vowel phoneme in the accented syllable tends to follow the generalizations we have studied concerning its sound. Would you expect the words below to conform to these generalizations? _____ <div align="center">met rain rate cat hope boy</div>
accented	**3.** Dictionaries, in showing pronunciation, do not place accent marks on one-syllable words. It is taken for granted that they are _____.
ex chang' ing, play' ful slow' ly, cold' est	**4.** <div align="center">**In general, prefixes and suffixes (affixes) form separate syllables. The accent usually falls on or within the root word.**</div> Place the accents in these words. <div align="center">ex chang ing play ful</div> <div align="center">slow ly cold est</div>
suffix	**5.** The root word (*play*) is more likely to be accented than the prefix (*re-*) or _____ (*-ed*) in *replayed*.
pre cook', un bend' able move' ment, re wrote'	**6.** Show the syllable division and place the accent for each word below. <div align="center">precook unbendable</div> <div align="center">movement rewrote</div>
accent snow' man, some' thing, cow' boy	**7.** A **compound word** is made up of two or more words that combine to form an entirely new word. **In compound words, the primary _____ usually falls on or within the first "word."** Rewrite these compound words to show the syllables; place the accents. snowman _____ something _____ cowboy _____

	8. Accents within sentences will not be considered here. However, note that a change in accent in each of the following sentences changes the meaning. Place the accent on *black* or *bird* in each sentence:
black', bird'	*I see a black bird; I think it is a crow.*
black' bird	*The blackbird built its nest in the marsh.*
	9. We have noted that (1) one-syllable words are accented; (2) accents usually
root	fall on or within the _____ word rather than on a prefix or a suffix;
first	and (3) the _____ "word" in a compound word is usually the accented one.

	10. **The placement of the accent may differentiate between a noun and a verb in words that are spelled alike. The accent usually falls on the first syllable of a noun.** Study the sentences below. Write *first* or *second* to show the syllable on which the accent falls in each of the underlined words.
first	*What is this <u>object</u>?* _____
second	*Do you <u>object</u>?* _____
first	*This is a <u>present</u> for you.* _____
second	*Please <u>present</u> this to your friend.* _____

	11. **When there is a double consonant within a word, the accent usually falls on the syllable that closes with the first letter of the double consonant:** *splen' did din' ner* Place the accent in each of these words.
bet' ter, thun' der, trum' pet	*bet ter thun der trum pet*
tim' ber, pen' sion, shel' ter, pep' per	**12.** Place the accents in the words below. *tim ber pen sion shel ter pep per*

	13. **In most multisyllabic words ending in the suffix *-tion, -sion*, or *-ic*, the primary accent falls on the syllable preceding the suffix.** Place the accent in these words.
ex ten' sion, mag net' ic, men' tion	*ex ten sion mag net ic men tion*
na' tion, car na' tion, no mad' ic, an gel' ic	**14.** Mark the primary accent in each word below. *na tion car na tion no mad ic an gel ic*

nā′ shən, kär nā′ shən *nō măd′ ĭk, ān jĕl′ ĭk*	**15.** Pronounce the words in frame 14. Using your knowledge of phonemes, rewrite the words to show pronunciation. na tion _____ car na tion _____ no mad ic _____ an gel ic _____
preceding first preceding	**16.** We expect the primary accent in a multisyllabic word ending in the suffix *-tion, -sion,* or *-ic* to fall on the syllable _____ the suffix. Pronounce the words below aloud. poet nomad donate concept poetic nomadic donation conception The accent is on the _____ syllable of these root words. When a word ends in *-tion, -sion,* or *-ic,* the accent is on the syllable _____ the suffix.
main tain′, be neath′, *ex plain′*	**17.** Let us make another generalization: **When the vowel phoneme in the last and closed syllable of a word is composed of two vowel letters, that syllable is *most often* accented.** Mark the accents in these words. main tain be neath ex plain
ex ceed′, con ceal′ *de cay′, com plain′*	**18.** Divide the words below into syllables and mark the accents. exceed _____ conceal _____ decay _____ complain _____
CV CVVC′ VC CVVCC′ CVC CVVC′ V CCVVC′	**19.** Mark the accent in the "words" below. CV CVVC VC CVVCC CVC CVVC V CCVVC
When the vowel phoneme in the last and closed syllable of a two-syllable word is composed of two vowel letters, that syllable is most often accented.	**20.** State the generalization that applies to the "words" in frame 19.

first	**21.** We have noted that (1) when a word is used as different parts of speech, the accent is usually on the _____ syllable of the noun; (2) the accent usually falls on the syllable that closes with the first letter of a double
consonant	_____ ; (3) when the last (and closed) syllable of a word has two
vowel	_____ letters, that syllable is most often accented; and (4) the
-tion, -sion, -ic	accent falls on the syllable preceding the _____ suffix.
fin' ish, prac' tice, scoun' drel *cen' ter, mon' key, lis' ten*	**22.** <div align="center">**When there is no other clue, the accent most often falls on the first syllable of a two-syllable word.**</div> Study these words to see if they follow this generalization. Place the accents.<div align="center">*fin ish prac tice scoun drel* *cen ter mon key lis ten*</div>
accented	**23.** Let us review all the generalizations concerning the placement of the accent. Consider the word *day*. A one-syllable word is considered to be _____.<div align="center">(accented, unaccented)</div>
sun' set compound first	**24.** Rewrite the word *sunset* and place the accent. _____ In _____ words, the accent usually falls on the _____ "word."
catch' ing root suffix	**25.** Rewrite the word *catching* and place the accent _____ The accent usually falls on the _____ word rather than on the prefix or _____ .
un faith' ful root	**26.** Consider this word: *unfaithful*. Place the accent. _____ Sometimes a root word has more than one affix, or the word has so many syllables that two or more syllables are stressed. The primary accent, then, usually falls on or within the _____ word.
reb' el noun	**27.** Consider the word *rebel* in the sentence: *He is a rebel.* Place the accent. _____ . Certain words that are spelled the same sometimes function as different parts of speech. The accent on the first syllable generally indicates that it is a _____ .

noun verb con tent'	**28.** The word *con' tent* is a _____. The word *con tent'* is a _____. How would you place the accent in this sentence? *After many revisions, the novelist was finally <u>content</u> with the manuscript.*
glit' ter consonant closes consonant	**29.** Consider this word: *glitter.* Place the accent. _____ When there is a double _____ within a word, the accent usually falls on the syllable that _____ with the first letter of the (closes, opens) double_____.
ob tain' last	**30.** Consider this word: *obtain.* Place the accent. _____ When two vowel letters appear within the last and closed syllable of a two-syllable word, the _____ syllable is most often accented. (first, last)
or gan' ic, at ten' tion -tion -sion, -ic	**31.** Divide the words *organic* and *attention* into syllables. Use what you have learned thus far to place the accent. Complete the generalization: **In most multisyllabic words ending in the suffix _____ ,** **_____ , or _____ , the primary accent falls on the** **syllable that precedes the suffix.**
for get' ting, con' tract, de mand' ed, ap pear' ance, o' pen ing, can teen', show' boat	**32.** Using what information you have and remembering that it is not customary to place accent marks on one-syllable words, place accent marks in all the appropriate places in the following: *I was for get ting my con tract which de mand ed my ap pear ance at the o pen ing of the can teen on the show boat.*

Study Guide
Syllable Accents

Syllable Defined
The **syllable** is the unit of pronunciation. There is one vowel phoneme in each syllable (unit of pronunciation). Each syllable may have more than one vowel letter but only one vowel phoneme (*boy, pause*).

Accent or Stress
One syllable in a multisyllable word receives more emphasis or greater stress than the other syllable(s). The accent, or stress point, affects the vowel sound.

Accent Mark
An accent mark indicates the primary stress (*ti′ ger*). In multisyllabic words, more than one syllable may be stressed. The secondary accent is shown by (′) (*cen′ ti pede′*).

Vowels in Accented Syllables
Vowels behave differently in accented and unaccented syllables. The vowel is most clearly heard in the accented syllable (*pa′ per, plan′ et*).

Vowels in Unaccented Syllables
We have a tendency to give most vowels in unaccented syllables the soft, short, indistinct schwa sound (*pen′ cil, pĕn′ səl*) or the short *i* (*brace′ let, brās′ lĭt*).

Clues to Placement of Accent
One-Syllable Words   We consider one-syllable words to have a primary accent (*bed′, boy′*). It is the convention for dictionaries to omit the accent mark for one-syllable words.

Prefixes and Suffixes   In general, prefixes and suffixes (affixes) form separate syllables. The accent usually falls on or within the root word (*play′ ful, slow′ ly*).

Compound Words   In compound words, the primary accent usually falls on or within the first "word" (*cup′ cake, snow′ man*).

Nouns and Verbs   The placement of the accent may differentiate between a noun and a verb in words that are spelled alike. The accent usually falls on the first syllable of a noun (*ob′ ject*) and on the second syllable of a verb (*ob ject′*). (*His con′ duct was excellent. He will con duct′ the tour.*)

Double Consonants   When there is a double consonant within a word, the accent usually falls on the syllable that closes with the first letter of the double consonant (*let′ ter, trum′ pet*).

Words Ending with -*tion*, -*sion*, or -*ic*   In most multisyllable words ending in the suffix -*tion*, -*sion*, or -*ic*, the primary accent falls on the syllable preceding the suffix.

Two Vowels in the Final Syllable   When the vowel phoneme in the last syllable of a word is composed of two vowel letters, that syllable is most often accented (*ex plain′, be neath′*).

When There Is No Clue to Accent   When there is no other clue, the accent most often falls on the first syllable of a two-syllable word (*fin′ ish, prac′ tice*).

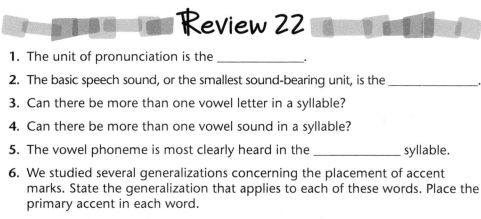

Review 22

1. The unit of pronunciation is the _____.

2. The basic speech sound, or the smallest sound-bearing unit, is the _____.

3. Can there be more than one vowel letter in a syllable?

4. Can there be more than one vowel sound in a syllable?

5. The vowel phoneme is most clearly heard in the _____ syllable.

6. We studied several generalizations concerning the placement of accent marks. State the generalization that applies to each of these words. Place the primary accent in each word.

   a. *in ter change a ble*   e. *na tion*
   b. *cow boy*   f. *dol lar*
   c. *fast*   g. *con ceal*
   d. *con vict* (noun)   h. *pa per*

See the Answers to the Reviews section for the answers to Review 22, page 237.

 ## Clues to Syllable Division

A single vowel in a closed syllable generally represents its short sound.	**1.** We have established some guidelines to help us decide on which syllable an accent might fall. We still have this problem: Where do the syllable divisions occur? There are generalizations to help—but with many exceptions. First, we need to review two generalizations concerning vowel phonemes. State the generalization that applies to the vowel sound in *met.*
A single vowel in an open syllable generally represents its long sound.	**2.** State the generalization that applies to the vowel sounds of *me* and *so.*
short	**3.** Let us attempt to divide the word *pupil* into syllables. If you divided it *pup il,* the first vowel would be expected to have its _____ sound.
long, open	**4.** If you divided it *pu pil,* the first vowel would be expected to have its _____ sound: It is in a(n) _____ syllable. (open, closed)
last (unaccented), *pū′ pəl*	**5.** Write the correct pronunciation of *pupil,* placing the accent and using the schwa in the _____ syllable _____.

When there is no other clue in a two-syllable word, the accent most often falls on the first syllable.	**6.** Which generalization concerning the placement of the accent would seem to apply?
le gal, (lē′ gəl)	**7.** Now write *legal* as it would appear in the dictionary. The entry word should show syllabication only. Follow this by rewriting the word to show pronunciation, using the key symbols and omitting silent letters (if any). _____ _____

vowel	**8.** Let us make a generalization:
	
	   If the first vowel in a two-syllable word is followed
	   by a single consonant, that consonant *often*
	   begins the second syllable.
	
	In other words, the syllable division is between the first _____ and the single consonant.

si lent, (sī′ lənt) *mi nus, (mī′ nəs)* *lo cal, (lō′ kəl)*	**9.** Follow the above generalization and write these words as they would appear in the dictionary entry word followed by pronunciation. silent _____ _____ minus _____ _____ local _____ _____
open CV′ CVC	**10.** We have designated CV to represent an open syllable for the purpose of determining the vowel phoneme (page 110). But how might we represent the open-syllable clue to syllable division? We will use V/CV to indicate the open-syllable clue. The first syllable in the word *pupil* (*pu pil*) is a(n) _____ syllable. Using C to represent consonant and V to represent vowel, we might represent *pupil* as CV′ CVC. Show the syllable division, mark the accent, and indicate the consonants and vowels in *bagel*. _____
si′ lo, CV′ CV *ba′ con, CV′ CVC* *do′ nut, CV′ CVC* *sea′ son, CVV′ CVC*	**11.** Show the syllable division and indicate each vowel (V) and consonant (C) in the words below. silo _____ _____ bacon _____ _____ donut _____ _____ season _____ _____

vowel open, closed	**12.** Study the words in frame 11. We can see that V/CV indicates that the first syllable is an open syllable. The open syllable ends with a _____ phoneme. The second, unaccented syllable may be _____ (*ha lo*) or _____ (*ba con*).
ha′ lo, CV′ CV *ba′ con,* CV′ CVC	**13.** Place the accents and indicate the vowels and consonants in *halo* and *bacon.*

silent	**14.** Let us review another generalization:
	
	    When two like consonants appear together, the second
	
	            is generally _____ (as in *ribbon*).

short long short	**15.** Examine the word *puppet.* If we divide it *pup pet,* we would expect the first vowel to have its _____ sound. If we divide it *pu ppet,* we would expect the *u* to be _____. The *u* in the word *puppet* should be_____.
closed *pŭp pet*	**16.** For the *u* to have the correct sound in the word *puppet,* it should appear in a(n) _____ syllable. Write the word *puppet,* (closed, open) dividing it correctly. Mark the *u.* _____
pup pet *p* *pŭp′ ət* or *pŭp′ ĭt* short	**17.** Now write *puppet* as it would appear in the dictionary—first the entry word, using syllabication but the correct spelling. _____ Follow this with the correct pronunciation. Omit the second _____. _____ Sometimes in an unaccented syllable, the vowel is not a schwa but rather a related sound, the soft _____ *i.* (short, long)

consonants
 	
consonants
	18. We can make a generalization:
	
	    When two vowel letters are separated by two _____,
	
	    the syllable division is generally between the _____.

closed short VC/CV	**19.** The first syllable in *after* (*af ter*) is _____. Therefore, we expect (open, closed) the vowel sound in this syllable to be _____. We will use _____ to represent the closed-syllable generalization for (V/CV, VC/CV) syllable division.

	20. The closed-syllable generalization (expressed VC/CV) gives us a clue for syllable division. Study the words below.
	normal better bandit hammer
closed	The first syllable is _____. We divide the syllable between the two
	(open, closed)
consonants	adjacent _____. How do we represent the closed-syllable generalization
VC/CV	for syllable division? _____
	21. Observing the open- and closed-syllable generalizations, divide the words below into syllables and place the accents.
mat' ter, sig' nal	*matter* _____ *signal* _____
shel' ter, gos' sip	*shelter* _____ *gossip* _____

	22. Study the words at the right.		**1**	**2**	**3**
	Divide each word into syllables and place the accent (2), and indicate the vowels and consonants (3).	*panda*	*pan' da*	CVC' CV	
cri' sis, CCV' CVC		*crisis*	_____	_____	
chi' na, CCV' CV		*china*	_____	_____	
pen' guin, CVC' CVVC		*penguin*	_____	_____	

V/CV	**23.** Let us review: We can use _____ to represent the open-syllable generalization for syllable division. The syllable division is between the single
vowel	_____ and the single consonant.
VC/CV	We can use _____ to represent the closed-syllable generalization. The
consonants	syllable division is between the two _____.
	24. Note the relationship among the sounds of the vowels, the syllable division, and the accent.
open	When we divide the word *diner,* the first syllable is a(n) _____
	(open, closed)
	syllable with the division between the first vowel and the consonant. The vowel
long, first	has its _____ sound, and the accent is on the _____ syllable.
	25. When we divide *dinner,* the first two letters are the same, but the pronunciation is different:
closed	The first syllable is _____, the sound represented by the first
short, first	vowel is _____, and the accent is on the _____ syllable.

	26. The syllable division between consonants is more dependable than the division between the single vowel and single consonant.
	There are many words in which the single consonant ends the first syllable: *ex it, nov ice, hon or, fac et.*
closed	In these words, the first syllable is _____ and the vowel has
	(open, closed)
short	its _____ sound.
	27. When in doubt, however, try this generalization first:
	If the first vowel in a two-syllable word is followed by a single consonant, that consonant
second	*often* begins the _____ syllable,
	as in *di ner.*
tī ger	**28.** Divide *tiger* into syllables: _____. Mark the vowel in the first syllable to show pronunciation. If *tiger* were spelled with two *g*s, would it be
yes	expected to rhyme with *bigger?* _____
yes	**29.** Study the words below. Is each a multisyllable word? _____
yes	Is there a single vowel in the first syllable? _____ Is the single vowel
yes	followed by two consonants? _____
	If so, divide the words between the consonants. Mark the first vowel in each to show its pronunciation. Mark the accent.
lĕt' ter, nŭm' ber	letter _____ number _____
ĕf' fort, măt' ter	effort _____ matter _____
If the first vowel in a two-syllable word is followed by a single consonant, that consonant *often* begins the second syllable.	**30.** State the generalization for the syllabication of *pilot.*
When two vowels are separated by two consonants, *generally* the word is divided between the consonants.	**31.** State the generalization for the syllabication of *member.*

hōp¢, hŏp, hŏp′ pĭng	**32.** Show the pronunciations of these words by dividing them into syllables, marking the vowels, placing the accents, and drawing a slash through silent letters.
	hope _____ hop _____ hopping _____
	If we did not double the *p* to form *hopping*, we might expect the first vowel
long	to represent a _____ *o*. This would not be our intention.
	<div style="text-align:center">(long, short)</div>
	33. Let us make a generalization:
	<div style="text-align:center">**Divide a compound word between the two "words" that form the compound, as in cowboy (cow boy).**</div>
sun shine	Divide *sunshine* into syllables. _____
compound	**34.** The words below are _____ words.
	<div style="text-align:center">sunshine seashore backyard seahorse</div>
two	Each of these compound words consists of _____ one-syllable words.
	<div style="text-align:center">(How many?)</div>
two	Therefore, each of these compound words has _____ syllables.
	<div style="text-align:center">(How many?)</div>
	35. We expect each "word" in a compound word to represent one or more syllables. Now let us consider the compound word *battleship*.
two	How many syllables do you identify in *battle*? _____
bat tle	Divide *battle* into syllables. _____
one	How many syllables do you identify in *ship*? _____
three	Therefore, *battleship* consists of _____ syllables.
	<div style="text-align:center">(How many?)</div>
bat′ tle ship	Place the primary accent: _____.
	36. Use the compound-word generalization and other generalizations to divide the words below into syllables. Place the accents.
match′ book, rain′ drop	matchbook _____ raindrop _____
fire′ crack er, pan′ cake	firecracker _____ pancake _____
	37. Remember that a two-letter grapheme, a consonant digraph, acts as a single letter.
	***Generally* do not syllabicate between the letters of a consonant digraph.**
th	The word *together* is not *to get her* because the digraph _____ is not to be divided.

dol′ phin, kitch′ en
pan′ ther, cash′ ew
	38. Show the syllables and mark the accent in the words below.
	
	    dolphin _____ *kitchen* _____
	
	    panther _____ *cashew* _____

blend (Cluster is also correct.)	**39.** Consonant blends (clusters) represent phonemes that are blended together when pronounced. **Consonant blends (clusters) are *often* in the same syllable.** The word *secret* is not *sec ret* because the consonant _____ is not divided.

em blem, lob ster
sis ter, com plete
sister
	40. Divide the words below into syllables.
	
	    emblem _____ *lobster* _____
	
	    sister _____ *complete* _____
	
	The word _____ is an exception. In *sister* the *s* and the *t* do not form a blend. The syllables in *sister* are divided between the *s* and *t* consonants.

blends	**41.** Let us summarize.
	
	       **We *generally* do not syllabicate between the letters
	       in a consonant digraph or consonant blend,**
	
	as in *dolphin* (*dol phin*) and *complete* (*com plete*).
	
	Consonant digraphs are more reliable clues to syllabic division than
	
	consonant _____. Apply the generalization first. If this does not produce a word that makes sense, try dividing the syllable between the consonants*uster*.

go′ pher, mer′ chant, *mar′ shal, bush′ el*	**42.** Observing the consonant digraph and other generalizations, divide the words below into syllables. Mark the accented syllable. *gopher* *merchant* *marshal* *bushel*
phoneme phoneme	**43.** Remember that long vowel digraphs represent one _____ (*freedom, train, boat, day, green, seat*). We generally do not divide syllables between vowel letters that represent one _____.
do not	**44.** A vowel diphthong represents a glide from one sound to another (*announce*). Therefore, we _____ divide syllables between the (do, do not) letters in a diphthong.

	45. We can make another generalization: **We *generally* do not syllabicate between the letters in a diphthong or long vowel digraph that represent one phoneme,** as in *royal* (*roy al*) and *freedom* (*free dom*).
fea ture *voy age* We generally do not syllabicate between the letters in a diphthong or long vowel digraph that represent one phoneme.	**46.** How would we divide the word *feature* into syllables? _____ How would we divide *voyage* into syllables? _____ State the generalization for the syllabication of letters in a vowel digraph or diphthong.
slŭg′ gish, măm′ mal *mē′ ter, lā′ ter* *mō′ tive, lăd′ der* yes	**47.** We are studying generalizations that pertain to syllable division. In this study, we are using words we already know. Now pretend you do not know the words below. Divide them into syllables following the open-syllable, long and closed-syllable, shor generalizations. Mark the vowel in the first syllable to show pronunciation. Place the accent. sluggish _____ mammal _____ meter _____ later _____ motive _____ ladder _____ Are all of these words marked the way they really are pronounced? _____
pī′ rət (or ĭt), păn′ thər *grā′ vē, hap′ pən*	**48.** Pretend you do not know the words below. Divide them into syllables according to the generalizations we've been studying. Mark the vowels to show pronunciation. Place the accents. Follow the directions carefully. pirate _____ panther _____ gravy _____ happen _____
yes	**49.** Reread the words in frame 48. Are they all marked the way they are really pronounced? _____. If any are not, correctly divide them into syllables and mark the vowel in the first syllable.
often	**50.** If the first vowel is followed by a single consonant, that consonant _____ begins the second syllable. (always, often) (Take time to check your results. Are you getting them all correct? Are you applying what you have learned? Do you complete a frame, writing all the answers, before you move the mask down? You should be able to see the results of your study. May you have a great feeling of self-satisfaction!)

root syllables	**51.** We have observed that the accent is generally on the _____ word rather than on the prefix or suffix. It is natural, then, to expect prefixes and suffixes to form _____ separate from the root word.
un fold, cord less, judged, draw ing	**52.** **Prefixes and suffixes _usually_ form separate syllables from the root word.** Divide the words below into syllables. unfold _____ cordless _____ judged _____ drawing _____
judged loaded, guarded, dieted, gated d, t, lōd əd	**53.** _Most_ prefixes and suffixes form separate syllables from the root word. _____ in the frame above is a one-syllable word. We have learned that –ed does not form a separate syllable when it represents /d/ (_judged_) or /t/ (_missed_). Indicate the words in which -ed forms a separate syllable. loaded laughed guarded dieted gated The –ed forms a separate syllable when it is added to root words that end in a _____ or a _____. Rewrite _loaded_ to show pronunciation. _____

sī' dər, gär' dən ing,
stā' shən
ŭn tīm' lē, wĭn' dō, əb
tān'
	54. Observing the generalizations divide the words below into syllables and mark them to show pronunciation. Place the accents.
	
	     cider _____ gardening _____ station _____
	
	     untimely _____ window _____ obtain _____

two ble, cle, ble	**55.** Examine the words _table, circle,_ and _marble._ Each of these words has _____ syllables. Write the last syllable in each word. We can show the pronunciations of these syllables as _bəl_ and _kəl_. ta _____ cir _____ mar _____
consonant	**56.** A helpful generalization is: **If the last syllable of a word ends in _le_ preceded by a** **_____, that consonant usually begins the last syllable.**

pur ple, can dle, mar ble
cir cle, ta ble, bri dle
	57. Divide the words below into syllables.
	
	     purple _____ candle _____ marble _____
	
	     circle _____ table _____ bridle _____

consonant, unaccented schwa	**58.** Study the words in frame 57. The final syllable in each word consists of a _____ and _le_ (C + _le_). This syllable is _____. (accented, unaccented) The vowel sound in the C + _le_ syllable is a _____.

ga ble, (gā′ bəl)	**59.** Write the complete pronunciation of *gable* as it would appear in the dictionary. _____ , (_____)
pronunciation (or meaning)	**60.** Now let us examine a word that is the same as *gable* except for an *m* that precedes the *ble.* Read this sentence: *Do not gamble with your health.* The letter *m* affects the _____ of the word.
b gam ble	**61.** The last syllable in *gamble* ends with *le* preceded by the consonant _____ . Show how we would divide the word. (Note that other generalizations correctly apply to this word.) _____
gam ble, (găm′ bəl)	**62.** Now write *gamble* as it would appear in the dictionary. _____ (_____)
consonants consonant root compound before diphthong blend (cluster)	**63.** The syllable divisions are most commonly made: **A.** between two _____ (as in *ladder*). **B.** between a single vowel and a single _____ (as in *paper*). **C.** between prefixes, suffixes, and _____ words (as in *unhelpful*). **D.** between words that form a _____ word (as in *snowman*). **E.** _____ the C + *le* (as in *stable*). (before, after) Syllable divisions are not made between letters representing a single phoneme—that is, between letters in a long vowel digraph (as in *cheetah*) or a _____ (as in *appoint*). They generally are not made between the letters in a consonant digraph (as in *gopher*) or a consonant _____ (as in *secret*). When letters do not form a blend or digraph (*cos tume*), the letters are in separate syllables and the syllable division is between the two letters.
syllable are not	**64.** We have seen that syllables are units of pronunciation. The arrangement of vowels and consonants within the _____ affects the pronunciation. We have noted that generalizations about syllabication are helpful but _____ infallible. (are, are not)
ā′ bəl change a ble chānj′ ə bəl	**65.** Sounds may change with the lengthening of the word: Divide *able* into syllables. Mark it to show pronunciation. _____ Divide *changeable* into syllables. _____ Rewrite it to show pronunciation. _____

Study Guide
Syllable Division

Four Clues to Pronunciation
The four important clues to the pronunciation of a word are (1) the vowel phonemes, (2) the consonant phonemes, (3) the position of the vowel in the syllable, and (4) the accented syllable.

First Vowel Followed by a Single Consonant
If the first vowel in a two-syllable word is followed by a single consonant, that consonant often begins the second syllable (*lo' cal, si' lent*). The V/CV pattern represents the long vowel, open-syllable pattern. We should note that in some words that are spelled with this pattern the first vowel is short (*lim' it*). Try the V/CV open-syllable pattern first.

Two Vowels Separated by Two Consonants
When two vowels are separated by two consonants, the syllable division is generally between the consonants (*pup' pet, mag' net*). The VC/CV pattern represents the short vowel, closed-syllable pattern. Syllable division between consonants is more dependable than the division between the single vowel and single consonant.

Prefixes and Suffixes
In general, prefixes and suffixes form separate syllables from the root word (*play' ful, un smil' ing*).

Last Syllable C + le
If the last syllable of a word ends in *le* preceded by a consonant, that consonant usually begins the last syllable (*ta' ble, han' dle*).

Compound Words
Divide compound words between the "words" that form the compound (*check' list, moon' light*).

Consonant Digraphs
In general, do not divide syllables between consonant digraphs (*cash' ew, pan' ther*). Consonant digraphs are more dependable than the consonant blends.

Consonant Blends
Consonant blends are *often* in the same syllable (*se' cret*). However, in some words the letters do not form a blend (*fab' ric*). In order to divide a word you do not recognize into syllables, first divide the syllables so the letters are in the same syllable. If this syllable division does not result in a familiar word, the letters do not represent a blend in the word. In this case, divide the syllables between the consonant letters.

Vowel Digraphs (oo), Long Vowel Digraphs, and Vowel Diphthongs That Represent One Phoneme
In general, do not syllabicate between the letters in a vowel digraph (*har' poon*), a long vowel digraph (*ex' ceed, free' dom*), or a diphthong (*trow' el, thou' sand*).

long	**66.** In *able,* the *a* represents the _____ sound. In *changeable,* the
schwa	second *a* represents the _____ sound; it is now in one of the
unaccented	_____ syllables.
	(accented, unaccented)

67. To check our understanding, let us use symbols. Study the key below. Divide the following "words" into syllables, marking the vowels as they would be found most commonly and as though all syllables were accented.

Key: C is <u>c</u>onsonant
V is <u>v</u>owel (other than *e*)
¢ is silent *e*
ph is digra<u>ph</u>
bl is a <u>bl</u>end

Cv̆C Cv̆ph	C v C C v ph _____
v̆C Cv̆C	v C C v C _____
blĭC Cv̄	bl v C C v _____
Cv̆ph Cv̄ph¢	C v ph C v ph ¢ _____
Cv̄ Cv̆C	C v C v C _____

Which "word" demonstrates the V/CV long vowel, open-syllable

Cv̄ Cv̆C	generalization? _____ What is another way to divide this "word" if
Cv̆C v̆C	the first vowel is short? _____
Did you succeed?	

Review 23

1. Examine the following vowel-consonant word patterns. In each one, place a slash where the syllable division would most likely occur. Make sure that there is a vowel in each syllable. Give the reason you divided the word as you did. There are no digraphs (consonant or vowel), diphthongs, or blends in these words.

   a. CVCVCC (Assume the first vowel is long.)
   b. CVCCVC
   c. CVCCV
   d. CCVCVCC (Assume the first vowel is long.)

2. How would you expect the following words to be divided? Why? (Pretend that you do not know the words; then you cannot say, "I can hear the pronunciation unit.")

   a. *playful*
   b. *capable*
   c. *father*

See the Answers to the Reviews section for the answers to Review 23, page 237.

Recap III

26 consonants phonemes	**1. Phonics** is the study of the relationship of letters and letter combinations to the sounds they represent. There are _____ letters in our alphabet, classified as vowels and _____. These letters and combinations represent the 44 sounds, or _____, used in the American-English language. (This is oversimplified but adequate in this step of the process of teaching children to read.)
phoneme phoneme 44 phonemes	**2.** How easy the development of independence in decoding would be if each letter represented only one _____ and each phoneme was represented by only one letter! You know that is not the case; however, you have gained an understanding of the patterns within the inconsistencies. You have also developed a one-to-one correspondence between grapheme and _____ by selecting a key symbol to represent each of the _____ _____ of the language.

pronunciation	**3.** Another relationship is that of the syllable to the word. A **syllable** is a unit
phoneme	of _____. Each syllable must have one and only one vowel
	_____. Each word has one syllable that receives the greatest amount
accented	of stress. We call this the _____ syllable. If a word has only one
accented	syllable, that is the _____ syllable. There is a strong relationship
vowel	between the _____ and the accented syllable.
vowel	The _____ in the unaccented syllable often is represented by the
	(vowel, consonant)
ə (schwa), i (ĭ)	soft, short sound of _____ or by the _____.

	4. You have become acquainted with the clues that help you
syllables	(1) to divide a word into _____ and
accented	(2) to determine which syllable is _____.
	The following frames present specific words, selected to illustrate your knowledge of the syllable–accent generalizations as well as to review other learning.

	5. On the blanks after each word in the following frames, (1) rewrite it as an entry word in the dictionary (useful for end-of-the-line hyphenation); (2) rewrite, adding the accent; and (3) in parentheses, using all your knowledge of phonemes, rewrite the word showing pronunciation. To make this study more effective, as you work, say the generalizations of syllables, accents, and other understandings to yourself. Also fill in the other blanks as indicated.
	Using the word *seesaw* as an example, say to yourself, "*Seesaw* is a
compound	_____ word; the syllable division comes between the words of which it is composed." (Fill in the first of the three blanks below.) "The accent usually
first, compound	falls on or within the _____ word of a _____ word." (Fill in blank two.) On blank three, mark the word for pronunciation.
see saw, seé saw, (sē′ sô)	*seesaw* _____ _____ _____

s	**6.** Continue your conversation about *seesaw:* "We represent the consonant phonemes in *seesaw* with the grapheme _____. The first syllable has
two	_____ vowel letters. We know that each syllable can have only
one	_____ vowel phoneme. When there are two adjacent vowel letters in
long, silent	a syllable, generally the first is _____ and the second is _____.
ē	So the phoneme in the first syllable is represented by _____. In the second 'word,' the vowel phoneme is *w*-controlled. The key symbol is
ô, ball	_____; the key word is _____." (But maybe you prefer to use *ought (ôt)* as the key word. Do you?) The third blank, frame 5, reads
(sē′ sô)	_____. Examine the footnote. Turn to Appendix A, page 239. Read items V 10 and 9. Did you use them in your conversation? How about S 1 and A 3 on page 240?
	V 10, V 9, S 1, A 3*
	7. The second word in your study is *citrus.* (Caution: Although you can achieve correct results immediately, don't do it that way. This is your opportunity to review by yourself your understandings of the generalizations on
s	syllables, accents, and so on, including "*c* usually represents the _____
i	phoneme when followed by _____.")
	Selected references to Appendix A are given below. Check your "conversation" after each frame. Did you include these generalizations? Also note irregularities in consonant and vowel phonemes.
cit rus, cit′ rus, (sĭt′ rəs)	*citrus* _____ _____ _____
	C 2, V 3, V 14, S 5, A 5*
un but ton ing, *un but′ ton ing,* *(ən bŭt′ ən ĭng or ŭn bŭt′ ən ĭng)*	**8.** Continue with the words as given in each of the following frames. *unbuttoning* _____ _____ _____
	V 3, V 14, S 2, S 5, A 2*
ad mi ra tion, *ad mi ra′ tion,* *(ăd mə rā′ shən)*	**9.** *admiration* _____ _____ _____
	S 2, A 6*
wrin kle, wring′ kle, *(rĭng′ kəl or rĭŋ′ kəl)*	**10.** *wrinkle* _____ _____ _____
	C 1a, S 3, A 8*

*Key to generalizations (Appendix A): C: Consonants, p. 239; V: Vowels, p. 240; S: Syllable Division, p. 241; A: Accent Clues, p. 240.

(1) *an nex, an nex',* *(ə nĕks')* 2. *an nex, an' nex,* *(ăn' ĕks)*	**11.** We will (1) *annex* the land on which the new (2) *annex* was built. (1) _____ _____ _____ (2) _____ _____ _____ A 4*
fi nal, fi' nal, (fī' nəl)	**12.** *final* _____ _____ _____ S 4*
weath er, weath' er, *(wĕth' ər)*	**13.** *weather* _____ _____ _____ S 6*
con tain, con tain', (kən tān')	**14.** *contain* _____ _____ _____ C 2, V 10, A 7*
yo gurt, yo' gurt, (yō' gərt) consonant	**15.** *yogurt* _____ _____ _____ Is this *y* a vowel or a consonant? _____ C 6, S 5, A 5*
reading (Children should know the words at the hearing level.)	**16.** Turn to Appendix A. Restudy the generalizations to check your thinking. I hope you are saying "I did very well." ("Perfect"—?) The problem we face is that you know these words. If you were attacking words not in your _____ (reading, listening) vocabulary, you would have a better test of your phonics ability.
onset, rime consonant vowel, follow(s)	**17.** Another way to analyze the syllable is to divide it into the _____ and the _____. You know that the **onset** is the _____ letter(s) that begin(s) the syllable, and the **rime** is the _____ and the consonant letter(s) that _____ the vowel.

*Key to generalizations (Appendix A): C: Consonants, p. 239; V: Vowels, p. 240; S: Syllable Division, p. 241; A: Accent Clues, p. 240.

	18. Using your knowledge of the onset and the rime in the syllable, divide the word *magnet* into syllables. Then analyze the two syllables as the onset and rime.
mag, net	The word *magnet* consists of the two syllables: _____ and _____.
m	The first syllable, *mag,* consists of the onset _____ and the rime
ag	_____.
n	The second syllable, *net,* consists of the onset _____ and the rime
et	_____.
sounds (phonemes)	**19.** You have studied the relationship of letters and letter combinations to the _____ they represent and have built a depth of understanding in the
phonics	content of _____. You will use that content to help those learning to read to develop skill in the recognition and identification of words. It must be pointed out that the use of phonics is the basis of **one** of the word-identification skills (skills needed to attain independence in reading) and that
reading	the mastery of the total _____ process requires the development of still other sets of skills, including the understanding of the material read. Reading is a complicated process!

*Key to generalizations (Appendix A): C: Consonants, p. 239; V: Vowels, p. 240; S: Syllable Division, p. 241; A: Accent Clues, p. 240.

Reference

National Governors Association Center for Best Practices & Council of Chief State School Officers. (2010). *Common Core State Standards for English Language Arts & History/Social Studies, Science, and Technical Subjects: Reading: Foundational Skills—Phonological Awareness, Phonics and Word Study.* Washington, DC: Author. Retrieved May 15, 2012, from http://www.corestandards.org/assets/CCSSI_ELA%20Standards.pdf

Part Eight

Morphemes, Prefixes, Suffixes, Contractions, and Compound Words

Common Core State Standards for English Language Arts

Reading Standards: Foundational Skills—Phonics and Word Recognition

Standard 3   *Know and apply grade-level phonics and word analysis skills in decoding words.*

FIRST GRADE

f. Read words with inflectional endings.

SECOND GRADE

d. Decode words with common prefixes and suffixes.

THIRD GRADE

a. Identify and know the meaning of the most common prefixes and derivational suffixes.

FOURTH GRADE

a. Use combined knowledge of all letter-sound correspondences, syllabication patterns, and morphology (e.g., roots and affixes) to read accurately unfamiliar multisyllabic words in context and out of context.

FIFTH GRADE

a. Use combined knowledge of all letter sound correspondences, syllabication patterns, and morphology (e.g., roots and affixes) to read accurately unfamiliar multisyllabic words in context and out of context.

These standards describe a learning sequence that begins in first grade when children are expected to read words with inflectional suffixes. Second graders are required to decode unfamiliar words with prefixes and to decode words with suffixes that were not studied in the first grade. Building on the foundation established in the first and second grades, children in the third grade are expected to identify common prefixes and derivational suffixes, and to know the meaning of these word parts. The standard for the fourth and fifth grades (standard a) describes children who are skilled at reading unfamiliar words with one or more prefixes and suffixes. Knowledge of prefixes and suffixes is especially important for reading fourth and fifth grade text. In fact, fifth grade text may have as many as twice the number of words with prefixes and suffixes as fourth grade text. Knowledge of these meaningful parts in word structure helps children read unfamiliar words and increase their reading vocabulary. A large reading vocabulary, in turn, is a major factor affecting children's ability to understand grade-level text and meet grade-level standards.

Introduction

phonemes	**1.** The graphemes we have studied thus far represent _____. Now we will turn our attention to groups of graphemes that represent sound and meaning.
re, place, ment meaning	**2.** Many words in the English language consist of more than one unit of meaning. The reader uses **structural analysis** to discover the meaning of these words. For the purpose of illustrating structural analysis, let us assume that *replacement* is an unfamiliar word. You might logically divide *replacement* into three meaningful units: _____, _____, and _____. Now pronounce *replacement*. Consider the contribution each unit makes to the _____ of *replacement*. You have now successfully used structural analysis.
yes	**3.** **Structural analysis is a word identification skill that involves the use of prefixes, suffixes, root words, the "words" in compound words, and the apostrophes in contractions to discover word meaning.** Would you expect the reader to use structural analysis to identify the word *unusually?* _____
meaning	**4.** Structural analysis is a useful tool for discovering the _____ of words. Knowledge of word meaning, in turn, is essential for the comprehension of text.
morpheme	**5.** We will begin our study with the **morpheme**. **A morpheme is the smallest unit of meaning.** We cannot divide a morpheme into smaller, meaningful units. A _____ may be a whole word, *ship,* or a meaningful word part, as the *-ment* in *shipment*.
free	**6.** We will study two types of morphemes: free morphemes and bound morphemes. A **free morpheme** can stand alone as a single word. We cannot divide a free morpheme into smaller units without affecting meaning. **A free morpheme can exist on its own.** *Paint* is a _____ morpheme. We cannot divide *paint* into smaller, meaningful units.
-ing	**7.** A **bound morpheme** cannot stand alone. This morpheme is always attached to another morpheme. The bound morpheme in *playing* is _____. **A bound morpheme must be added to another morpheme.**

one, one	**8.** Recognizing that we are oversimplifying the situation, we will consider an English **word** to be a free morpheme or a free morpheme to which one or more bound morphemes are attached. *Chewable* consists of _____ free morpheme(s) and _____ bound (How many?) (How many?) morpheme(s).
chew	_____ is a *free* morpheme.
-able	Write the *bound* morpheme. _____ The bound morpheme and the free morpheme together form the word
chewable	_____.
free, bound	**9.** We will continue our study by examining the word *preheated*. *Heat* is a _____ morpheme. The *pre-* and *-ed* are _____ morphemes. Therefore, a word may consist of a free morpheme (*heat*) or a free morpheme with one or more bound morphemes (*preheated*).
compound	**10.** How, then, do we classify a word like *pancake*. *Pancake* is a _____ word.
no	Does *pan* have the same meaning as *pancake*? _____ How about
no	*cake?* _____ *Pancake* cannot be divided into smaller parts and still retain its meaning.
free	Therefore, *pancake* is a _____ morpheme.
free **bound**	**11.** Let us restate our definition of an English word: **For the purposes of teaching reading, a word may consist of a** **_____ morpheme (a morpheme that can stand alone), such** **as *jump*, or a free morpheme and one or more _____** **morphemes (morphemes that must be added to another morpheme),** **such as the *-ing* in *jumping*. (A word may also contain one or more** **word parts borrowed from other languages.)** Therefore, we will consider *jump, jumped,* and *jumping* to be words. Do we
no	consider *-ing* to be a word? _____
sadly, *restore*, *powerful*, *misstep*, *unfairly*, *shipment*	**12.** Study the words below. *sadly restore powerful misstep unfairly shipment* Each word consists of a free morpheme and one or more bound morphemes. Draw a single line under the free morpheme and a double line under the bound morpheme(s).

	13. We have defined a word from the perspective of the teacher of reading. Some teachers' manuals or curriculum guides use the term **root word** as a synonym for a free morpheme; other instructional materials use **base word**. We will use root word in our study. You may use either term—root word or base word—in your answers.
one, *late*	*Lately* consists of _____ root word(s). The root word is _____. (How many?)

Review 24

1. We have defined a morpheme as _____.

2. *Cat* is a free morpheme because _____.

3. Circle the free morphemes in the list below.

   dog   -ing   desk   pre-   hat   -ly   dis-   table

4. For the purposes of teaching reading, we define an English word as

   _____.

5. Underline the bound morphemes in the words below:

   laughable   untimely   enact   dangerous   childish

6. **a.** A bound morpheme must be attached to another _____.

   b. A bound morpheme _____ stand alone.
   (can, cannot)

See the Answers to the Reviews section for the answers to Review 24, page 238.

Morphemes, Prefixes, Suffixes, Contractions, and Compound Words

beginning	**1.** The bound morphemes are divided into two groups: prefixes and suffixes. *Pre-* means before. Therefore, a **prefix** is placed at the _____ of a (beginning, end) root word (free morpheme). **A prefix is placed before a root word.**
not, not	**2.** A prefix may change the meaning of a root word (free morpheme) or make its meaning more specific. The prefix *il-* denotes "not." Therefore, *illegal* means "_____ legal," and *illogical* means "_____ logical." It is a common practice to add a trailing hyphen to a prefix when it is not attached to a root word (*mis-*).

fill again root word (or free morpheme) bound	**3.** *Re-* means "again." Therefore, *refill* means "to _____ ." *Fill* is a _____ . *Fill* has meaning in and of itself. The prefix *re-* is a _____ morpheme. *Re-* cannot stand alone; it must be added to a free morpheme (root word).
unusual, reopen, midweek, misfit, precondition	**4.** Place a check beside each word below that contains a prefix. *unusual union reopen midweek misfit precondition*

union
 	
is not
 	
is
 	
root words (or free morphemes)
	5. Which word in frame 4 does not contain a prefix? _____
	
	The *un* in *union* _____ a prefix. *Union* is the smallest meaningful unit.
	               (is, is not)
	
	The *un-* in *unusual* _____ a prefix. Therefore, we can conclude that
	               (is, is not)
	
	union and *usual* are _____ .

prefix	**6.** Complete the following:
	
	     A _____ **is a bound morpheme that is placed before a root word
	     to change its meaning or to make its meaning more specific.**

end
 	
-ment, bound
	7. A **suffix** is placed at the _____ of a root word (free morpheme)—that is, after the free morpheme. Write the suffix in
	
	encouragement. _____ A suffix is a _____ morpheme.
	                      (free, bound)
	It is common practice to place a leading hyphen before a suffix that is not attached to a root word.
	
	      **A suffix is a bound morpheme placed at the
	      end of a root word (free morpheme).**

un- *-ive,* response *happy,* no *un-, -ly, -est, -er*	**8.** We will use **affix** to refer to a prefix or a suffix. A root word with affixes, then, has more than one prefix or suffix. *Unresponsive* contains two affixes, one prefix and one suffix. Write these two affixes. _____ and _____ The root word is _____ Consider *unhappily, happiest,* and *happier.* The root word (free morpheme) is _____ . Do these words have the same meaning? _____ Write the affixes in the words below. *unhappily* _____ *happiest* _____ *happier* _____ Note that these affixes contribute to the meaning of the root word (free morpheme).

Study Guide
Prefixes for Word Study

Prefix	Prefix Meaning	Examples
anti-	against	antibiotic, antitrust
de-	away from	defrost, debug
dis-*	opposite of, lack of	displace, disagree
em-, im-, in-	into, in	empower, imbed, inbound
en-	cause to be, on, put into	enable, enlarge
fore-	front, before	forefoot, forefather
il-, im-, in-, ir	not	illegal, imperfect, inaccurate, irrelevant
inter-	between	interstate, interact
mid-*	middle	midday, midline
mis-*	wrong, bad	misfortune, miscue
non-*	not	nonstop, nonfat
out-*	more	outdo, outperform
over-*	too much	overdue, overweight
pre-*	before	preview, prepay
pro-	forward, before	proactive
re-*	again	rewrite, reread
semi-	half, partly	semicircle, semifinal
sub-*	under	subway, substandard
super-*	above, exceeding the norm	superhighway, supertanker
trans-	across	transatlantic, transplant
un-*	not	unfair, unsafe
under-	in a lower place	underpay, underrate

The most frequently used prefixes are **un- (unlucky), re- (remove), in-** (meaning "not," as in **incomplete**), and **dis- (dislike)**.

* These prefixes are often taught in elementary school. Check your teachers' manual or curriculum guide to identify other prefixes to include in your classroom literacy program.

9. A root word (free morpheme) may have more than one affix. Study the words below. Complete the table with (1) the root word, (2) the number of affixes, and (3) the affix or affixes.

	Root Word	Number of Affixes	Affix(es)
	recovered	_____	_____	_____
	immature	_____	_____	_____
	unfailingly	_____	_____	_____
	nonmagnetic	_____	_____	_____
	misaligned	_____	_____	_____
	prejudged	_____	_____	_____

cover, 2, re-, -ed

mature, 1, im-

fail, 3, un-, -ing, -ly

magnet, 2, non-, -ic

align, 2, mis-, -ed

judge, 2, pre-, -ed

affix

We can see that more than one _____ may be added to a single root word.

---

10. We will recognize two types of suffixes: **inflectional suffixes** and **derivational suffixes**.

An inflectional suffix changes number, affects verb tense, indicates comparison, or denotes possession.

The -s in *raindrops* is

number

an inflectional suffix. The -s denotes a change in _____.

---

11. Underline the inflectional suffixes added to the words below:

watch<u>ed</u>, bigg<u>er</u>, cut<u>est</u>,

rock<u>s</u>, bark<u>ing</u>

watched _____   *bigger* _____   *cutest* _____

rocks _____   *barking* _____

---

12. We will recognize two types of inflectional suffixes: **comparative suffixes** and **superlative suffixes**.

The comparative suffix -er compares two things.

comparative

The -er in *smaller* is a _____ suffix. For example, "My puppy is *small<u>er</u>* than your puppy."

---

13.   The superlative suffix -est denotes a comparison of three or more things.

superlative

The -est in *tallest* is a _____ suffix. For example, "John is the tall<u>est</u> boy in the class."

bigger

Write the word in frame 11 that has a comparative suffix. _____

cutest

Which word in frame 11 has a superlative suffix? _____

14. Use the following terms to fill in the blanks below.

    comparative   superlative   number   verb tense   possession

number

verb tense

possession

superlative

comparative

The -s in *bicycles* denotes a change in _____.

The -en in *eaten* indicates a change in _____.

The 's in *John's* indicates _____.

The -est in *tallest* is a _____ suffix that denotes a comparison among three or more things.

The -er in *taller* is a _____ suffix that denotes a comparison of two things.

---

15. Rewrite the words below, adding the inflectional suffix.

Sam's, softest

warmer, books

sewing, laughed

number, verb tense

possession, comparison

comparative

superlative

Sam + 's = _____   soft + est = _____

warm + er = _____   book + s = _____

sew + ing = _____   laugh + ed = _____

These suffixes change _____ (*books*), affect _____ (*sewing, laughed*), indicate _____ (*Sam's*), and show _____ (*warmer, softest*). The -er in *faster* is a _____ suffix; the -est in *fastest* is a _____ suffix.

---

16.   **A derivational suffix affects meaning and may change the part of speech.**

The -able in *breakable* changes a verb (*break*) into an adjective (*breakable*).

derivational

Therefore, the suffix -able is a(n) _____ suffix. A derivational suffix affects the meaning of the root word. The meaning of *breakable* is related to the meaning of the root word, but their meanings are different. The word *breakable* is "derived" from the original word, *break*.

---

noticeable, dirty, massive, fitness, joyous, historic

17. Study the words below. Underline the suffix in each one.

noticeable   dirty   massive   fitness   joyous   historic

Do these suffixes affect meaning and change the grammatical category of words?

yes, derivational

_____ Therefore, these word endings are _____ suffixes.

18. How can we distinguish between inflectional suffixes and derivational suffixes? An inflectional suffix does not change a word's part of speech.

Note that the -ed in *danced* indicates the past tense of the verb *dance*.

inflectional

Therefore, the -ed is a(n) _____ suffix.
             (inflectional, derivational)

Adding -ic to *history,* a noun, changes into *historic,* an adjective. Therefore,

derivational

-ic is a(n)_____ suffix.
           (inflectional, derivational)

Study Guide
Suffixes for Word Study

Suffix	Suffix Meaning	Examples
-able, -ible	capable of, quality of	*breakable, collectible*
-age	act of, state of	*storage, leakage*
-al	relating to	*coastal, tropical*
-ance	act of, quality of	*assistance, acceptance*
-ed	past	*played, cried*
-en	relating to	*frozen, strengthen*
-ence	act of, quality of	*patience, dependence*
-er	more	*bigger, nearer*
-er, -or	one who	*baker, actor*
-ess	female	*waitress, actress*
-est	most	*kindest, farthest*
-ful	quality of	*beautiful, helpful*
-hood	state of	*parenthood, childhood*
-ian, -ant, -ent	a person who	*historian, assistant, student*
-ic	of, having to do with	*heroic, historic*
-ing	act of, instance of	*jumping, writing*
-ish	something like	*babyish, ticklish*
-ism	doctrine, practice, condition	*heroism, formalism*
-ist	someone who	*cyclist, biologist*
-ive	being able to, having	*active, negative*
-ize	having the nature of	*materialize, motorize*
-less	without	*careless, fruitless*
-like	similar to	*childlike, lifelike*
-ly	manner of	*neatly, totally*
-ment	result, product	*agreement, improvement*
-ness	quality of	*darkness, happiness*
-ous	full of, state of	*dangerous, famous*
-s, -es	plural	*swings, matches*
-ship	showing status	*membership, flagship*
-sion, -tion	act, state of	*action, celebration, invade, invasion*
-ty	state of, characteristic	*ability, validity*
-ure	act of, process of	*closure, legislature*
-ward	in the direction of	*northward, backward*
-y	quality of, condition	*easy, rainy*

These suffixes are often taught in elementary school. Check in your curriculum guide or teachers' manual.

19. We have established that affixes affect the meanings of root words and may also change their grammatical categories. Let us now consider an element of word structure that does not affect word meaning: the apostrophe in a contraction.

A contraction is a shortened form of two or more words.

A **contraction** combines two or more words into a single word. An apostrophe denotes one or more missing letters—for instance, *is not* becomes

does not

isn't. Word meaning _____ change.
                 (does, does not)

---

20. Each of the word pairs below may be combined to form a common contraction. Write the contraction.

we're, wasn't, I've

    we are _____   *was not* _____   *I have* _____

she'd, they'll, let's

    she would _____   *they will* _____   *let us* _____

---

21. We have noted that compound words are free morphemes. Combine each set of words below to form a compound word.

searchlight, pineapple ✓

    search + light = _____   *pine + apple* = _____

buttercup ✓, limelight ✓

    butter + cup = _____   *lime + light* = _____

lamppost, mousetrap

    lamp + post = _____   *mouse + trap* = _____

backpack, sandman ✓

    back + pack = _____   *sand + man* = _____

Place a check beside each compound word in which the meaning of the "words" *do not* give us a clue to the meaning of the compound word. We

cannot

_____ assume that the two "words" in a compound will give us
    (can, cannot)
reliable clues as to the meaning of the compound. We expect the accent to

first

fall within the _____ "word" of a compound word.
           (first, second)

Study Guide

Contractions for Word Study

not	is	will
aren't (are not)	he's (he is)	he'll (he will)
can't (cannot)	here's (here is)	I'll (I will)
couldn't (could not)	how's (how is)	it'll (it will)
didn't (did not)	it's (it is)	she'll (she will)
doesn't (does not)	she's (she is)	they'll (they will)
don't (do not)	that's (that is)	you'll (you will)
hadn't (had not)	there's (there is)	we'll (we will)
hasn't (has not)	what's (what is)	what'll (what will)
haven't (have not)	when's (when is)	where'll (where will)
isn't (is not)	where's (where is)	
mustn't (must not)	who's (who is)	
needn't (need not)		
shouldn't (should not)		
wasn't (was not)		
weren't (were not)		
won't (will not)		
wouldn't (would not)		

have	had	would
could've (could have)	he'd (he had)	he'd (he would)
I've (I have)	I'd (I had)	I'd (I would)
might've (might have)	she'd (she had)	it'd (it would)
should've (should have)	they'd (they had)	she'd (she would)
they've (they have)		they'd (they would)
we've (we have)		we'd (we would)
would've (would have)		
you've (you have)		

are	has	Other Contractions
they're (they are)	he's (he has)	I'm (I am)
we're (we are)	it's (it has)	let's (let us)
who're (who are)	she's (she has)	o'clock (of the clock)
you're (you are)		

22. Let us review what we have learned thus far:

meaning

A. A morpheme is the smallest unit of _____.

free

B. A _____ morpheme can stand alone. It has meaning in and of

yes

itself. Is *drink* a free morpheme? _____ Is *-ing* a free

no

morpheme? _____

root

C. We will call the free morphemes _____ words. *Dog* is an
example of a root word.

bound

D. A _____ morpheme cannot exist alone. It must be attached to
another morpheme. *Re-* and *-ous* are bound morphemes.

beginning

E. A prefix is placed at the _____ of a root word (free morpheme).
(beginning, end)

end

F. A suffix is placed at the _____ of a root word (free morpheme).
(beginning, end)

Inflectional

G. _____ suffixes change number, affect verb
(Inflectional, Derivational)
tense, indicate possession, or denote comparison.

Derivational

H. _____ suffixes affect meaning and may change
(Inflectional, Derivational)
the part of speech.

comparative

I. The _____ suffix *-er* is used to compare two things.

superlative

J. The _____ suffix *-est* is used to compare more than two things.

contraction

K. A _____ combines two words into a single word; a(n)

apostrophe

_____ denotes one or more missing letters.

compound word

L. A _____ consists of two or more root words that, when
combined, form an entirely new word. The new word is a free morpheme.

Review 25

1. A _____ is placed at the beginning of a root word.

2. A _____ is placed at the end of a root word.

3. The term _____ refers to both prefixes and suffixes.

4. Draw a single line under the affix or affixes (bound morphemes) in each word below.

   climbing   likeable   prehistoric   impolite

   previewed   treatment   illogical   uncovered

5. Underline the prefix in each word below.

   distrust   midair   impure   unsafe

   nonstop   subplot   retie   demerit

6. Write the suffix or suffixes in each word below. Work carefully, and refer to the Study Guide. Some root words have more than one suffix.

   parenthood   joyous   motorists   heroism

   actor   massive   musician   uselessly

7. Write an *I* beside each word that contains an inflectional suffix and a *D* beside each word that contains a derivational suffix.

   furious _____   attracting _____   wolves _____

   sculptor _____   penniless _____   boyish _____

8. Most contractions are shortened forms of words in which a(n) _____ denotes one or more missing letters. Does a contraction have the same meaning as the words written separately? _____ Write the contraction for each word pair below:

   could have _____   where is _____

   do not _____   they are _____

   we will _____   what will _____

   he had _____   we would _____

9. A compound word is a _____ morpheme. Using what you have learned, rewrite the compounds words below to show pronunciation. Use key symbols; omit silent letters; show syllable division; and indicate the accented syllable.

   crosswalk _____   eyesight _____

   cornbread _____   landlocked _____

   treadmill _____   wholesale _____

See the Answers to the Reviews section for the answers to Review 25, page 238.

Spelling Generalizations for Adding Prefixes and Suffixes to Words

	1. *mismatched* *reapplied* The root words (free morphemes) in the two words above are
match apply	_____ and _____.
no	Do *mis-* and *-ed* affect the spelling of *match?* _____
yes	Do *re-* and *-ed* affect the spelling of *apply?* _____ How do we know when adding an affix will affect the spelling of a word? Fortunately, there are guidelines to help us spell words with prefixes and suffixes.
	2. We will begin our study with affixes that usually do not affect the spelling of a root word. Study the words below. Write the prefix for each one.
dis-, mis-	*dishonest* _____ *misfit* _____
im-, pre-	*impatient* _____ *preschool* _____
ir-, in-	*irregular* _____ *indirect* _____
no	Do these prefixes affect the spellings of these words? _____
	3. We can make a generalization:
does not	**Adding a prefix** _____ **affect the spelling of the root word.** (does, does not)
	4. Consider the words below. Underline the suffix in each one.
ship<u>ment</u>, harm<u>ful</u>, friend<u>ly</u>	*shipment* *harmful* *friendly*
kind<u>ness</u>, cord<u>less</u>, child<u>hood</u>	*kindness* *cordless* *childhood*
consonant	**5.** Each of the suffixes in frame 4 begins with a _____. Note, (consonant, vowel)
consonant	too, that each word ends with a _____. (consonant, vowel)
no	Do the spellings of these root words change? _____
	6. Complete this generalization:
consonant	**The spelling of a root word often does not change when** **we add a suffix that begins with a** _____ **to a** **root word that ends in a consonant.**

7. Next let's consider generalizations for adding -s and -es to root words.

Rewrite each word below by adding -s or -es, as indicated in columns 1 and 2.

	Column 1: Word + -s		Column 2: Word + -es
hat	_____	baby	_____
bike	_____	bus	_____
play	_____	dish	_____
ball	_____	catch	_____
car	_____	box	_____
jump	_____	buzz	_____

hats   babies

bikes   buses

plays   dishes

balls   catches

cars   boxes

jumps   buzzes

---

8.   We add an -s to most words to form the plural. There are situations, however, that call for adding -es. Refer to your answers in the frame above to fill in the blanks below.

babies

Add -es to a word that ends in a y preceded by a consonant (_____) or to a word

buses, dishes, catches

that ends in an s (_____), sh (_____), ch (_____),

boxes, buzzes

x (_____), or z (_____).

---

9. Let us summarize the -s and -es generalizations:

-es

Add _____ to words that end in a y preceded by a consonant and to

-s

words that end in s, sh, ch, x, or z. Add _____ to most other words.

---

10. Another spelling question is whether to change the final y to i before adding a suffix.

Solve each word "equation" below by adding the indicated suffix.

beautiful, busily

beauty + ful = _____   busy + ly = _____

happiness, pitiless

happy + ness = _____   pity + less = _____

laziness, furious

lazy + ness = _____   fury + ous = _____

tried, worrier

try + ed = _____   worry + er = _____

---

11. Let us take a closer look at the words in frame 10. Do these words end in a y? _____

yes

Does a consonant precede the final y?_____

yes

Does the y change to i when a suffix is added? _____

yes

We can make a generalization:

Change the final y to i when a consonant precedes the y.

	12. Study the words below.
	stayed annoyed payment joyful
yes	Do these root words end in a *y*? _____
yes	Does a vowel precede the *y*?_____
no	Does the *y* change to *i*?_____
is not	The spelling of the word _____ usually affected when a vowel (is, is not) precedes the final *y*.
	Do not change the final *y* to *i* when a vowel precedes the y.
	13. Apply the *y*-to-*i* guidelines to solve the word "equations" below.
annoying, drier	annoy + ing = _____ dry + er = _____
buried, plays	bury + ed = _____ play + s = _____
envious, merciless	envy + ous = _____ mercy + less = _____
happiness, tried	happy + ness = _____ try + ed = _____
	14. Now let us consider *-ing* as a suffix. Rewrite the words below by adding *-ing*.
trying, copying, hurrying	try _____ copy _____ hurry _____
applying, emptying, studying	apply _____ empty _____ study _____
	15. Do the words in the frame above end in a *y* preceded by a consonant?
yes, no	_____ Does the *y* change to *i* before adding *-ing*? _____
	Do not change the final *y* to *i* before adding *-ing* to a word that ends in a *y* proceeded by a consonant.
	16. Why do we keep the *y* when adding *-ing* to the words in frame 14? Let us conduct an experiment to investigate this exception.
	Add *-ing* to *copy*, but this time change the *y* to *i*. The new spelling is
copiing	_____.
yes	Would you also expect to keep the *y* when adding *-ist* to *copy*? _____
copyist	Write this word. _____
yes	Does this hold for adding *-ish* to *baby*? _____ Write this word.
babyish	_____ Keeping the *y* when adding a suffix that begins with an *i* avoids an unnecessary *i* in spelling (*copiing*). Furthermore, keeping the *y* provides a more accurate representation of pronunciation.

	17. We can restate our exception to the *y-to-i* generalizations accordingly:
	Do not change the final *y* to *i* before adding a suffix that begins with an *i* to a word that ends in a *y* preceded by a consonant.
	We should note that there are exceptions to this generalization. The
does not	generalization _____ apply to *summary* (*summarize*). (does, does not)
	18. Let us review the final *y-to-i* generalizations.
	Change the final *y* to *i* before adding a suffix to a word
consonant	**that ends in a *y* preceded by a _____.**
	Do not change the final *y* to *i* when a word
vowel	**ends in a *y* preceded by a _____.**
	Do not change the final *y* to *i* when adding a suffix that begins
consonant	**with an *i* to a word that ends in a *y* preceded by a _____.**
	19. We have established that the final *y* is usually changed to *i* when a root word ends in a *y* preceded by a consonant. But what happens when a word ends in the letter *e?* We shall use *time* as an example.
	Place a check beside the correctly spelled word(s) below.
timer, timing	timer timing timeed
	Dropping the final *e* (*timer, timing, timed*) ensures that we do not add an
vowel	unnecessary _____.
	20. Solve each word "equation" below by adding the indicated suffix.
baking, hoped	bake + ing = _____ hope + ed = _____
closer, saved	close + er = _____ save + ed = _____
nicest, latest	nice + est = _____ late + est = _____
settled, tumbling	settle + ed = _____ tumble + ing = _____
yes	**21.** Do the suffixes in the frame above begin with vowels? _____
yes	Do the words end in a silent *e?* _____
	Drop the final silent *e* before adding a suffix that begins with a vowel.
yes	Should we drop the *e* before adding *-ist* to *cycle*? _____ Write
cyclist	the new word. _____

	22. How does the final-*e* generalization apply to the suffixes -*able* and -*ous* when a word ends in *ce* or *ge*? Rewrite the words below by adding the indicated suffix.

	-*able*		-*ous*	
noticeable, courageous	notice	_____	courage	_____
replaceable, advantageous	replace	_____	advantage	_____
manageable, outrageous	manage	_____	outrage	_____

When applied to words that end *ce* or *ge*, the -*able* and -*ous* suffixes are too irregular to have a final-*e* spelling generalization.

soft	**23.** The final *e* in each word in the frame above indicates that the *c* and the *g* represent _____ sounds (page 57). Write the key symbols for (hard, soft)
s, j	the soft sounds of *c* _____ and *g* _____.
	In the absence of the final *e*, we are inclined to pronounce the *c* and the *g*
hard, *k, g*	as _____ sounds: key symbols _____ and _____. (hard, soft)

24. To better understand the final-*e* generalization, we will consider suffixes that begin with consonants. Rewrite each word below by adding the indicated suffix.

	-*ly*		-*less*		-*ment*	
likely, useless, agreement	like	_____	use	_____	agree	_____
nicely, ageless, excitement	nice	_____	age	_____	excite	_____
lively, hopeless, movement	live	_____	hope	_____	move	_____
lately, tireless, shipment	late	_____	tire	_____	ship	_____

consonant	**25.** Each suffix in frame 24 begins with a _____. Each word
e	ends with an _____.
	Keep the final *e* when adding a suffix that begins with a consonant.

	26. What happens when -*y* is added to words that end in a silent *e*? Rewrite the words below by adding -*y*.
hazy, shady, wavy, nosy, shiny	haze _____ shade _____ wave _____ nose _____ shine _____

long	**27.** The *y* in frame 26 represents a _____ vowel phoneme: key (short, long)
ē, eraser	symbol _____ ; key word _____.
vowel	The -*y* acts as a _____ (see page 113). Therefore, we expect to drop the final *e* before adding -*y*.

	28. We can make these generalizations regarding root words that end in silent *e:*
	When adding a suffix to a word spelled with a final, silent *e,*
	a. drop the final *e* before adding a suffix that begins with a
vowel	_____.
consonant	**b.** keep the final *e* when adding a suffix that begins with a _____.
	When applied to words that end in *ce* or *ge,* the *-able* and *-ous* suffixes are too irregular to have a final-*e* spelling generalization.

29. Let us turn out attention to *consonant doubling.* When should we double the final consonant of a *one-syllable* word before adding a suffix? Rewrite each word below by adding the indicated suffix.

-ed	*-ing*	*-er*	*-est*
jog	*run*	*dim*	*big*
_____	_____	_____	_____

jogged, running, dimmer, biggest

30. Examine the words in the frame above. Each of these one-syllable words consists of one vowel followed by a single consonant. The vowel

phoneme is _____.
(short, long)

short

The vowel–consonant pattern is _____ (page 100).
(VC, VCe)

VC

Each suffix begins with a _____.

vowel

31. Rewrite each word below by crossing out the silent consonant.

flatten _____   shipping _____   thinner _____

biggest _____   hidden _____   hugged _____

flatten, shipping, thinner biggest, hidden, hugged

32. You may wish to use the expression *one–one–one* to help you remember this generalization:

Double the final consonant when a suffix that begins with a vowel is added to a root word

that has _____ syllable and _____
(How many?)   (How many?)

one, one

vowel and ends in _____ consonant.
(How many?)

one

pin	**33.** We will use *pinned* to illustrate one–one–one. The word is _____.
yes	Does the *-ed* begin with a vowel? _____ Is the final consonant
yes	doubled? _____
one, one	*Pin* has _____ syllable(s) and _____ vowel(s), and it ends in
	(How many?) (How many?)
one	_____ consonant(s).
	(How many?)

	34. Study the words below. Pronounce the words in lines 1 and 2. Then write the words to show pronunciation.
hŏpt, mŏpt, tăpt	**Line 1** *hopped* _____ *mopped* _____ *tapped* _____
hōpt, mōpt, tāpt	**Line 2** *hoped* _____ *moped* _____ *taped* _____

	35. The vowel-consonant pattern of the one-syllable words in line 1 is
VC	_____. Doubling the final consonant (line 1 in the frame above)
short	indicates that a word has a _____ vowel phoneme. Not doubling
long	the final consonant (as in line 2) indicates a _____ vowel pronunciation. If we did not double the final consonant in words line 1,
long	the sound of the vowel would be _____.

	36. What happens when we add a suffix that begins with a consonant? Complete the word "equations" below.
badly, jobless	bad + ly = _____ job + less = _____
madness, fitful	mad + ness = _____ fit + ful = _____
spotless, sadly	spot + less = _____ sad + ly = _____
	We do not double the final consonant of a one-syllable word when we add a suffix that begins with a consonant.

	37. Continuing our study of the final-consonant-doubling generalization, rewrite each word below by adding the indicated suffix. Note that each suffix begins with a vowel and each word consists of one syllable.
	-ed **-ing** **-er**
	hunt _____ rest _____ help _____
hunted, resting, helper	seat _____ read _____ sweet _____
seated, reading, sweeter	melt _____ farm _____ camp _____
melted, farming, camper	

consonant, vowel	**38.** Study the words in the previous frame. Each one-syllable word ends in. more than one _____ or has more than one _____.
CVCC, CVVC	Indicate the vowel–consonant pattern of *jump* _____ and of *sweet* _____. Use a C to represent each consonant and a V to represent each vowel.
no	**39.** Would we expect to double the final consonant before adding -*est* to *fast?* _____
fastest	Write the new word. _____
	Would we expect to double the final consonant before adding -*est* to *fat?*
yes	_____
fattest	Write the new word. _____
	Do not double the final consonant when a one-syllable word ends in two or more consonants or includes two vowels.
	40. Let us recap what we have learned about the final-consonant-doubling generalization when applied to *one-syllable* words:
	Double the final consonant before adding a suffix that
vowel	**begins with a _____ to a *one-syllable* word that ends in one vowel followed by one consonant (as in *running*).**
Do not	**_____double the final consonant when a suffix begins with a consonant (as in *sadly*), when the one-syllable word ends in two**
consonants, vowels	**_____ (*jumped*) or has two_____(as in *sweeter*).**
	41. Now let us consider *multisyllable* words. The final-consonant-doubling guideline is most reliable when applied to one-syllable words. Pronounce the two-syllable words below. Rewrite each word by adding the suffix indicated.
	com mit' *be gin'*
committed, beginner	commit + ed = _____ begin + er = _____

VC (CVC is also correct.)	**42.** Notice that the final syllable in each *multisyllable* word above represents the _____ vowel–consonant pattern. These syllables have one vowel followed by one consonant.
last	The accent—indicated by '—is placed on the _____ (first, last)
vowel	syllable. Each suffix begins with a _____.
short	We expect the vowel to respresent a _____ sound. (long, short)
	We usually double the final consonant before adding a suffix that
vowel	**begins with a _____ when the last syllable of a *multisyllable* word is accented and ends in one vowel followed by one consonant(as in *beginner*).**
	43. Rewrite each word below by adding the *-ed* suffix.
	$cov'\ er$ $o'\ pen$
covered, opened	cover + ed = _____ open + ed = _____
first	The accent in *cover* and *open* is placed on the _____ (first, last)
	syllable.
	44. Study the multisyllable words below. Each suffix begins with a
consonant	_____.
	com mit' + ment = commitment
	for get' + ful = forgetful
do not	**We usually _____ double the final consonant** (do, do not)
	before adding a suffix to the final, unaccented
	syllable of a *multisyllable* word (as in *opened* and *forgetful*).
	Does this generalization apply to a suffix that begins with a consonant?
yes	_____
	45. Let us consider multisyllable words that end in *l*. Solve the word "equation" below:
canceled or cancelled	$can'\ cel$ + ed = _____
	Would it surprise you to learn that dictionaries show more than one way to spell some root words when a suffix beginning with a vowel is added to a final, unaccented syllable that ends in *l?* It is customary not to double the *l* in American-English spelling (*equaled*). Doubling the *l* is more likely in British-English spelling.

Study Guide

Spelling Generalizations for Adding Prefixes and Suffixes to Words

Prefixes

The spelling does not change when a prefix is added to the beginning of a root word.

Suffixes Beginning with a Consonant

The spelling of a root word often does not change when adding a suffix that begins with a consonant.

Final y

Change the final *y* to *i* before adding a suffix to a word that ends in a *y* preceded by a consonant (*applies*). Do not change the *y* to *i* before adding a suffix to a word that ends in a *y* preceded by a vowel (*joyful*) or when adding *-ing* (*copying*).

-es and -s

Add *-es* to form the plural of most words that end in a *y* preceded by a consonant (*babies*) or an *s* (*kisses*), *sh* (*dishes*), *ch* (*benches*), *x* (*boxes*), or *z* (*quizzes*).
Add *-s* to most other words to form plurals.

Final e

Drop the final *e* before adding a suffix that begins with a vowel (*timer*). Keep the *e* when adding a suffix that begins with a consonant (*timely*). When applied to VCe root words, the *-able* and *-ous* suffixes are too irregular to apply a final-*e* spelling generalization.

Final Consonant Doubling

Double the final consonant before adding a suffix that begins with a vowel to a *one-syllable* word that ends in a single vowel followed by a single consonant (a VC pattern, as in *hopped*). Double the final consonant when the last syllable of a *multisyllable* root word has one vowel followed by one consonant (VC) and receives the greatest stress or accent (*be gin' ner*).

   Do not double the final consonant when adding a suffix to a *one-syllable* word that ends in two or more consonants (as in *melted*) or has two vowels (as in *eaten*). Do not double the final consonant when a suffix begins with a consonant (as in *sadly*). (Remember, the final *e* in *hope* was dropped before the *-ed* was added.) Do not double the final consonant when the last syllable of a *multisyllable* word is not accented (*o' pen ing*) or the suffix begins with a consonant (*for get' ful*).

	46. Let us summarize the final-consonant-doubling generalizations.
	We usually double the final consonant before adding a suffix that begins with a vowel:
vowel	A. to a *one-syllable* word that ends in one _____ followed by one consonant (as in *running,* frame 40) or
accented	B. when the last syllable of a *multisyllable* word is _____ and ends in one vowel followed by one consonant (as in *be gin' ner,* frame 42).
	We usually do not double the final consonant before adding a suffix:
consonant	A. that begins with a _____ to a *one-syllable* word (as in *sadly,* frame 40),
	B. to a one-syllable word that includes two vowels (as in *sweeter,* frame 40),
	C. to a one-syllable word that ends in two (as in *jumped,* frame 40), or
unaccented	D. when the last syllable of a *multisyllable* word is _____ (as in *o'pen ed,* frame 44).
	47. We have been studying generalizations for the spelling of
words (or words)	_____ to which affixes are attached.
	These generalizations would be more accurate if each included a cautionary word such as *often, occasionally, sometimes,* or *usually.* For the sake of simplicity, a caution is not explicitly stated for each generalization.
are not	However, we acknowledge that the generalizations _____ infallible.
	We refer to the dictionary or spellchecker when we are in doubt as to the correct spelling. Occasionally, the dictionary may indicate more than one acceptable spelling (*likable, likeable*).

Review 26

1. State the final-consonant-doubling generalization for a one-syllable word that ends in a single vowel followed by a single consonant.

2. We usually _____ the final *e* before adding a suffix that begins with
   (keep, drop)

   a vowel to a word that ends in a silent *e*.

3. Add the indicated suffix to each word below:

   -er   *-ed*   *-est*

   nice _____   *dine* _____   *close* _____

   bake _____   *hike* _____   *fine* _____

4. Rewrite each word by adding *-s* or *-es*, as appropriate.

   bird   *dish*   *toy*   *mix*   *marry*   *boss*   *quiz*

5. Complete these generalizations:

   a. Add *-es* to words that end in a *y* preceded by a _____ or

      to words that end in an _____, _____,

      _____, _____, or _____.

   b. Add _____ to all other words.

6. Solve these word "equations" by adding the indicated suffixes.

   silly + est = _____   *copy + ed =* _____

   deny + ed = _____   *lazy + ness =* _____

7. State the generalization that applies to adding suffixes to the words in question 6.

8. Solve the word "equations" below:

   camp + ed = _____   *recent + ly =* _____

9. State the generalizations for adding suffixes to the words in question 8.

See the Answers to the Reviews section for the answers to Review 26, page 238.

Recap IV

three,	**1.** We have studied the meaningful parts in word structure. Let us begin our recap with the word *recounted.* We recognize _____ meaningful parts in *recounted:* one (How many?)
free, bound	_____ morpheme and two _____ morphemes. The free
count	morpheme is _____.
re-, -ed	The bound morphemes are _____ and _____.
morpheme	**2.** A free morpheme can exist alone. A bound morpheme cannot exist alone. A bound morpheme must be attached to another _____.
beginning	**3.** You have studied two groups of bound morphemes: prefixes and suffixes. A prefix is placed at the _____ of a root word; a suffix is (beginning, end)
end	placed at the _____ of a root word. (beginning, end)
mis- understood	**4.** *Misunderstood* consists of the prefix _____ and the root word _____.
un- believe, -able	*Unbelievable* consists of the prefix _____, the root word _____, and the suffix _____.
inflectional derivational	**5.** You have learned that a(n) _____ suffix changes number, affects verb tense, indicates comparison, or denotes possession. A(n) _____ suffix affects meaning and may change the part of speech. Place an *I* after each word below that includes an inflectional suffix. Place a *D* beside each word that includes a derivational suffix.
D, I, D, D	*angelic* _____ *babies* _____ *studious* _____ *active* _____
I, D, I, I	*Maria's* _____ *writer* _____ *nicest* _____ *widen* _____

	6. Generalizations help us determine how to spell a word when we add a suffix. Use your knowledge to match each of the following words with the correct generalization below.
	payable shipment watches staying babies
	happily making clapped preset
happily	**A.** _____ Change the y to i before adding a suffix to words that end in a y preceded by a consonant.
payable	**B.** _____ Do not change the final y to i when adding a suffix to words that end in a y preceded by a vowel.
babies	**C.** _____ Change the y to i and add -es to words that end in a y preceded by a consonant.
watches	**D.** _____ Add -es to words that end in s, sh, ch, x, or z.
making	**E.** _____ When words end in a silent e (VCe), drop the e when adding a suffix that begins with a vowel.
clapped	**F.** _____ Double the final consonant before adding a suffix to one-syllable words that end in a single vowel followed by a single consonant (VC).
shipment	**G.** _____ The spelling of root words usually does not change when we add a suffix that begins with a consonant to words that end in a consonant.
staying	**H.** _____ Do not change the y to i when adding a suffix that begins with an i.
preset	**I.** _____ The spelling of root words is not usually affected by a prefix.
contraction	**7.** A _____ is two words combined into one word; an apostrophe replaces the missing letter (or letters).
compound word	A _____ consists of two or more "words" (free morphemes) combined to form a word with a meaning that is different from the meanings of the two "words" separately. The compound word is a free morpheme (rainbow).
sea	**8.** The compound word seashore consists of the "words" _____ and
shore, sea shore	_____. Show the syllable division and place the accent. _____
fire' crack er	Divide firecracker into syllables and place the accent. _____ Firecracker
three	has _____ syllables. The first "word," fire, consists of
	(How many?)
one	_____ syllable(s).
	(How many?)
two	The second "word," cracker, consists of _____ syllable(s).
	(How many?)

sounds (phonemes)	**9.** You have studied the relationship of letters and letter combinations to the _____ they represent. You have also studied the meaningful parts in the structure of English words.
sound, meaning	The prefix *re-* is an example of a word part that represents both _____ and _____.
sound	The syllable *rab* in *rabbit* (*rab' bit*) represents only _____.
comprehend (understand)	**10.** Structural analysis helps the reader understand the meaning of words with more than one meaningful part. Knowledge of word meaning, in turn, helps the reader _____ text.
reading	**11.** You have studied phonics and structural analysis. They form the basis of **two** of the word-attack skills needed to attain independence in _____.
	Mastery of the reading process requires the development of still other sets of skills, including the use of context clues and the understanding of the material read. Reading is a complicated process!

You are now ready for the posttest. Show your mastery of the content of phonics and word structure! Best wishes.

References

National Governors Association Center for Best Practices & Council of Chief State School Officers. (2010). *Common Core State Standards for English Language Arts & History/Social Studies, Science, and Technical Subjects: Reading: Foundational SkillsPhonological Awareness, Phonics and Word Study.* Washington, DC: Authors. Retrieved May 15, 2012, from http://www.corestandards.org/assets/CCSSI_ELA%20Standards.pdf

Self-Evaluation II

A Posttest

This test is designed to help you evaluate your growth in the field of phonics and word analysis. Read each item, including **all** the choices. Indicate the answer you consider best by circling the appropriate letter (a, b, c, d, or e) or by marking the appropriate letter on an answer sheet. Please respond to every item. The answer page for the posttest (p. 229) cross-references the page in the text that addresses the correct answer for each test item. Time: 30 minutes.

I. Multiple Choice. Select the best answer.

1. Which of the following most adequately completes this sentence?

   The consonant phonemes in the American-English language are represented by

   a. the consonant–vowel combinations.

   b. the distinctive speech sounds we associate with each of the 21 consonant letters of the alphabet.

   c. 18 of the consonant letters of the alphabet plus 7 digraphs.

   d. the single-letter consonants plus their two- and three-letter blends.

   e. The American-English language is too irregular to represent the consonant phonemes with any degree of accuracy.

2. The second syllable of the nonsense word *omethbin* can be expected to rhyme with

   a. *see.*

   b. *pet.*

   c. *wreath.*

   d. *breath.*

   e. *kin.*

3. The open syllable in the nonsense word *phattoe* can be expected to rhyme with

   a. *fa* of *fatal.*

   b. *day.*

   c. *fat.*

   d. *dough.*

   e. Both a and b

4. How many phonemes are represented in the nonsense word *ghight?*

   a. one

   b. two

   c. three

   d. four

   e. six

5. The sound of the schwa is represented by

   a. the *a* in *carry.*

   b. the *e* in *meet.*

   c. the *i* in *lighted.*

   d. the *o* in *falcon.*

   e. the *u* in *rule.*

6. *Y* as the only vowel and final letter in a one-syllable word is most likely to represent the same sound as

   a. the *e* in *be*.

   b. the *oy* in boy.

   c. the *y* in *gym*.

   d. the *i* in *limb*.

   e. the *y* in *cycle*.

7. Generally, when two like consonants appear together in a word or syllable,

   a. one is sounded with the first syllable and the other with the second.

   b. both are sounded when the preceding vowel is *e*.

   c. both are sounded when the following vowel is *i*.

   d. only one is sounded.

   e. neither is sounded.

8. A requirement of a syllable is that

   a. it contain no more than one vowel letter.

   b. it contain no more than one vowel phoneme.

   c. it contain at least one consonant phoneme.

   d. it contain no more than one phoneme.

   e. None of the above.

9. An example of a closed syllable is found in the word

   a. *low*.

   b. *sofa*.

   c. *doubt*.

   d. *high*.

   e. None of these.

10. The letter *w* is most likely to be a consonant when

    a. it follows *o* in a syllable.

    b. it has the sound of *i* as in *light*.

    c. it is the first letter in a word or syllable.

    d. it is the last letter in a word or syllable.

    e. None of the above.

11. The letter *q* could be removed from the alphabet because it can adequately and without conflict be represented by

    a. *ch* as in *chair*.

    b. *k* as in *kite*.

    c. *cu* as in *cubic*.

    d. All of the above

    e. The idea is foolish; *qu* represents a distinctive consonant phoneme.

12. If *e* was the only vowel in an open syllable, that *e* would most likely represent the same sound as

    a. the *y* in *baby*.

    b. the *e* in *mice*.

    c. the *e* in *break*.

    d. the *e* in *net*.

    e. the *e* in *fine*.

13. Which of the following has an incorrect diacritical mark?

    a. *bǎll*.

    b. *fěll*.

    c. *wǐsh*.

    d. *drǒp*.

    e. *cǔt*.

14. Which of the following has an incorrect diacritical mark?

    a. *spāde*.

    b. *hēad*.

    c. *sīde*.

    d. *lōne*.

    e. *fāil*.

15. When *o* and *a* appear together in a syllable, they usually represent the same sound as

    a. the *a* in *bacon*.

    b. the *o* in *done*.

    c. the *o* in *force*.

    d. the *o* in *ghostly*.

    e. the *a* in *camel*.

16. The symbol *s* is used in the dictionary to show the pronunciation of the sound heard in

    a. *should*.
    b. *has*.
    c. *sure*.
    d. *zoo*.
    e. *waltz*.

17. If *o* was the only vowel in an accented, open syllable, that *o* would most likely represent the same sound as

    a. the *o* in *ton*.
    b. the *o* in *ow* in *now*.
    c. the *o* in *gone*.
    d. the *ou* in *dough*.
    e. None of these.

18. A consonant blend (or cluster) is illustrated by

    a. the *ch* in *chin*.
    b. the *ng* in *sing*.
    c. the *bl* in *black*.
    d. the *ph* in *graph*.
    e. a, c, and d.

19. When the single vowel *i* is followed by a single consonant and a final *e* in an accented syllable, the *i* will most likely have the sound of

    a. the *i* in *readily*.
    b. the *i* in *active*.
    c. the *y* in *cry*.
    d. the *e* in *sea*.
    e. the *y* in *happy*.

20. If *a* was the single vowel in an accented syllable ending with a consonant, that *a* would most likely represent the same sound as

    a. the *ay* in *daylight*.
    b. the *a* in *have*.
    c. the *a* in *many*.
    d. the *a* in *wall*.
    e. the *a* in *car*.

21. When *c* is followed by *i*, it will most likely represent the same sound as

    a. the *c* in *cube*.
    b. the *c* in *chime*.
    c. the *c* in *cello*.
    d. *c* followed by *o*.
    e. None of these.

22. The word *if* ends with the same sound as

    a. the *ph* in *phrase*.
    b. the *f* in *of*.
    c. the *gh* in *cough*.
    d. All of the above.
    e. Both a and c.

23. When *oi* appears in an accented syllable, it represents the same sound as

    a. the *ou* in *mouse*.
    b. the *ow* in *how*.
    c. the *ew* in *new*.
    d. the *oy* in *boy*.
    e. a and d.

24. When the letter *g* is followed by *a*, it will most likely represent the same sound as

    a. the *j* in *jam*.
    b. the *g* in *go*.
    c. the *g* in *gnat*.
    d. the *g* in *bring*.
    e. the *g* in *giant*.

25. We usually do not double the final consonant before adding a suffix to a one-syllable word that

    a. ends in a consonant blend.
    b. ends in a silent *e*.
    c. includes a long vowel phoneme.
    d. ends in a consonant digraph.
    e. All of these.

26. Which underlined item illustrates a free morpheme?

    a. un*just*
    b. *dancer*
    c. *historic*
    d. *nervous*
    e. None of these.

27. Which word includes a derivational suffix?

    a. *diver.*
    b. *biggest.*
    c. *books.*
    d. *faster.*
    e. *falling.*

28. The final *y* changes to *i* before a suffix is added to a word that

    a. ends in a vowel followed by the letter y.
    b. has two or more vowels.
    c. ends in a consonant followed by the letter y.
    d. ends in two consonants.
    e. consists of no more than one syllable.

29. Double the final consonant before adding a suffix to a one-syllable word to indicate that the

    a. vowel is a schwa.
    b. vowel represents a long sound.
    c. vowel is a diphthong.
    d. vowel is unaccented.
    e. vowel is short.

30. Which nonsense word below illustrates a closed syllable?

    a. *aeth.*
    b. *pluft*
    c. *ghoumt.*
    d. b and c.
    e. All of the above.

31. Which word includes both a free and a bound morpheme?

    a. *happily.*
    b. *handle.*
    c. *cowboy.*
    d. *unison.*
    e. *level.*

32. The guideline for adding a suffix to a word that ends in an e is illustrated by

    a. *nicer.*
    b. *riding.*
    c. *hopeful.*
    d. *safest.*
    e. All of the above.

33. Which word below includes an inflectional suffix

    a. *famous.*
    b. *active.*
    c. *parenthood.*
    d. *lovable.*
    e. *swimming.*

34. Add −*es* to a word that ends in

    a. the letters *sh.*
    b. the letters *ch.*
    c. the letter *x.*
    d. a and b.
    e. All of the above.

35. The apostrophe in a contraction denotes

    a. possession.
    b. one or more missing letters.
    c. emphasis placed on a syllable.
    d. pronunciation of the vowel.
    e. None of the above.

36. Which of the words below shows the correct syllable division?

    a. *hand' writ ing.*
    b. *fire' fighter.*
    c. *re' lation.*
    d. *choco' late.*
    e. *qual' ify.*

37. A compound word is illustrated by

    a. *preteen.*
    b. *personality.*
    c. *yardstick.*
    d. *employment.*
    e. *relay.*

38. A consonant digraph is illustrated by

    a. the *qu* in *quick.*
    b. the *ch* in *porch.*
    c. the *gh* in *high.*
    d. a and c.
    e. None of these.

39. The contraction *he's* is composed of which of the following two words?

    a. *he was.*
    b. *he will.*
    c. *he is.*
    d. *he has.*
    e. Both c and d.

40. When *ou* appears in an accented syllable, it represents the same sound as

    a. the *ow* in *crow.*
    b. the *oi* in *boil.*
    c. the *ow* in *cow.*
    d. the *oy* in *toy.*
    e. the *ew* in *new.*

41. A suffix may

    a. affect the meaning of a word.
    b. change the part of speech.
    c. make the meaning of a word more specific.
    d. a and c.
    e. All of the above.

42. The CVVC (or VV) vowel-vowel pattern is illustrated by

    a. *foil.*
    b. *school.*
    c. *mouse.*
    d. *road.*
    e. All of the above.

43. The VCe (vowel–consonant–e) pattern is best illustrated by

    a. *able.*
    b. *meet.*
    c. *cable.*
    d. *globe.*
    e. *large.*

44. The VC (vowel–consonant) pattern is best illustrated by

    a. *toe.*
    b. *far.*
    c. *trash.*
    d. *oil.*
    e. *he.*

45. *W* is part of a diphthong in

    a. *who.*
    b. *snow.*
    c. *answer.*
    d. *flower.*
    e. *subway.*

II. **Multiple Choice.** In the following items, where does the accent fall in each word or nonsense word given at the left? Indicate your answer by selecting the last two letters of the accented syllable.

Look at the example: *showboat*. The first "word" in a compound word is generally accented: *show'boat*. Look for the last two letters of *show, ow,* in the row to the right. You would circle b or mark b on your answer sheet.

Example:

showboat	**a.** ho	**(b.)** ow	**c.** bo	**d.** at

46. tenlaim	**a.** te	**b.** en	**c.** nl	**d.** la	**e.** im
47. grottome	**a.** ro	**b.** ot	**c.** to	**d.** om	**e.** me
48. religherly	**a.** re	**b.** rl	**c.** gh	**d.** er	**e.** ly
49. damapantion	**a.** am	**b.** ma	**c.** pa	**d.** an	**e.** on
50. present (verb)	**a.** re	**b.** es	**c.** se	**d.** nt	**e.** pr

III. **Multiple Choice.** There are three words in each item (a, b, c). Select the word in which you hear the same sound as that represented by the underlined part of the word at the left. You may find that the sound is heard in all three words; if so, mark d. If none of the words contains the sound, mark e.

51. tent	**a.** missed	**b.** listen	**c.** catch	**d.** All	**e.** None
52. pleasure	**a.** vision	**b.** sabotage	**c.** rouge	**d.** All	**e.** None
53. tanker	**a.** banner	**b.** singer	**c.** nose	**d.** All	**e.** None
54. gem	**a.** edge	**b.** soldier	**c.** jelly	**d.** All	**e.** None
55. that	**a.** bath	**b.** theory	**c.** this	**d.** All	**e.** None
56. chill	**a.** chute	**b.** chord	**c.** question	**d.** All	**e.** None
57. hook	**a.** pool	**b.** moose	**c.** tooth	**d.** All	**e.** None
58. ace	**a.** bead	**b.** said	**c.** lab	**d.** All	**e.** None
59. now	**a.** snow	**b.** joyous	**c.** cow	**d.** All	**e.** None
60. sock	**a.** sure	**b.** sugar	**c.** city	**d.** All	**e.** None
61. chain	**a.** character	**b.** machine	**c.** chalk	**d.** All	**e.** None

IV. **Multiple Choice.** Select the letter(s) at the right that represents the onset in each one-syllable word.

62. might	**a.** mi	**b.** ight	**c.** m	**d.** gh	**e.** igh
63. blank	**a.** ank	**b.** la	**c.** lan	**d.** bl	**e.** bla

Select the letter(s) at the right that represents the rime in each one-syllable word.

64. spill	**a.** ill	**b.** sp	**c.** ll	**d.** spi	**e.** s
65. thick	**a.** th	**b.** ick	**c.** ck	**d.** k	**e.** thi

V. Multiple Choice. Select the word in each row that is **incorrectly** divided into syllables.

66. **a.** tot al   **b.** li lac   **c.** fa tal   **d.** ma trix   **e.** bo ny

67. **a.** fin ger   **b.** cot ton   **c.** gamb ol   **d.** for get   **e.** an gry

68. **a.** par don a ble   **b.** re sist i ble   **c.** in vent ion   **d.** in fu sion   **e.** ex hale

69. **a.** saw dust   **b.** to get her   **c.** side walk   **d.** shark skin   **e.** loop hole

VI. Multiple Choice. Complete each sentence by selecting the word for which the correct pronunciation is indicated.

70. When I picked my vegetables, I dropped a

    a. *răd ′ ĭsh.*   **b.** *kăr ′ ŏt.*   **c.** *kŭ kŭm ′ bĕr.*   **d.** *pĕ.*   **e.** *kăb ′ ôg.*

71. I went to the park for a

    a. *kăn ′ cûrt.*   **b.** *rās.*   **c.** *wôlk.*   **d.** *pĭk ′ nək.*   **e.** *păr ′ tē.*

72. The wall is

    a. *thĭn.*   **b.** *stŭck ′ ŏŏd.*   **c.** *pĭngk.*   **d.** *lōu.*   **e.** *krăk ′ əd.*

73. The tree we planted was a(n)

    a. *fĭr.*   **b.** *ăzh.*   **c.** *sprōōs.*   **d.** *bərtch.*   **e.** *cē kwoi ′ ə.*

74. I went to the grocery store for

    a. *ôr ′ ĭng əz.*   **b.** *brēd.*   **c.** *jăm.*   **d.** *pō tā ′tōz.*   **e.** *kăn ′ dy.*

75. I washed the

    a. *wôls.*   **b.** *wĭnd ′ ōs.*   **c.** *kown ′ tər.*   **d.** *nīvz.*   **e.** *sĭnk.*

(See p. 229 for answers to Self-Evaluation II.)

Self-Evaluation II: Number correct _____

Self-Evaluation I: Number correct _____

Answers to the Pretest and Posttest

Answers to Self-Evaluation I: A Pretest

Note: The number(s) following each answer refers to the page on which information that addresses the question is found.

1. c (pp. 168)	26. e (pp. 194)	51. d (pp. 66)
2. b (pp. 32)	27. e (pp. 207)	52. b (pp. 77)
3. a (pp. 60)	28. e (pp. 204)	53. b (pp. 55)
4. a (pp. 39)	29. e (pp. 200)	54. c (pp. 48)
5. c (pp. 100)	30. c (pp. 212)	55. c (pp. 58)
6. d (pp. 110)	31. e (pp. 210)	56. c (pp. 41)
7. a (pp. 212)	32. b (pp. 199)	57. d (pp. 120)
8. c (pp. 116)	33. c (pp. 194)	58. e (pp. 130)
9. c (pp. 16)	34. c (pp. 202)	59. b (pp. 127)
10. d (pp. 100)	35. b (pp. 186)	60. b (pp. 60)
11. d (pp. 85)	36. a (pp. 202)	61. c (pp. 81)
12. a (pp. 97)	37. e (pp. 203)	62. d (pp. 157)
13. d (pp. 108)	38. b (pp. 127)	63. a (pp. 157)
14. b (pp. 108)	39. a (pp. 100)	64. b (pp. 159)
15. d (pp. 110)	40. b (pp. 106)	65. a (pp. 159)
16. c (pp. 35)	41. b (pp. 133)	66. b (pp. 177)
17. a (pp. 100)	42. b (pp. 127)	67. a (pp. 178)
18. e (pp. 133)	43. b (pp. 100)	68. c (pp. 184)
19. d (pp. 65)	44. c (pp. 113)	69. d (pp. 181)
20. b (pp. 110)	45. a (pp. 127)	70. b (pp. 120)
21. e (pp. 52)	46. b (pp. 171)	71. e (pp. 132)
22. e (pp. 57)	47. b (pp. 171)	72. e (pp. 118)
23. b (pp. 55)	48. e (pp. 172)	73. b (pp. 132)
24. a (pp. 207)	49. d (pp. 171)	74. a (pp. 48)
25. d (pp. 194)	50. d (pp. 170)	75. c (pp. 81)

Answers to Self-Evaluation II: A Posttest

1. c (pp. 32)	**26.** e (pp. 194)	**51.** a (pp. 48)
2. d (pp. 100)	**27.** a (pp. 200)	**52.** d (pp. 64)
3. d (pp. 110)	**28.** c (pp. 207)	**53.** b (pp. 81)
4. c (pp. 16)	**29.** e (pp. 212)	**54.** d (pp. 55)
5. d (pp. 116)	**30.** e (pp. 100)	**55.** c (pp. 77)
6. e (pp. 113)	**31.** a (pp. 194)	**56.** c (pp. 74)
7. d (pp. 39)	**32.** e (pp. 210)	**57.** e (pp. 130)
8. b (pp. 168)	**33.** e (pp. 199)	**58.** e (pp. 106)
9. c (pp. 100)	**34.** e (pp. 207)	**59.** c (pp. 127)
10. c (pp. 60)	**35.** b (pp. 202)	**60.** c (pp. 57)
11. b (pp. 35)	**36.** a (pp. 186)	**61.** c (pp. 74)
12. a (pp. 110)	**37.** c (pp. 202)	**62.** c (pp. 157)
13. a (pp. 97)	**38.** b (pp. 72)	**63.** d (pp. 157)
14. b (pp. 108)	**39.** e (pp. 203)	**64.** a (pp. 159)
15. d (pp. 133)	**40.** c (pp. 127)	**65.** b (pp. 159)
16. e (pp. 65)	**41.** e (pp. 204)	**66.** a (pp. 177)
17. d (pp. 110)	**42.** d (pp. 133)	**67.** c (pp. 178)
18. c (pp. 85)	**43.** d (pp. 106)	**68.** c (pp. 184)
19. c (pp. 106)	**44.** c (pp. 100)	**69.** b (pp. 181)
20. b (pp. 100)	**45.** d (pp. 127)	**70.** a (pp. 100)
21. e (pp. 57)	**46.** e (pp. 172)	**71.** b (pp. 107)
22. e (pp. 52)	**47.** b (pp. 171)	**72.** c (pp. 81)
23. d (pp. 127)	**48.** c (pp. 170)	**73.** c (pp. 129)
24. b (pp. 55)	**49.** d (pp. 171)	**74.** c (pp. 100)
25. e (pp. 212)	**50.** d (pp. 171)	**75.** d (pp. 41)

Answers to the Reviews

These reviews give you an indication of your mastery (or lack of mastery) of the material. *Work to achieve 100% on each review!* Your success depends largely on your self-motivation. It takes **very** little more effort to achieve mastery than to fail, even while writing each answer. The difference depends on your mind-set. Good luck!

 ## Review 1

1. phoneme
2. 44
3. segment (or separate), blend
4. segmenting
5. blending
6. grapheme
7. rhyme
8. a. phonemic awareness
   b. phonemes (or sounds), graphemes (or letters)
   c. phonemic awareness, phonics

Scores:

 ## Review 2

1. no
2. phonemes (The key symbols represent sounds, never letters.)
3. *m*
4. *m*
5. 2, digraphs
6. letters
7. digraph, 1

Scores:

 ## Review 3

1. 5, 5
2. 3, 3
3. digraphs

4. *c, q, x.* They are represented by other letters; they have no distinctive phonemes of their own.
5. symbols, words
6. *m, k, r, v*
7. *u,* silent, *w*
8. *m v r, k w v r*
9. When we see a *v* in a word, we know it represents the same sound as that heard at the beginning of *van.*

Scores:

 ## Review 4

1. a. *no*
    b. *saf*
    c. *mel*
    d. *plara*
    e. *gaeve*
    f. *kef*
    g. *sim*
    h. *tovom*
    i. *rok*
    j. *rim*
    k. *kwimel*
    l. *klopem*
    m. *vout*
2. a. *blos̸som*
    b. *dumb̸*
    c. *k̸nob*
    d. *doub̸t*
    e. *g̸hastly*
    f. *pol̸len*
3. We are apt to add a vowel sound pronounced as "uh."
4. The key symbols represent the sounds of our language. Each sound is represented once. *Q* would be a duplication.

Scores:

If you have missed any items in previous Reviews, retake them now. Write the second score following the first. Do you show improvement?

 ## Review 5

1. a. *b*   i. *z n*
    b. *t f*   j. *h f t*
    c. *h j*   k. *p l n d*
    d. *v*   l. *k w l t*
    e. *f n*   m. *z r*
    f. *t t*   n. *s l*
    g. *g s t l*   o. *k l m*
    h. *r m*

2. **a.** *don't, ride, moved*
    b. *fine, graph, photo, off*
    c. *wedge, soldier, Roger*
    d. *knot, stranger*
    e. *his, puzzle, does*

Scores:

If you missed any, turn to the appropriate pages and restudy. Select a previous Review. Write the answers. Did you better your score or maintain a perfect score? Be sure you write your scores for each Review and "review of Reviews."

 # Review 6

1. A *g* followed by *e, i,* or *y* generally has the sound of /j/; a *g* followed by *a, o, u,* or any consonant or at the end of a word represents /g/ as in *goat.*

2. **a.** *j n t*   **h.** *m ch*
    b. *b ng k*   **i.** *y l*
    c. *g r l*   **j.** *w*
    d. *b g*   **k.** *k w k*
    e. *s r k s*   **l.** *r t*
    f. *k k*   **m.** *y t*
    g. *h*   **n.** *n k*

3. *girl*
4. C followed by *e, i,* or *y* generally has the sound of /s/; *c* followed by *a, o, u,* or any consonant or at the end of a word usually represents /k/.
5. The consonants *w* (as in *wagon,* /w/) and *y* (as in *yo-yo,* /y/) appear before the vowel in a syllable.

6. **a.** *g*   **f.** *k*
    b. *j*   **g.** *f*
    c. *j*   **h.** *k*
    d. *k*   **i.** *k*
    e. *j*   **j.** *f*

7. *n, nut,* /ng/

Scores:

 # Review 7

1. **a.** *e, i, y; k, a, o, u*
    b. *k*
    c. *ks, gz, z*
2. **a.** hard, *a, o, u*
    b. soft, *j, e, i, y*
3. **a.** some
    b. *z*
4. *d, t*
5. *v*
6. *ch, sh*

7. **a.** *s, sh, z, zh; z, s, zh*
   b. *c, z; z, s, x* (any two)
   c. *k, g, h;* silent; *t,* silent
8. **a.** graphemes, phoneme
   b. phonemes, grapheme
   c. phoneme

Scores:

 ## Review 8

1. digraph
2. *k k, h, zh, wh, wh ch, th, th, sh, sh g, w sh, v zh, ng*
3. *weather, which, bring, wish, both, through* (If you omitted the *wh* of *which*, you are correct also.)
4. letter; 7; digraphs; *sh, ch, wh, zh, th, th, ng*
5. *gh* in *tough, ck* in *luck, ph* in *phoneme*
6. *f, k, f*
7. *sungk, skwash, now* (no), *grafik, feazant, kouf*

Scores:

Continue those reviews of Reviews to improve your scores or maintain perfect scores!

 ## Review 9

1. **a.** *sh v r*
   b. *g z*
   c. *sh r*
   d. *sh r*
   e. *t r zhr*
   f. *k r k t r*
   g. *l zh r*
   h. *th t*
   i. *s k l z*
   j. *g s t s*
   k. *ch r j*
   l. *sh t*
   m. *k w k*
   n. *l sh n*
   o. *d v zh n*
   p. *sh k g*
   q. *m j k*
2. The digraph does not appear in the spelling of a word.

Scores:

 ## Review 10

1. *ng* (swing), *wh* (whale), *zh* (measure), *th* (mother), *sh* (flash), *ch* (porch)
2. *breath*
3. (1) — (*l* is silent), (2) *yo-yo,* (3) *sun,* (4) *table,* (5) *jeep,* (6) — (*b* is silent), (7) *fish,* (8) — (*h* is silent), (9) *van,* (10) *goat,* (11) — (*h* is silent), (12) *lion,* (13) — (not a consonant), (14) *ring,* (15) *lion,* (16) *kite*
4. is not, does not
5. consonant
6. *this, father, feather, them*
7. *wheel, white, whip, whistle*
8. Each grapheme functions as a consonant and as a vowel. *W* and *y,* as consonants, appear at the beginning of a word or syllable.

Scores:

Review 11

1. The following are spaced only to make them more distinct, not to indicate syllables. If you get these, you're good!
   a. *ma ng go, mang gle, man j y*
   b. *pin, pi ng, pi ng k, pi ng-po ng*
   c. *ban, ba ng, ba ng k, ba ng k i ng*
   d. *ran, ra ng, ra ng k, ra ng k i ng*
2. a. *b, d, f, g, h, j, k, l, m, n, p, r, s, t, v, w, y, z*
   b. digraphs; *sh, ch, wh, zh, th, th, ng*
3. *C* has no distinctive sound of its own. It is represented by the *s* and *k*.
4. *q, x*
5. *Ph* is represented by *f*.
6. *hole, hi, kwik, gofer, holy, fone, thach, that, taut, kom, glisening, ech, rusle, dout, not, bujet, rap, thingking*

Scores:

There were some tricky words in this review. Sincere congratulations if you had them all correct. If you did not, make sure you understand the principle involved. Restudy the appropriate section. Plan to "review this Review" soon.

 ## Review 12

1. You hear the sounds represented by the letters in the blend (cluster is also correct); a digraph represents a new sound.
2. The blends are represented by phonemes we already know.
3. *zh (pleasure), th (the), ng (nearing), th (through), ch (changed), wh (wheel), sh (shoulder)*. Note: The *thr* in *through* also forms a blend consisting of the digraph (*th*) and the (*r*).
4. *egzit* or *eksit, sity, kuickly* or *kwikly,*
5. */st/* in *started*, */pl/* in *pleasure*, */tr/* in *trip*, */dr/* in *driver*, */thr/* in *through*, */kw/* in *quickly* (The *l* and the *d* in *shoulder* represent phonemes that are in different syllables—*shoul der*.)

Scores:

 ## Review 13

1. *a, e, i, o, u, w, y*
2. *w, y*
3. C, V, V, C, V, C
4. consonant digraph
5. more
6. 19

Scores:

Review 14

1. **a.** When there is a single vowel in a closed accented syllable, that vowel phoneme is usually short.
   b. When a word or an accented syllable has two vowels, one of which is a final *e,* and the two vowels are separated by two consonants, the first vowel often represents the short sound and the final *e* is silent.
2. *bĕd, nĕxt, lōt, căt, trĭp, skĭn, mōp, ŭs, sĕnd, bŭg*
3. VC, VC (or CVC), VCCe (or CVCCe), VC (or CVC), VC, VCCe (or CVCCe)
4. VC (or CVC), VCCe
5. *e, i, y*

Scores:

 Review 15

1. *ē, ī, ō, ū,* macron
2. *i (ī), e (ē)*
3. *e.* When a word or accented syllable has two vowels, one of which is the final *e,* the *e* is silent and the first vowel usually represents its long sound.
4. accented, long
5. end, long
6. sound (or phoneme)
7. *dine* C *n; tack* C *k; <u>way</u>* V *ā; watch* C *ch; table* C *l; <u>go</u>* V *ō; tight* C *t; enough* C *f*
8. *bītҽ, bĭt, căn, cănҽ, pĕt, Pētҽ, cŭt, cūtҽ, mŏp, mŏpҽ*

Scores:

 Review 16

1. schwa
2. It saves assigning separate diacritical marks to each vowel to indicate a phoneme all share.
3. *regal, handmade* or *handmaid, celebrate, episode, damage*
4. *ĭ* (short *i*)

Scores:

 Review 17

1. short, *ă, ĕ, ĭ, ŏ, ŭ*
2. long, *ā, ē, ī, ō, ū*
3. *schwa, ə, agree (ə grē).* It saves assigning separate diacritical marks to each vowel to indicate a phoneme all share.
4. **a.** ball (*bôl*)
   b. fur (*fûr*)
   c. father (*fäṭhər*)
   d. care (*kâr*)
5. following, *r, l, w*

Scores:

(How did you do? You can feel a *real* sense of accomplishment if you had all of these correct. They are not easy!)

Review 18

1. oi, ou
2. vowel
3. owl-ou, cow-ou, moist-oi, oyster-oi
4. h<u>ous</u>, b<u>oi</u>, <u>ou</u>ns, ĕnj<u>oi</u>, n<u>oi</u>z, br<u>ou</u>

Scores:

 Review 19

1. A digraph is a two-letter grapheme that represents a single phoneme.
2. o͞o, o͝o
3. You cannot tell. The only clue is that it is most often o͞o as in food.
4. to͞oth, spo͞on, bo͝ok, lo͞os, sto͝od, mo͞o, sho͝ok
5. klo͞od
6. bo͞ot, fŭj, doun, toi, sho͝ok, kōkō, nīt, fro͞ot, thrō, thro͞o, t̸hō, thôt, kwĭt, bo͝ok, smo͞ot̸h, fo͞ol, brĕth, brē̸th, nīt, koin

Scores:

 Review 20

1. oi, ou, house
2. o͞o, o͝o, ho͝ok
3. When two vowels appear together in a word or accented syllable, the first may represent the long sound and the second is usually silent.
4. When a one-syllable word has an ending pattern VCe, the first vowel is generally long and the e is silent.
5. letter, phoneme

Scores:

 Review 21

1. wr, c, sh, h, st, s, b, sch, st, g
2. ask, ouch, am, old, if
3. vowel, consonant(s)
4. ain, ent, ice, amp, our, ild, ought, ince, ouse, ip
5. train, flour, bought, since, house
6. **a.** and
   b. ight
   c. ail
   d. ink
   e. ock
   f. ake
7. **a.** red, bed
   b. light, fight, right
   c. cow, how, now

8. rime, rhyme;
   a. *said, head;*
   b. *kite;*
   c. *snow*

Scores:

 Review 22

1. syllable
2. phoneme
3. yes
4. no
5. accented
6. a. The accent usually falls on or within the root word. *in ter change' a ble*
   b. In compound words, the accent usually falls on the first "word." *cow'boy*
   c. One-syllable words are accented. We usually do not indicate the accent in one-syllable words. *If we were to indicate the accent, we would record* fast'.
   d. When a word functions as different parts of speech, the accent is usually on the first syllable of a noun. *con' vict* (noun)
   e. The primary accent is usually on the syllable preceding the -*tion* ending. *na' tion*
   f. The accent usually falls on the syllable that closes with the first letter of a double consonant. *dol' lar*
   g. When two vowel letters are within the last syllable of a two-syllable word, that last syllable is most often accented. *con ceal'*
   h. When there is no other clue, the accent most often falls on the first syllable of a two-syllable word. *pa' per*

Scores:

 Review 23

1. a. CV/CVCC   The syllable division is between the single vowel and the single consonant.
   b. CVC/CVC   The syllable division is between the two consonants when there are single vowels on both sides of the two consonants.
   c. CVC/CV   The syllable division is between the two consonants when there are single vowels on both sides of the two consonants.
   d. CCV/CVCC   The syllable division is between the single vowel and the single consonant.

2. a. *play ful*   Suffixes and prefixes generally make separate syllables. This root word has one syllable.
   b. *ca pa ble*   The syllable division is between the single vowel and single consonant. If the last syllable of a word ends in *le* preceded by a consonant, that consonant usually begins the last syllable.
   c. *fa ther*   We usually do not divide between letters of a digraph; we treat the digraph as though it were one consonant. The division is between the single vowel and the digraph.

Scores:

Review 24

1. the smallest unit of meaning in our language
2. We cannot divide it into smaller, meaningful parts.
3. *dog, desk, hat, table*
4. a free morpheme or a free morpheme with one or more bound morphemes
5. *use<u>able</u>, <u>un</u>timely, <u>en</u>act, <u>un</u>need<u>ed</u>, child<u>ish</u>*
6. **a.** morpheme
   b. cannot

Scores:

 # Review 25

1. prefix
2. suffix
3. affix or affixes
4. *climb<u>ing</u>, like<u>able</u>, <u>pre</u>historic, <u>im</u>polite, <u>pre</u>viewed, treat<u>ment</u>, <u>il</u>logical, <u>un</u>covered*
5. *<u>dis</u>trust, <u>mid</u>air, <u>im</u>pure, <u>un</u>safe, <u>non</u>stop, <u>sub</u>plot, <u>re</u>tie, <u>de</u>merit*
6. *parenthood, -hood; joyous, -ous; motorists, -ist, -s; heroism, -ism; actor, -or; massive, -ive; musician, -ian; uselessly, -less, -ly*
7. *furious, D; attracting, I; wolves, I; sculptor, D; penniless, D; boyish, D*
8. *apostrophe, yes, could've, where's, don't, they're, we'll, what'll, he'd, we'd*
9. free, *kros'wok, ī'sīt, korn'brĕd, lănd'lŏkt, trĕd'mĭl, hōl'sāl*

Scores:

 # Review 26

1. When a one-syllable word ends in a single vowel followed by a single consonant, we usually double the final consonant before adding a suffix that begins with a vowel.
2. drop
3. *nicer, baker, dined, hiked, closest, finest*
4. *birds, dishes, toys, mixes, marries, bosses, quizzes*
5. **a.** consonant, *s, sh, ch, x, z*
   b. *s*
6. *silliest, copied, denied, laziness*
7. Usually change the final *y* to *i* when a consonant precedes the final *y*.
8. *camped, recently*
9. Do not double the final consonant when a one-syllable word with a short vowel phoneme ends in two or more consonants.

Scores:

Appendix A

Generalizations for Phonics and Word Study

 ## Consonant Generalizations

1. Consonant letters are fairly reliable: There is a high relationship between the letter and the sound (/ /) we expect it to represent (p. 31). However, there are irregularities:

   a. A letter may represent more than one phoneme (pp. 52, 67). Some common patterns are:

c:	/k/, /s/	n:	/n/, /ng/
d:	/d/, /t/	s:	/s/, /sh/, /z/, /zh/
g:	/g/, /j/	z:	/z/, /s/, /zh/

   The symbol η also represents the pronunciation of /ng/. You will observe that some dictionaries use the η.

   b. A phoneme may be represented by more than one letter (pp. 44, 52, 67, 82). Some common patterns are:

/f/:	f, gh, ph	/s/:	s, z
/j/:	j, g, dg, d	/w/:	w, u
/k/:	k, ch, q	/z/:	z, s

   c. A letter may represent no phoneme; that is, it may be silent. When two like consonants appear together, the second usually is silent (pp. 39, 44, 52, 67). Some common silent letter patterns occurring in the same syllable are:

b following m	k followed by n
b followed by t	l followed by m, k, d
c following s	p followed by s, t, n
c followed by k	t following f; followed by ch
g followed by n	

   h following k, g, r; following a vowel; as the initial letter in certain words

2. When the letter c or g is followed by e, i, or y, it usually represents its soft sound as in *city* or *gem;* when c or g is followed by any other letter or appears at the end of a word, it usually represents its hard sound as in *cup* or *go* (p. 67).

3. The suffix *-ed* usually forms a separate syllable when it is preceded by t or d. When *-ed* does not form a separate syllable, the d may represent /t/ or /d/ (pp. 48, 52).

4. The letter q always represents /k/ (pp. 37, 44).

5. The letters *c, q,* and *x* have no distinctive phonemes of their own (p. 34).
6. The consonants *w* and *y* are positioned before the vowel in a syllable. The consonant *y* is never silent (pp. 61, 67).
7. We use two-letter combinations (digraphs) to represent the seven consonant phonemes not represented by single letters (*ch, sh, ṯẖ, th, wh, zh, ng*) (pp. 72, 82).

 ## Vowel Generalizations

1. A letter may represent more than one phoneme (p. 95).
2. A phoneme may be represented by more than one vowel letter (p. 95).
3. A single vowel in a closed accented syllable usually represents its short sound (pp. 101, 103).
4. A letter may represent no phoneme; that is, it may be silent (pp. 102, 114, 137).
5. When a one-syllable word or accented syllable contains two vowels, one of which is a final *e,* the first vowel usually represents its long sound and the final *e* is silent (pp. 106, 114).
6. A single vowel in an open accented syllable often represents its long sound (pp. 110, 114).
7. When *i* is followed by *gh* or when *i* or *o* is followed by *ld,* the vowel usually represents its long sound (pp. 112, 114).
8. If the only vowel letter in a word or syllable is followed by *r,* the vowel sound will be affected by that *r* (pp. 124, 125).
9. If the only vowel in a word or syllable is an *a* followed by *l* or *w,* the sound of the *a* is usually that heard in *ball* (pp. 124, 125).
10. When two vowel letters appear together in a one-syllable word or in an accented syllable, the first vowel often represents its long sound and the second is silent. This holds true most often for *ai, oa, ee, ey,* and *ay* combinations (pp. 133, 134, 137).
11. The vowel *y* always follows the vowel or is the only vowel in a syllable and is silent or represents the phonemes we associate with *i* or *e* (pp. 103, 114).
12. Although a syllable may have more than one vowel letter, there is only one vowel phoneme in a syllable (pp. 133, 175).
13. Vowels behave differently in accented and unaccented syllables. The vowel is most clearly heard in the accented syllable (pp. 169, 175).
14. The vowel in most unaccented syllables represents the ə or ĭ (pp. 116, 118).

Accent Clues

1. The vowel phoneme is the most prominent part of the syllable (p. 175).
2. When a word contains a prefix and/or a suffix, the accent usually falls on or within the root word (pp. 170, 175).
3. The accent usually falls on or within the first word of a compound word (pp. 170, 175).
4. In a two-syllable word that functions as either a noun or a verb, the accent is usually on the first syllable when the word functions as a noun and on the second syllable when the word functions as a verb (pp. 171, 175).
5. When there is a double consonant within a word, the accent usually falls on the syllable that ends with the first letter of the double consonant (pp. 171, 175).
6. In most multisyllabic words ending in the suffix *-tion, -sion,* or *ic,* the primary accent falls on the syllable preceding the suffix (pp. 171, 175).
7. When the vowel phoneme within the last and closed syllable of a two-syllable word is composed of two vowel letters, that syllable is usually accented (pp. 172, 175).

8. When there is no other clue in a two-syllable word, the accent most often falls on the first syllable (pp. 173, 175).

Syllable Division

1. In a compound word, the syllabic division usually comes between the "words" of which it is composed (pp. 181, 186).
2. Prefixes and suffixes usually form separate syllables from the root word (pp. 184, 186).
3. If the last syllable of a word ends in *le* preceded by a consonant, that consonant usually begins the last syllable (pp. 184, 186).
4. If the first vowel in a two-syllable word is followed by a single consonant, that consonant often begins the second syllable (pp. 177, 180, 186).
5. When two vowel letters are separated by two consonants, the syllabic division usually occurs between the consonants (pp. 178, 186).
6. In syllabication, digraphs are treated as representing single phonemes (pp. 181, 182, 186).

Spelling Words with Prefixes and Suffixes

1. The spelling of a root word is not usually affected by adding a prefix (*unreal*) (pp. 206, 215).
2. The spelling of a root word often does not change when we add a suffix that begins with a consonant to a root word that ends in a consonant (*gladly*) (pp. 206, 215).
3. Add *-es* to words that end in a *y* preceded by a consonant and to words that end in *s, sh, ch, x,* or *z* (*berries, buses, crashes, churches, taxes, buzzes*). Add *-s* to most other words (pp. 207, 215).
4. Usually, change the *y* to *i* before adding a suffix to a word that ends in a *y* preceded by a consonant (*worried*). Do not change the *y* to *i* when a word ends in a *y* preceded by a vowel (*played*). Do not change the *y* to *i* before adding *-ing* to a word that ends in a *y* preceded by a consonant (*worrying*) (pp. 207, 208, 209, 215).
5. When a root word ends in a final silent *e,* drop the *e* before adding a suffix that begins with a vowel (*liked*). Keep the final silent *e* when a suffix begins with a consonant (*likely*) (pp. 209, 210, 211, 215).
6. Double the final consonant before adding a suffix to a one-syllable word that ends in a single vowel followed by a single consonant (*hopped*). Double the final consonant before adding a suffix that begins in a vowel to the final, accented syllable of a multisyllable word that ends in one vowel followed by one consonant (*be gin' ner*). Do not double the final consonant when a suffix begins with a consonant (*badly*). Do not double the final consonant when a one-syllable word has two vowels (*sweeter*) or ends in two consonants (*jumped*). Do not double the final consonant when the last syllable of a multisyllable word is unaccented (*o' pen ing*) (pp. 215, 216).

Appendix B

Graphemes, Key Symbols, and Key Words

Grapheme	Key Symbol	Key Word	Grapheme	Key Symbol	Key Word
Single Consonants			**Short Vowels**		
b	b	*boat*	a	ă	*apple*
c	no key symbol	no key word	e	ĕ	*edge*
d	d	*dog*	i	ĭ	*igloo*
f	f	*fish*	o	ŏ	*ox*
g	g	*goat*	u	ŭ	*umbrella*
h	h	*hat*			
j	j	*jeep*			
k	k	*kite*	**Long vowels**		
l	l	*lion*	a	ā	*apron*
m	m	*moon*	e	ē	*eraser*
n	n	*nut*	i	ī	*ice*
p	p	*pig*	o	ō	*overalls*
q	no key symbol	no key word	u	ū	*unicorn*
r	r	*ring*			
s	s	*sun*			
t	t	*table*	**Schwa** (vowels in unaccented syllables)		
v	v	*van*	a	ə	*comma*
w	w	*wagon*	e	ə	*chicken*
x	no key symbol	no key word	i	ə	*family*
y	y	*yo-yo*	o	ə	*melon*
z	z	*zipper*	u	ə	*circus*

Grapheme	Key Symbol	Key Word	Grapheme	Key Symbol	Key Word
Consonant Digraphs			**Diphthongs**		
ch	ch	*chair*	oi, oy	oi	*oil*
sh	sh	*ship*	ou, ow	ou	*house*
th	th	*thumb*			
th	t̶h̶	*that*	**Digraphs**		
wh	wh	*whale*	oo	o̅o̅	*food*
	zh	*treasure*	oo	ŏŏ	*hook*
ng	ng	*king*			
			Long Vowel Digraphs*		
Other Single Vowels			ai	ā	*apron*
a	â	*care*	ay	ā	*apron*
u	û	*fur*	ea	ē	*eraser*
a	ä	*father*	ee	ē	*eraser*
a	ô	*ball*	oa	ō	*overalls*
			ow	ō	*overalls*

The long vowel digraphs do not have key symbols or key words. The long vowel digraphs represent the long vowel sounds that are already assigned. The long vowel digraphs are listed here so as to give a full representation of the patterns you have studied.

Glossary

Note: The number following each entry refers to the page on which the word is introduced.

Accented syllable   A syllable that receives greater stress than the other syllables in a word. 175

Affix   A term used when referring to either a prefix or a suffix. 197

Base word   A synonym for root word (free morpheme) that is used in some teachers' manuals and curriculum guides. 196

Beginning sound awareness   The understanding that each word begins with a phoneme and the ability to separate the beginning phoneme from the rest of the word (/*map*/ begins with /*m*/). 21

Blending   The ability to combine smaller speech units into larger units. When applied to phonics, blending describes the ability to combine individual phonemes together to pronounce a word. Blending is essential for using phonics (/*m*/ + /*a*/ + /*n*/ = /*man*/). 20

Bound morpheme   A unit of meaning that must be added to another morpheme; a bound morpheme cannot stand on its own. *Un-* and *-ing* are examples of bound morphemes. 197

Breve   A diacritical mark (˘) used to indicate the short sound of a vowel, as the /*ĕ*/ in *red*. 97

Closed syllable   A syllable that ends in a consonant phoneme (/*trip*/). 100

Comparative suffix   The *-er*, an inflectional suffix, is used to compare two things, as in "My piece of cake is larger than your piece." 199

Compound word   A word made up of two or more shorter "words" (*cowboy* and *rainbow*). A compound word is a free morpheme. 202

Consonant   One of the two classifications of speech sounds. There are 21 consonant letters and 25 consonant sounds. (*See* Vowel.) 30, 33

Consonant blend   A combination of two or more adjacent consonant phonemes that are blended together when pronounced, as the /*bl*/ in /*blue*/. It is common practice in many teachers' manual and curriculum guides to refer to the consonant letters that represent these phonemes as consonant blends, as the *bl* in the word *blue*. Consonant cluster and consonant blend are used interchangeably in this text. 85

Consonant cluster   Two or more consonant letters appearing together in a syllable that, when sounded, form a consonant blend. Consonant clusters are taught as units rather than as single graphemes (e.g., *bl* as representing two blended phonemes rather than as an isolated /*b*/ and an isolated /*l*/. 85

Consonant digraph   A two-letter consonant grapheme that represents a phoneme not represented by the single letters, such as the *sh* in *shoe*. 72

Contraction   The combination of two words into a single word in which an apostrophe denotes one or more missing letters (*isn't*). 202

Decoding   Translating graphemes into the sounds of spoken language so as to pronounce a visually unfamiliar word. Teachers may refer to this process as "sounding out" words. 15

Derivational suffix   A unit of meaning added to the end of a word that modifies its meaning and may change its grammatical category. The suffix *-able* changes a verb (*like*) to an adjective (*likeable*). 200

Diacritical mark   A special mark or symbol added to a letter to indicate pronunciation. The breve, a u-shaped symbol placed over a vowel to indicate a short pronunciation, and the macron, a line placed over a vowel to indicate a long pronunciation, are two of the most common diacritical marks. 97

Digraph   A grapheme composed of two letters that represents one speech sound (phoneme). 30

Diphthong   A single vowel phoneme resembling a glide from one sound to another; represented by the graphemes *oi* (*noise*), *oy* (*toy*), *ou* (*found*), and *ow* (*now*): key symbols are *oi* and *ou*; key words are *oil* and *house*. 127

Free morpheme   The smallest unit of meaning that can stand alone. A free morpheme cannot be divided into smaller units and still retain its meaning (*play*). 194

Grapheme   The written symbol used to represent the phoneme. It may be composed of one or more letters, and the same grapheme may represent more than one phoneme. 16, 19

Inflectional suffix   A unit of meaning added to the end of a word that changes its number, affects verb tense, indicates possession, or denotes a comparison (*cats, playing, Tom's, smaller*). 199

Key symbol   One of the 44 specific graphemes representing the 44 phonemes of the American-English language (as presented in this text), thus achieving a one-to-one correspondence between key symbol and phoneme: one symbol for each phoneme and one phoneme for each symbol. 31

Key word   One word selected for each of the 44 phonemes that identifies the specific phoneme. 34

Long vowel   One of the five vowels represented by *ā, ē, ī, ō,* and *ū* that, in the context of the teaching of phonics, are indicated by a macron (ˉ) and "say their names." Key words: *apron, eraser, ice, overalls,* and *unicorn*. 105

Long vowel digraph   Two adjacent vowel letters that represent one phoneme, as the *ee* in *street* or the *oa* in *road*. These digraphs do not have key symbols. Their key symbols have already been assigned to the single-letter long vowels. The long vowel digraphs are also called vowel teams or vowel pairs. 132

Macron   A diacritical mark (ˉ) used to indicate the long sound of a vowel. 105

Morpheme   The smallest unit of meaning in the English language (*re-, play, -ed*). 194

Onset   One or more consonant letters that precede the vowel phoneme in a syllable (the *c* in *cat*, the *ch* in *chat*, the *chr* in *chrome*). 157

Open syllable   A syllable that ends in a vowel phoneme (*play, blue*). 109

Phoneme   The smallest unit of sound that distinguishes one word from another. This program identifies 44 phonemes. 16, 18

Phoneme addition   Attaching one or more phonemes to a word or word part (adding /t/ to /able/ to pronounce /table/). 22

Phoneme deletion   Removing one or more phonemes from a word or word part (removing /s/ from /stop/ to pronounce /top/). 23

Phoneme substitution   Deleting one or more phonemes from a word or word part and then replacing the deleted phoneme(s) with one or more different phonemes (deleting the /t/ from /sat/ and replacing it with a /d/ to pronounce /sad/). 23

Phonemic awareness   The ability to conceptualize speech as a sequence of phonemes (sounds) combined with the ability to consciously manipulate the phonemes of the English language. Children who are phonemically aware can separate words into their individual phonemes; add, subtract, substitute, and rearrange the phonemes in words; and blend phonemes together to pronounce words. 20

Phonetics   The science of speech sounds. 127

Phonics   The study of the relationships of the letters and letter combinations in written words (the graphemes of the English language) to the sounds they represent in spoken words. The study of phonics provides the content for developing skill in the decoding of unfamiliar words. 12

Phonological awareness   The understanding that spoken language consists of words, syllables, rhymes, and phonemes. 20

Prefix   A bound morpheme placed at the beginning of a root word (free morpheme), as the *re-* in *replay*, to change the meaning of the root word or to make word meaning more specific. 196

R-controlled vowel   A vowel followed by the letter *r* in a syllable or one-syllable word. The *r* affects the pronunciation of the vowel. The vowel is neither long nor short. 124

Rime   The vowel and consonant letter(s) that follows the vowel in a one-syllable word or a syllable (the *at* in *sat* or the *ild* in *child*). 159

Rhyme   Commonality in the vowel and consonant sounds at the end of words, as heard in /red/, /bed/, and /said/. 20

Rhyme awareness   The understanding that spoken words rhyme, and the ability to recognize rhyming words and to think of rhyming words. 20

Root word   The free morpheme to which a prefix or suffix may be attached. Some teachers' manuals use the term *root word* for parts borrowed from other languages, most often the Greek and Latin languages. In our study, we use root word as a synonym for *free morpheme*. 196

Schwa   A vowel phoneme in an unaccented syllable that represents a soft "uh" and is indicated by the key symbol ə, which resembles an inverted *e*. Key words: *comma, chicken, family, button, circus*. 116

Segmenting   The process of separating a large unit of spoken language into smaller units. In the context of using phonics, segmenting is the ability to separate spoken words into individual phonemes. Segmenting is an essential skill for the use of phonics. 20

Short vowel   The vowel letters *ă, ĕ, ĭ, ŏ,* and *ŭ* that, in the context of the teaching of phonics, are indicated with a breve (˘), and are heard in the key words *apple, elephant, igloo, ox,* and *umbrella*. 97

Silent letter A name given to a letter that appears in a written word but is not heard in the spoken word: *knight* has six letters, but only three are sounded; *k*, *g*, and *h* are silent. 39, 44

Slash marks Slanting lines / / enclosing a grapheme indicating that the reference is to its sound, not to the letters. 16

Structural analysis The use of prefixes, suffixes, root words, the "words" in compound words, and the apostrophes in contractions to read and understand the meaning of unfamiliar words. 194

Suffix A bound morpheme placed at the end a word (*played*). 197

Superlative suffix The inflectional suffix *-est*, which is used to compare more than two things. 199

Syllable The unit of pronunciation. The English syllable has only one vowel phoneme. There are as many syllables in a word as there are vowel phonemes; there is only one vowel phoneme in a syllable. 175

Syllable awareness The understanding that spoken words consist of syllables and the ability to segment multisyllable words into syllables and to blend syllables into words. 20

Unaccented syllable A syllable that does not receive stress when pronounced. Most vowels in unstresssed syllables represent a schwa, a soft "uh" (ə), or a short *i* (I). 169

Voiced *th* The initial phoneme heard in the key word *that*, in which the vocal cords vibrate during the production of the phoneme. 77

Voiceless *th* The initial phoneme heard in the key word *thumb*, in which the vocal cords do not vibrate during the production of the phoneme. 77

Vowel One of the two classifications of speech sounds. The vowels are *a, e, i, o, u*, and sometimes *w* and *y*. (*See* Consonant.) 30

Vowel digraph A two-letter vowel grapheme that represents one sound. In this text, the vowel digraphs are the o͞o in *food* and the o͝o in *hook*. 129

Vowel pair Two adjacent vowel letters that usually represent a long vowel phoneme associated with one of the letters, such as the /ā/ in *rain* that is represented by the *ai* grapheme. *Long vowel digraph* and *vowel team* are other names for these two-letter vowel combinations. 132

Vowel team Two adjacent vowel letters that usually represent a long vowel phoneme associated with one of the letters, such as the /ē/ in *meet* that is represented by the *ee* grapheme. *Long vowel digraph* and *vowel pair* are other names for these two-letter vowel combinations. 132

Word For the purposes of teaching reading, we define a word as a single free morpheme (*play*) or a free morpheme and one or more bound morphemes (*replaying*). 195

Word awareness The understanding that spoken language consists of word-length units and the ability to separate sentences and phrases into words. 20

Word family Words with the same rime (*at*) and rhyming sound (*cat, fat, hat*). 160